I am on a different trajectory today because of Kris Taylor's work and writings. I experienced her teachings, particularly chapters 1 through 4, which shifted my thinking completely about my leadership, career, and life. I am now CEO of my own company and loving every minute of it.

- Angela Nuttle, President of Corporate OD Strategies

Kris Taylor takes the latest theory on organizational change and clearly translates into an action plan that inspires people to push through the fear of change and embrace the possibilities. She is a gifted visionary thinker, writer and speaker who has honed her craft through years of real world situations that make her the "real deal". If organizational change is your key priority Kris Taylor is your guru.

- MaryAnn Rivers, CEO, The Droste Group, Inc.

We are moving into an era that cannot simply value and take action from the "do what's right for me/my family/my organization" platform anymore and still be successful in the long term. Addressing the need for practices of self-awareness as an access for being effective in this new era of "we", Kris Taylor captures artfully the shift in context from "me" to "we' even in what looks like similar behaviors in her newest book for leaders.

- Andrea Bednar, Founder & CEO, PoP Associates

Kris is a phenomenal change management expert, and I've been fortunate to work with her directly. She brings her whole self to her writing and work. Her writing on Gratitude was life changing for me, and arrived just when I needed it. Kris doesn't separate personal life experiences from her work. She finds a way to fold them in – something not many people can do – and it makes her work that much more powerful.

- Susie Wolf, Director, Global Employee Communications, Eli Lilly and Company

Acknowledgements

This book is a compilation of my life experiences in leading, learning and implementing change in businesses, academic and non-profit arenas. Each step in my journey was shaped by others in powerful and sometimes unseen ways – and their influence is infused in this writing. With special gratitude to:

My Mom and Dad who encouraged me to excel academically and to explore the world

Dot Kroehler of Community Action Program of Lancaster County, who first taught me the basics of leadership and instilled in me that my actions as a leader shaped the outcomes of the programs I was responsible for

Carmen Gatti, my partner in Developmental Day Care Systems, who discovered with me that visions can be realized, that one can create something really amazing and that passion trumps technical know how

My husband, Dan, who never stood in the way of my next "big" thing, no matter what that was

My two children, Brad and Nicole, who bless my life with love, with laughter, and with the profoundness of the continuity of life

Steve Oswalt, HR Manager at RR Donnelley, who demonstrated thoughtful leadership infused with caring and courage (and who stuck his neck out on me more than once)

Co-workers at RR Donnelley who worked with me side by side to develop people, to deliver good products and to help move the organization forward

Chip Neidigh, of Catalyst OC, who lives high trust relationships and challenges my ideas and approaches – and makes them richer and better as a result

Mike Donahue and the folks around the table in the peer groups he facilitates, who have shown me the way to grow myself and my business and in the process, to recognize the power of peer groups

My clients, who most often become partners and friends, that allow me to enter their world and who are open to ways to create the changes they desire

My associates, who enter into this work of change and leadership with integrity, heart and spirit

My colleagues at Purdue, who nurture the entrepreneurial (and creative) spirit in myself and others

The folks who have helped make this book a reality – from ideas, to inspiration, to hands on work: Lou Russell, Elaine Biech, Lori Tatum, Abby Thompson, Karen Demerly, Elaine Todd, and Nicole Gebhardt

Deanna Brown and the women of Cultural Connections, who open my eyes to the world and how very interconnected we are

My granddaughter, Aubrey, who brings joy, love and delight into my life every moment and who fuels my passion to leave the world a better place

Cover design by Lori Tatum.

Published by Evergreen Leadership.

ISBN 978-0-9906163-0-6

Introduction

This book is written for leaders of all kinds and levels – CEOs and community board leaders, directors in large companies and non-profits, selected leaders and elected leaders, entrepreneurs and educators, those that lead as a living and those that lead because there is something that needs to be done. It is for those who want to make this world a better place, in some form or fashion. It is for those who seek a path to leadership that is more holistic, more nurturing, more sustaining for those it serves and sustainable over time.

These concepts flow from my work, both inside and outside of organizations. I've led in for profit and not for profit organizations. Of course that means I've also been led by those above me in those places. At times I led well. At other times, not. At times I've worked with amazing leaders. And sometimes that was not the case.

In addition, over the past ten years, I've had the good fortune to be invited in to a variety of organizations to work with their leaders as they implemented change. This book is a summation of what I've learned and what I am continuing to learn.

This is truly an unprecedented time. I'm certain others have said that across the ages, but nowhere in history can I find a time where so many disruptions were occurring in the speed at which they are occurring today. We all see the changes that computers and the internet have wrought. We live a life that is more global, more diverse and more connected than ever before. We exist in a time where technology, knowledge and information are on an exponential growth curve. We live on a planet threatened by our collective actions, but without collective will to change the course.

When asked to describe today's environment, I hear these words: fast paced, uncertain, scary, opportunistic, global, confusing, shifting, chaotic, ever changing, uncertain, overwhelming – in a word turbulent.

The impact to leaders and organizations is far reaching. In every organization I encounter, there is a crying need for people who can lead and not merely manage. Leaders I work with are frazzled, overwhelmed and feeling overworked. The pace is breakneck, with things seeming to move at warp speed with little respite. Our increasing technology has not freed time as touted, but enabled work to creep into every moment of our lives. Global competition has forced a leveling that means there are fewer people doing more work and being paid less. Budgets get cut, headcount reduced and demands increase. Clearly there needs to be a better way.

Yet, in all the companies I work with, there are leaders who are thriving. Ones who are both grounded and visionary, who don't know the way but are confident that together we will find a way, who can move others forward in spite of uncertainty and turbulence. Leaders who focus on the most important things and let go of actions no longer needed. Leaders who build organizations by building the people within those organizations. Leaders who know deeply that leadership is about "we" not "me" and that the "we" is a big we – well past their shift, their department, their division, their business unit, and even beyond their organization.

I will be up front with you that I've NOT encountered one leader who has ALL the skills, attitudes and behaviors that are contained in this book. But consistently, leaders who are able to lead well in today's turbulent world possess many of the attributes discussed here.

So what are those attributes? Leaders who are leading well today are:

1. Firmly grounded and aware of who they are as a leader. Their values guide them, their strengths empower them and their passions fuel them. Self-awareness is not about narcissism, but is about being aware of how they show up, what their impact is on others and when they are at their best. It is also about knowing weaknesses, blind spots and personal pitfalls – so that they can be avoided or mitigated.
2. Able to envision and create better futures. They can create within organizations, bringing new products, services, processes or ways of working together into being.
3. Agile in their approach – willing to try new things, comfortable with small failures as the price for the bigger win, untethered by the current restraints.
4. Able to provide clarity and direction in the midst of uncertainty.
5. Willing to engage others in creating better futures. Knowing that collaborating with others results in better and richer outcomes.
6. Strong team builders
7. Continual learners who are skilled at developing themselves and those they lead. They are leaders who see learning opportunities daily – and not just when the company offers a seminar or a workshop.
8. Globally minded – recognizing that this is an interconnected world, that diversity brings richness and that thinking beyond themselves is necessary.
9. Able to shed what is no longer needed.
10. Take time to plan, reflect, and think – in other words, to slow down in order to go faster in the right direction. They are not going too fast to refuel, not arriving quickly and finding that where they have landed in the wrong place.
11. Grateful – and share their gratitude.

In 2011 I paused for a bit to gather my thoughts and observations about the rich learning from working with over 40 clients in the seven years since I had founded my change management firm. As a result, I created a leadership development program, Evergreen Leadership. The program teaches those skills most needed today in an integrated fashion – and is the basis for this body of work.

I chose the Evergreen metaphor for a specific reason. Evergreens carve out a unique niche in every eco-system on earth. While most plants repeat the process of dormancy, growth, blossoming, yield and decay – evergreens have a different adaptive mechanism to stay green and to avoid the extreme cycles of other plants. Evergreens shed and replace leaves on a continual basis. The greenery that they shed serves two purposes: to put needed nutrients back into the soil and to make the soil more acidic and hence, inhospitable to other plant forms – but perfect for evergreens. Some evergreens thrive in rain forests, others in drought stricken areas. No matter their environment, they are resilient and adaptive. "Evergreens carve out a unique niche in every eco-system on earth."

Evergreen leaders share many of the same traits that make evergreens in nature so resilient. Leaders in our programs learn to continually shed what is of no use to them and allow new, healthy growth to appear. Evergreen leaders can find a foothold in even some of the most inhospitable environments. Evergreen leaders nurture their soil and roots and create a climate where others can thrive. Evergreen leaders adapt to the conditions they find themselves in – and find ways to fit into their ecosystem.

I've taken the content from our Evergreen leadership development program, enriched it a bit and pulled it together in this guide. This book is a practical (and I stress practical) guide. It is based on theory, but takes current research and thinking and puts it into understandable, actionable steps.

The book is real world tested. It is filled with the learnings from my lifetime of work – in small companies, big companies, for profit and not for profits. The book is filled with what I have learned from others, what I've learned from my successes and my failures and from testing it in a variety of situations. The readings and exercises have been used by our change management clients and by leaders in our Evergreen Leadership Development Programs. They work.

This book is filled with exercises. I encourage you to actually do the exercises as you work through the book. You don't learn to lead by reading alone. Learning to lead requires testing your skills against your situation. One must do the work and then learn from the outcomes – it is the only way to learn, to improve and ultimately to master these skills.

The book will not teach you basic supervisory skills. But the book will teach you many things that are not typically taught in traditional leadership or management courses. It will teach you how to create a better future, how to connect others to support your vision, how to establish high performing teams in turbulent times, how to lighten your load and how gratitude can enhance your leadership and your life.

The concepts in this book supplement and enhance those typically taught in leadership courses. Leaders still need to problem solve, direct, allocate resources, manage, and execute. What this guide will teach you is how to deepen and balance your skill set – to be more holistic, more agile, more adaptable.

If you'd like help and support along the way, contact us about our Evergreen Leadership Circles, in which an experienced guide walks you and your team through the process. We have programs for executives, high potential leaders and for individuals.

I'd also love to hear how this work has changed your leadership and to learn what positive results it has brought to you. Feel free to contact us via our website: www.evergreenleadership.com or to stay in touch by subscribing to our blog at www.ktaylorandassoc.com/blog/ .

So I encourage you to read, think, reflect, experiment, practice, improve – all in the service of creating better futures – for yourself and for those you lead. Go forth and lead – the world needs you!

CHAPTER 1
Your Inner Core

1   Thriving Today

The journey to become a better leader in today's turbulent times begins on the inside. It may seem counterintuitive to focus inward when it is all we can do to stay afloat in the rush of activity in the outside world. Yet there are two key reasons we begin to hone your leadership skills by starting on the inside. The first is that regardless of the external environment, good leadership is grounded in deep self-awareness. Before you lead others, you must first have some degree of self-mastery. The second reason is directly related to the chaotic world in which you lead. There are three specific elements of deep self-awareness that will enable you to maintain personal stability and consequently to lead better in times of change. Let's explore each of them.

> *Every human has four endowments – self-awareness, conscience, independent will, and creative imagination. These give us the ultimate human freedom… The power to choose, to respond, to change.*
>
> Stephen Covey

2   Why Self-Awareness?

It may be easier to understand why deep self-awareness is important for leaders if you think back to leaders you've experienced. Most people have had multiple experiences that span a range from excellent leaders to very poor leaders. We have something to learn from all of them.

We'll start with poor, perhaps even horrible leaders. I've worked for some. I suspect you have as well. In general, some of the characteristics that made them bad include:

- Arrogance and insensitivity
- Ego driven pride
- Lack of vision
- Inability to inspire
- Inability to delegate effectively
- Poor communication skills
- Ineffective decision making skills

But no matter what their deficiency was, the far bigger challenge was all too often they could neither see, nor admit, their blind spots. Poor leaders generally follow this pattern. Without fail, they continue to bumble (or charge) ahead, impervious to the trail of bad results that follow in their wake. Feedback falls on deaf ears. Attempts to help or support them in improving are met with defensiveness and blame. Issues are externalized. Others are blamed for the lack of results. And as a result, performance suffers. People leave. Morale plummets. And yet, these leaders carry on, blind to their contribution to the situation and unwilling to take the hard look in the mirror that might save them and their team.

I hope that you've had more good leaders than poor. In my experience, some of the best leaders I've had the pleasure to work with (and for), were extremely self-aware. Their ability to reflect on their own leadership meant that they operated with a level of consciousness and care that was lacking in others. Knowing and owning their challenge areas made them stronger, rather than weaker, as it averted blind spots and gave them the ability to compensate. These

> *Just as your car runs more smoothly and requires less energy to go faster and farther when the wheels are in perfect alignment, you perform better when your thoughts, feelings, emotions, goals, and values are in balance.*
>
> Brian Tracy

leaders are more open to feedback, input and then consequently growth. As they admitted their own imperfections and idiosyncrasies, it freed others to do the same. They were human, approachable and teachable. And is seems that this personal insight carried into the group, and that these leaders were much more likely to relate to those they led as unique individuals, each with passions, strengths, challenges and a personal life.

Deep self-awareness brings a leader and those they lead many gifts, including:

- Awareness of blind spots or situations that have a tendency to trip them up
- Ability to be proactive rather than reactive
- Willingness to be humble and consequently, human
- A shift from ego centric to other centered
- Openness rather than defensiveness
- Ability to grow and learn
- Ability to anticipate opportunities and curb distractions

Consider this thought. If you were in need of a leader to guide you through a dark and shadowy place fraught with dangers, would you prefer one who had a blindfold on or one who had a bright lantern to show the way? Would you prefer a leader who had no clear understanding of their skills and also of their limitations? Or one who knew deeply what they knew, how they knew it and where their limitations were? I prefer light to shadow any day – and even more so when the stakes are high and the environment uncertain.

> *The key to growth is the introduction of higher dimensions of consciousness into our awareness.*
>
> Lao Tzu

Why Now More than Ever?

I'm not the first, nor will I be the last, to propose the idea that self-awareness is a core component of good leadership as well as a rich and full life. Yet at a time in which we are immersed in complexity, ambiguity and change, I submit to you that it has never been more important. Why is this?

I suspect, you have encountered individuals who were calm in the face of chaos. Who appeared to take it all in stride, not by giving up or by giving in, but by marching to their own inner wisdom and guidance. These are individuals who we might describe as "being comfortable in their own skin" or being impervious to the whirlwind around them. They achieve much, but never appear to be overextended or spinning out of control. These individuals seem to be guided by something you can't quite see, yet you can feel something deep within them.

Most likely, you have picked up this book because you find it challenging to lead when things feel so uncertain. Perhaps you find there are times you feel caught up in a swirling frenzy, an ever changing, fast moving rush of changes, shifts and activity. What was new and exciting 6 months ago is now passé. You've barely mastered the old technology before it is replaced by new and different. Expectations in your job are continually ratcheted up. You are running faster and harder and getting even more behind.

It is easy to be confused, dazed and disoriented in today's world. This chapter will help you do more than just survive in this complexity; in fact to thrive within the tumult around you. You can do this by developing a strong inner core, one that provides grounding and balance, no matter how turbulent the world around you.

> *The first step toward change is awareness. The second step is acceptance.*
>
> Nathaniel Branden

3   The Inner Core

There is ONE BIG differentiator that distinguishes those who are able to navigate change well and those who struggle. Those who thrive are able to do so because they have an "inner core." Even though things outside them may appear to be in a state of chaos – they have an internal ballast system them keeps them upright and floating. This also keeps them from spinning out of control.

That is not to mean that individuals with an inner core are immune from change or that they don't experience all the normal feelings that others do in times of flux. They, however, are able to operate from a deep source that helps provide much needed stability and a guidance system. It is almost like an internal GPS system. They can quickly right themselves when something pushes them off center. They are like the wobble people toys that, no matter how many times they are knocked over, spring right back to their original position.

Your inner core provides both stability and unbelievable strength. It is the strength from your core that enables you to remain balanced and strong. This is true, both physically, emotionally, socially and mentally. A quick physical example is using a balance board, an exercise tool that is a small board perched atop of a small ball. To stay upright on this board, one must have (and use) the core muscles of their trunk to maintain balance – much more difficult than one can imagine. So to the uninformed, balancing on this wobbly board is about foot movement. To those skilled, they know their stability comes from deep within the muscles of the abdomen, back and chest. They know it is not about the extremities – it is about their core. They know it is not about movement, but control. They know it takes both physical control and mental focus.

Having a strong core is important in many areas of our life. A strong core of supportive friends

A people that values its privileges above its principles soon loses both.

Dwight D. Eisenhower

and family is a way to maintain social stability – and researchers have shown even allows us to be in better health and live longer. This chapter looks at our psychological core – one that guides us at work, home and play.

Operating from this deep inner core allows you to have a strong sense of inner calm and focus when there is much turbulence around you. Yet don't be deceived by the calmness and interpret it as lethargy or inaction. In fact, it is the opposite. Working from your core enables you to exert great power without being forceful. It provides both strength and flexibility. It both grounds you and enables you to reach higher.

The first step is knowing what your inner core is. You can then intentionally operate from your core more and more. Initially it will take some detective work and then some practice and discipline. Yet over time your inner core will become your internal guidance system – and will always point you to your correct destination, even in stormy times.

3.1 What Comprises the Inner Core?

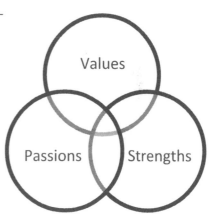

There are two primary elements of the inner core: your **values** and your **strengths**. All in all, these are relatively fixed in your early 20s and don't change very much through adulthood. It may be that some values become amplified due to life circumstances – but generally they are like concrete that has set with your unique handprints in it.

There is one additional element that adds power to your core: your **passions**. Passion brings intensity, focus, and energy to your core. However passions do change over time. The passions of your twenties give way to different ones in your thirties and forties. There may be some passions that stick with you through life and others that you discover along the way. Other passions may share a common theme (helping others, love of nature) and get realized in different ways as you age.

These three elements: values, strengths and passion work together in a synergistic way. Values provide direction, strengths provide ability and passion provides energy. When the three work in concert—you are guided by your values, fueled by your passions and able to execute well due to your strengths. This enables you to move through your life with grace and ease. Think about these three as a tightly woven braid – in which the combination of each one makes the whole much stronger, just like the woven strands of a heavy duty rope.

You are the most grounded, the strongest, the most energetic and the most likely to be successful in times of change when you:

- Can clearly articulate your core values and work with intention to honor them in tangible ways
- Know your strengths and spend most of your time using them
- Understand your passions and use them to fuel your day to day actions

"Management has a lot to do with answers. Leadership is a function of questions. And the first question for a leader always is: 'Who do we intend to be?' Not 'What are we going to do?' but 'Who do we intend to be?'"

Max DePree, Hermann Miller

---

4 A Deeper Dive

4.1 Values

Values begin to form at a young age – and are shaped by those that are most influential in our early years. Most often, this is your immediate family, your teachers and coaches, your community and your faith tradition. Depending on your life circumstances, any one of these may have a disproportionate influence on your value formation. You may be someone who comes from a strong family situation and perhaps were home schooled. In that case, your values might strongly reflect those of your family. Or perhaps your family was fragmented, but you had an exceptionally involved coach who invested time and energy in you. The values this coach taught you might supersede those of your family – and be an on-going source of inspiration and hope for you.

Values are deeply rooted – and as such are seldom top of mind. Just like an iceberg, there is more below the surface than we realize. Our values guide us and shape our beliefs and consequently our actions – yet often we would be hard pressed to list them quickly. Complicating the process of identifying our values is the fact that most of the common values articulated sound like good ones. Who does not want to value honesty or integrity or truth or beauty? The fact we have value judgments about values limits our ability to have a clear assessment about what they are for us as individuals.

Now comes the time to put this in practice. Begin now to do these activities that allow you to put these concepts into your own personal leadership practice.

When your values are clear to you, making decisions becomes easier.

Roy E. Disney

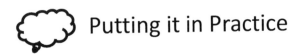 # Putting it in Practice

Values Exercise – Part 1: Create a Starting List

Quickly read through the following list of values. Circle any that are values for you personally. Then go back over your list and prioritize them until you have a shorter list of eight or fewer values. Note that values, by their nature, tend to refer to things that are inherently something of worth. The key here is determining your own personal order of magnitude. Feel free to add other values to your list that are not named here.

Agility	Faith	Marriage
Ambition	Family	Nature
Autonomy	Flexibility	Passion
Change	Focus	Patience
Community	Freedom	Peace
Compassion	Friendship	Perseverance
Competition	Fun	Philanthropy
Cooperation	Imagination	Reason
Creativity	Influence	Resilience
Curiosity	Knowledge	Respect
Discipline	Leadership	Security
Diversity	Learning	Strength
Endurance	Logic	Teamwork
Energy	Love	Trust
Environmentalism	Making a Difference	Uniqueness

4.2   Finding Your Core Values

I suspect that the process of narrowing your values to down to eight possible ones was difficult. Even still, we want to get even more focused and narrow. This is even more difficult. However, the truism that "actions speak louder than words" can come to our aid here. What we do, where we spend our time, our energy, our money, our effort are clear indicators of what we truly value. The person who says they value family, but spends 90% of their waking hours at work – most likely really and truly values work. The person who claims they value teamwork but has to control every task the team undertakes, may really value control rather than teamwork.

To learn more about ourselves and what our actions are telling us, compete this next exercise.

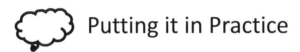 # Putting it in Practice

Values Exercise – Part 2: The Real World Test

Now that you have narrowed the values list down to 8 or fewer, we are going to test them in the real world. Your actions speak to your values with more clarity than your thoughts or intentions. List your highest order values on the worksheet below. Then jot down a few actions that would indicate some behaviors that would demonstrate the value in action. A few examples are provided to illustrate.

Then, in the next week, take 5 minutes at the end of the day to check times when you did something that exhibited that value. It may be the action you noted or a similar action. No matter what, give yourself the gift of honesty. This exercise is only for you.

Examples of Values and Actions

My Values	Examples of Actions that Demonstrate the Value	Week One						
		S	M	T	W	R	F	S
Health / Wellness	• Exercise • Prepare a healthy meal	✓		✓		✓	✓	
Excellence	• Taking time to improve something • Practicing a key skill		✓	✓		✓		
Creativity	• Time in a creative pursuit • Quiet time to dream	✓			✓	✓		
Friends / Family	• Saying no to other obligations to be with friends or family • Doing something nice for a friend, family member	✓	✓			✓	✓	✓
Helping Others	• Volunteer work • Doing extra work for a co-worker			✓		✓		✓

My Top Values		Week One						
		S	M	T	W	R	F	S
My Values	Examples of Actions that Demonstrate the Value							
	•							
	•							
	•							
	•							
	•							
	•							
	•							
	•							

4.3   A Values Based Perspective

Being able to clearly know and articulate your core values enables you to use them as a compass for both simple day-to-day decisions (Go to the kid's game or work an extra hour?) as well as those larger decisions (What type of work do I want to do?). An apt and often used image is to think of values as your "north star" or "true north" – referring to the enduring and fixed nature of values – and their ability to guide us, even in stormy seas, deep darkness or times of great confusion.

As your self-awareness becomes keener, you will begin to notice several things related to values:

1. You will feel a sense of unease when you are operating outside your value set. You might be unsettled or your intuition may be signaling that things are "not right".
2. Conversely, you will derive great inner satisfaction when you are working in ways that honor your core values. You feel light yet connected. You feel a deep sense of purpose and alignment.

The more you can tune into these internal signals, the more quickly you can recognize when you are in alignment with your core values and when you are not. And the earlier your ability to recognize those situations quickly, the speedier you can take action to course correct and drive to more alignment in your life.

A clear signal that your need to name and claim your personal values is when there is conflict in your life that seems almost impossible to reconcile. The conflict may be internal (your own decision making) or external (inability to reconcile with another person). When the conflict is thorny, emotional and long standing – chances are that competing values are at the root. Being able to discern the underlying values may not create an instant solution, but may enable the conversation to be centered on the issues that really matter – rather than petty differences or emotional rhetoric.

> "If we are to go forward, we must go back and rediscover those precious values - that all reality hinges on moral foundations and that all reality has spiritual control."
>
> Martin Luther King, Jr.

> The greatness of a man is not in how much wealth he acquires, but in his integrity and his ability to affect those around him positively.
>
> Bob Marley

Although the work of clearly articulating your core values may continue to deepen over time as your personal self-awareness grows, take some time now to list the five core values that you believe are the most important to you.

 Putting it in Practice

Values Exercise – Part Three: Identifying your Core Values

At the end of the week, review your tally sheet.

- What values do you consistently demonstrate?

- Which values did not get demonstrated on a daily basis? Why do you think that is so? Are these values that can be removed from your core list?

- Are there any values from the original list that should be added to your list, based on the actions you take, day in and day out?

- Based on your observations and analysis, list your top four core values.

My Core Values

1.

2.

3.

4.

4.4 Strengths

The second key element of your inner core is your strengths. You may or may not be able to clearly articulate them yet, but trust me; you have things that you are really very, very good at. Much better that the average, perhaps even stellar. In fact, you may be so good at them that you can't comprehend that others might struggle with them. These are the things that come naturally to you or that you learn easily. And as you practice them, progress is continual and almost effortless.

People's strengths are as individual as people themselves. Some strengths show up as skills that became evident in your schooling. Perhaps you were strong in math, science, art, writing or sports. Others become evident in the way you interact in the world – you may be very good at relationships or seeing the humor in things or problem solving. And others might be in how you organize your world – like being able to innovate or synthesize information or create detailed plans.

Knowing what your strengths are is only the first step. More importantly, you want to find ways to use your signature strengths daily. When you do, you'll find you are much more satisfied at the end of the day. This is because you are more productive and happier when working in your areas of strength. With focus, feedback and practice, you are able to continually improve your performance in this strength area. And you become even more productive and energized – and as a result get great results. It becomes a virtuous cycle – and in this cycle your inner core becomes even stronger and more resilient.

Chances are you can easily list many of the things that are challenge areas for you. We are taught, in our Western culture, to focus on what is wrong rather than what is right. If you brought home a report card with 2 A's, 3 B's and 1 D, it is likely that your parents (and by default you) spent

One we discover how to appreciate the timeless values in our daily experiences, we can enjoy the best things in life.

Jerome K. Jerome

You have power over your mind - not outside events. Realize this, and you will find strength.

Marcus Aurelius

more time focusing on the D (you area of weakness) than the 2 A's (your area of strength). In our culture, we spend much energy identifying and fixing our challenge areas and far too little cultivating our strengths.

We each will have some weaknesses that we need to focus on just enough so that they are not glaring liabilities. I am very ill at ease in large social events, far preferring an intimate conversation with one or two people, rather than two hundred. Yet it is a skill I've had to learn. I am not the life of the party – and that is not my goal. My goal is to get by without embarrassing myself or others. And that I can do!

As such, we can improve just enough in our areas of weakness so that we are not hindered by our lack of skill. Alternatively, we can find ways to compensate for our void. Perhaps others can do the thing at which you are not good – especially those that are good at that particular thing. We can design our life and our work so that it requires less and less of what we struggle with. I am reasonably good at math but horrible about attention to detail. I struggled with keeping the books for my business for years, hating every moment of it. And I would hate it even more when the mistakes I invariably made, would require hours of time to track down and correct. My life is better, my books are better and I am much happier now that I have someone who loves bookkeeping do my books.

There are two human tendencies that get in the way of being able to identify our strengths. The first is that our strengths come so easily and naturally to us, we can't imagine that the same thing does not happen with others. As such, we tend to underestimate our natural gifts. Secondly, many of us may lack the ability to accurately assess how others see and experience us – and as such, are blind to our strengths. These two tendencies are then magnified by cultural norms that focus on attention on what is weak or deficient, and

> *When you catch a glimpse of your potential, that's when passion is born.*
>
> Zig Ziglar

> *There is no passion to be found playing small - in settling for a life that is less than the one you are capable of living.*
>
> Nelson Mandela

train us to ignore what is brilliant and wonderful about us.

Just as true values are hard to identify, due to the fact they are so submerged in our psyche, strengths are hard to find because we've seldom focused on them. They are recognized by some of the side effects. When working in a strength area, we are:

- Extremely focused
- Find that time flies by
- Get good results without much effort
- Learn quickly
- Feel an inner sense of satisfaction
- Drawn to learning more

As you see in the following diagram, there is a virtuous circle when you are operating in a strength-based position.

The Strength Cycle

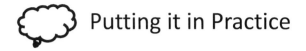 Putting it in Practice

Strengths Exercise – Part 1: Creating Your Personal Strengths List

To kick start the process of naming your strengths, spend some quiet time reflecting on these questions:

Take 15 to 30 minutes in a quiet place and reflect on these questions:

• What subjects did I excel at in school?

• What do others ask me to do on a regular basis, because I am good at it? Think about requests you get at home, work and in the community.

• List the 5 accomplishments that you are most proud of. What strengths did you use to make this happen?

• What are the top 5 strengths that you see in yourself?

Given the nature of our strengths, we often have an obstacle in self-identifying our own personal strengths. Because these gifts come easily to us, we can totally discount the fact that others may struggle. These are things that come naturally to us, as if by magic. As such, we don't see their uniqueness.

Asking others to identify the strengths they see in you is both enlightening and also affirming. The next exercise does just this – and I strongly encourage you to do this, even though it may feel a bit awkward.

Strengths Exercise – Part 2: Poll Those Who Know You Well

For this exercise, make a list of 10 people in your life who both know you well and whose opinion you value. Ensure that everyone on the list will be comfortable providing you with straightforward feedback. Now, ask those on your list to share their perceptions on your strengths. Generally, this works best when the individual has some time to think about it – so a request in writing (letter, email) works better than a conversation. You might set up your request in this way:

> *Dear (name):*
>
> *As a person who knows me well and whose opinion I value, I would like you to help me with a project I've undertaken. I am taking steps to better understand my unique and signature strengths. Once I've done that, I will be finding ways to incorporate more of those strengths in my day to day life and work.*
>
> *In your honest opinion, what are the things that you see that I do exceptionally well? What differentiates me from others you know? Where is it that I add unique value and do things in a way which are mine alone?*
>
> *How you format your response is up to you – it can be a bulleted list, a paragraph or two or a list of sentences. The most important thing is that you are honest with me.*
>
> *Thanks in advance for helping me get clarity about my strengths. I'd greatly appreciate a reply within the next week.*

Once you get your replies:

1. Compile them into one master list.

2. Read through them and highlight any responses or similar themes that you heard from more than one source.

3. Reflect on strengths that others noted, but that you did not list. Why might that be the case?

If this area of strengths intrigues you, you might want to do this optional exercise.

Optional Exercise: Complete a Strength Profile

StrengthsFinder

There are two strengths profile assessments that can provide helpful information about your strengths. The first is StrengthsFinder 2.0, which is a Gallop product based on the work of Marcus Buckingham. By purchasing the book, you will be provided an access code that can be used online to take the profile. The book can be purchased at most major bookstores or online at Amazon or Barnes & Noble. Gallop also has a strength profile for leaders, Strength Based Leadership, which works in a similar fashion.

The second option for a formal assessment tool is the Kolbe. The Kolbe A Index measures a person's instinctive method of operation (MO), and identifies the ways he or she will be most productive. It need only be taken once, since these innate abilities do not change over time. Kolbe offers a range of instruments, including assessments designed for youth. Kolbe A is delivered online. There is great support provided for those who have questions or would like help in interpreting their results.

4.5   Passion

The third element of your inner core is passion. Passion provides a powerful and unwavering source of energy.

Passions are as unique as you are. Some people are passionate about art, some about learning, some about fitness, some about social causes, and some about the outdoors.

Passions are much easier to identify than values or strengths, simply due to the energy factor. There is a burst of positive, clean energy when you are doing something you are passionate about. You look forward to eager anticipation the time you spend in your passion. You wake up early and can't wait to get started. You become absorbed in the activity and time appears to slow down or stop. You feel great and have a sense of accomplishment and positive energy, both during and after the activity.

Just like leaves, which are shed and then regenerate, passions can change over time – or at least be realized in a different way. A passion about being physically active may manifest itself differently in high school than it does at age 60. In high school you might have been an avid tennis player – and at age 60 you may love the game of golf. There are clearly some linkages – and most likely a core value about health or teamwork or physical activity or competition.

Please note that you may have strengths that are not passions – and passions that are not strengths. For example, I am good at math but detest doing lots of calculations and math related work. And I am passionate about music – but cannot sing a note nor play an instrument. As such, I find ways to outsource the math in my life (accountants, teaching assistants) and ways to bring music into my life (concerts and recordings). However, since they don't pass the test of being both a strength and a passion – they are not a part of my inner core.

A passion I do have is to help others learn. In college, I worked with youth and teenagers in the probation system. In my early career, I taught in early childhood settings. I then transitioned to learning roles in corporate environments and currently my business is built around helping people learn and grow. I get some of my greatest satisfaction from seeing others learn and benefit from our time together. One of my greatest joys is teaching at Purdue University. Teaching is a lifelong passion that has been realized in different ways over time – yet is a consistent element in all my life.

My mission in life is not merely to survive, but to thrive; and to do so with some passion, some compassion, some humor, and some style.

Maya Angelou

Passion is energy. Feel the power that comes from focusing on what excites you.

Oprah Winfrey

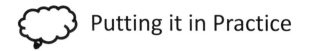 Putting it in Practice

Passion Exercise – Part 1: Uncovering Your Passion

The clue to passion is energy – that results in voluntary effort and a positive feeling. If you can't automatically name your passion (and many of us can't), you'll need to spend some time unearthing it, almost like an archeologist. There is still a flame of passion burning deep inside you – sometimes it takes a bit to uncover it from the rubble of your life.

- **Look around your house or apartment for clues.** What do you learn as you look around? Do your bookshelves groan with books? If so, what are the topics? Do you have an abundance of music? Of technology? Of sports gear? Of travel books? Of art? Is your house teeming with friends and family most of the time?
- **Where do you spend your free time?** When you have an hour, a day or a weekend to spend in any way that you want – what do you do with it? And if your life is so jam packed that you have no free time, what do you dream about doing?
- **What did you love as a child?** Picture yourself when you were 8 or 9 years old. It's the best Saturday ever. What are you doing?
- **Categorize your bucket list.** If you're a person that has created a list of things to do before you "kick the bucket" (or in your lifetime) – what categories constitute the majority of the items? It may be learning, helping others, relationships, giving back, adventure, travel. What themes are evident as you analyze your list?
- **Begin to monitor your personal energy.** Take note, through the day, the things that either energize you or conversely, sap your energy.

My Passions

1.
2.
3.
4.
5.

---

5 The Synergy of All Three

Knowing, and then leveraging, all three elements of your inner core: values, strengths, and passions, provides many benefits, as they all work together in synergy. Using a tree metaphor, your values are your roots: they hold you strong and nourish you. Your strengths are like a sturdy trunk – providing stature and structure. And your passions are like leaves, converting sunlight to energy.

Discovering each of the elements of your inner care may take some time and observation. Knowing is only the first step in creating a strong inner core. The most critical step is in using your inner core, day in and day out. You'll do this by:

- Ensuring that your daily actions align with your values;

- Finding ways to use your strengths in all you do;

- Finding ways to reduce the amount of time spent in areas of weaknesses;

- Consciously doing more and more of what you are passionate about.

There are no perfect circumstances in which our lives are always congruent with who we are and what we do well. But there clearly are people who are able to spend considerably more time in alignment with their core values, strengths and passions. They are in tune and aware. They shape circumstances to stay true to who they are and to enable themselves to bring their best forward. There are many others who are miserable – stuck in jobs they hate and relationships that drain them. I encourage you to be one of those people who has great clarity about who they are and who can draw from that, day in and day out, no matter what life throws at you, and manage to navigate the circumstances with grace and ease. I challenge you to complete the exercises in this chapter, do the reflective work, and build a strong inner core.

Passion is the genesis of genius.

Tony Robbins

Ability is what you're capable of doing. Motivation determines what you do. Attitude determines how well you do it.

Lou Holtz

Putting it in Practice

Final Exercise: Bringing it all Together

You've spent some time observing, thinking and reflecting on your values, strengths and passions. Make an inventory of them.

Values	Strengths	Passions	
			• What patterns do you see?
			• Circle the ones that you either manifest or get an opportunity to use on a daily basis.
			• What can you do to honor your values and use your strengths and passions more?

While you will continue to define your inner core over time, take a moment now to crystallize your best insights as to the elements of your inner core. I encourage you to create a summary version and keep it in a place where you see it frequently – on your desk, in your wallet, hanging on your refrigerator, on the dash of your car. Refer to it frequently – and continually explore how each element of your inner core is showing up on a day-to-day basis.

Name		
Date		
Values	Strengths	Passions

Additional Resources:

Buckingham, Marcus, and Curt Coffman. *First, break all the rules: what the world's greatest managers do differently*. New York, NY. Simon & Schuster, 1999.

Buckingham, Marcus, and Donald O. Clifton. *Now, discover your strengths*. New York: Free Press, 2001.

Loehr, James E., and Tony Schwartz. *The power of full engagement: managing energy, not time, is the key to high performance and personal renewal*. New York: Free Press, 2003.

CHAPTER 2
Leadership Starts on the Inside

1   Thinking Shapes Results

Now that you have better defined and are working increasingly from your inner core, we will continue to journey inward – starting with your "story" and then a bit deeper to your thoughts, feelings and beliefs. The reason is this: the more aware you are and the better you are able to manage what is happening on the inside, the better able you are to influence and guide what is happening on the outside. Managing yourself comes before leading others. Yet too often we are painfully unaware of what we think, feel and believe in a meaningful way. This unawareness means that the power that our thoughts, feelings and beliefs have to help us lead well remains untapped. It means that we are reactive rather than proactive. It means that we feel out of control and aren't sure why.

In this chapter, you'll start to explore the stories you tell about yourself. As you surface them, you'll discern if they are true and helpful – or inaccurate and detrimental. You'll learn how to create new stories, ones of possibilities that begin to shape the future you desire.

Whether you think you can or think you can't. Either way, you are right.

Henry Ford

1.1   We All Have a Story

As human beings, we are meaning making machines. **No matter what we experience, we assign meaning and significance to that event.** How we do that is shaped by our life experiences, our psychological makeup and our inner values and beliefs.

I suspect you've have the experience of being in the same meeting as someone else, hearing the exact same words and interacting with the exact same people. Yet after the meeting, you may be surprised at what the other person heard that you did not, saw that you did not, and intuited differently than you had. I often say that if there are six people in a meeting, there are six different meetings, each dependent on the person's view of the world, role, personality and disposition at the time.

Not only does each individual experience things differently, they also assign meaning based on what they believe happened. And those meanings turn into stories – often based on nothing more than a skeletal few observations and with meaning we assign and details we fill in.

I saw this vividly unfold in a van with seven women who were traversing over the mountains of southern India. The road had gotten bumpy. The driver spotted a local villager, pulled over, opened his window and had a rather lengthy conversation in the local language. Even though none of us knew this local language, we all observed with great interest the interaction. And at the conclusion of the exchange, there were seven different stories about the interaction, exactly one version for each person observing. One person was certain we were lost and the conversation was about directions. Another

We are what we think. All that we are arises with our thoughts. With our thoughts we make the world.

Buddha

The only person who can pull me down is myself, and I'm not going to let myself pull me down anymore.

C. JoyBell C.

speculated that the van had a mechanical problem and the driver was asking where a garage might be. Another insisted that it was about the conditions of the road and if a van of this size would be able to safely continue on. Another believed that this was someone known to the driver and they were reconnecting. The bottom line is – none of us knew – yet each of us took what we saw and heard and assigned meaning to it. The fact that the villager pointed to the road ahead convinced me it was about direction. Noticing that the interaction was friendly prompted the creation of the acquaintance story. Having just passed a mud slide in the road fueled the story about road conditions and navigability. There was a debate about whose story had the most credence – and each of us could point to all the reasons why. But the bottom line was clearly this: each one of us had made up a convincing story (to ourselves anyway) based on a little bit of information and a great amount of speculation.

And so it goes with our lives. We create stories all the time. About ourselves. About others. About situations. About motives. About reasons. About consequences. Some are harmless diversions and fleeting. But they can become invisible traps that give us a starring role in a story line that is unexamined for both accuracy and helpfulness.

We all have a story about our lives. In fact, we have multiple stories: about our work, our families, our interests, our health, our worldviews, and our lives. The story has a plot line, including how we got here and where we are going. We tell the story to ourselves – over and over, for months, years, and decades. With repetition, the stories become deeply engrained. And as they become engrained, we act them out. Perhaps unknowingly, but in concert with the story line. Author Jim Loeher says, "Our stories become our lives." This is so very true.

Your visions will become clear only when you can look into your own heart. Who looks outside, dreams; who looks inside, awakes.

C.G. Jung

I have been and still am a seeker, but I have ceased to question stars and books; I have begun to listen to the teaching my blood whispers to me.

Hermann Hesse, Demian

Here is an example of a story that affected my life for over 20 years. I attended a very small school in rural West Virginia, with only 23 students in my class. I was a happy child, in a solid family and I loved school. I had many neighborhood friends to ride bikes, explore the woods and play kick ball with. But I had one very special friend, Darryl, who was my best friend and with whom I spent countless hours with including sleepovers most weekends. For some reason, still unknown to me, that all changed when we got to the 7th grade and junior high. She didn't want to be my friend. I don't know why, but it was painfully clear. I was devastated, hurt and bewildered. I struggled to find new friends from the relatively small group of girls in my class. I did, but none were as special as my friendship with Darryl.

There was a story that I spun as a result, one that I didn't create this story with intention but it sprang to life like an ugly, pervasive and fast spreading weed. The story's main theme was that no one liked me. That turned to a story about being unlikable. This was in spite of the fact that I did have other friends – in fact many of them. Still deep within I harbored the story about not being liked, as the hurt from losing Darryl as a friend cut very deep.

I'd love to report to you that I matured and realized how foolish this story was by the end of my 7th grade year. That I shook off this story as unfounded and untrue. Not the case. This story haunted me through high school, college and up until my mid 30's. By that time it has calcified and become my truth.

And here is the thing you need to know about stories. They start when your brain pieces together various pieces of information, fills in lots of blanks and puts things in a coherent whole. And then they become solidified. Speculation begins to be seen as fact. You never question their truth. At times, the

Great men are they who see that spiritual is stronger than any material force—that thoughts rule the world.

Ralph Waldo Emerson

Thinking has become a disease….It is not so much that you use your mind wrongly, you usually don't use it at all. It uses you. That is the disease. You believe that you are your mind.

Eckhart Tolle

stories are deeply held within our psyche and can be virtually invisible. None the less, once you've created a story, you begin to act in concert with it. That means you act differently and invariably things happen that reinforce the story. Your brain says, "See. I told you so." And the story becomes even more entrenched, your actions more fully align with the story and it becomes a reinforcing loop.

In my case, I was hesitant to reach out and form deep relationships. I dreaded social situations. I felt awkward around others. I didn't invite others "in" to my life, as I feared they would find just how unlikable I was and I'd be hurt again. Silly, but true. I'm glad to report that I am "over" that story, but I will share that remnants still remain. As I meet new folks, I wonder if they will like me. Being liked is still important to me. Yet I am much more aware – and challenge myself when the story reemerges to discern fact from fiction.

The insidious thing for most people is that we are seldom aware of these stories and the power they exert on the life we lead. Since most of the story lives in our subconscious, it takes conscious effort to find and examine the story lines we are playing out.

Equally challenging is that in addition to the stories we have personally crafted, we internalize stories others tell about us. It may be our parents, our siblings, our extended families, our teachers or our friends and peers. Here are some I've seen reinforced over and over again in my family:

- The smart one
- The irresponsible one
- The one who is always late
- The one who is destined for great things
- The one who is too big for their britches
- The responsible one
- The wild child

The more tranquil we become, the greater is our success, our influence, our power for good.

James Allen

You've always been what you are. That's not new. What you'll get used to is knowing it.

Cassandra Clare

And as it is told, so it goes. We count on the family member with the assigned story to act in ways that are aligned with our story about them. When the irresponsible one makes a shift, we often can't see it. Yet we are always trolling for stories that reinforce our belief that they are irresponsible. And they become part of the family lore.

Here are two stories that you might recognize. Note how both individual may have had a similar background, yet the stories that evolved are dramatically different.

Story 1

"I came from a really poor family. It was tough, but we all worked together. We might not have had much, but we had each other. And I learned one thing — I can make it no matter what happens."

Story 2

"I'm one of those people who never get a break. My family was truly dysfunctional. I went to an inner city school where the teachers didn't care. I've had three marriages, all of which were disasters. I wish I had a different life — I just don't think it is likely to happen."

Changing our stories, no matter if they are of our own creation or those of others, is possible. In fact, it is needed if you wish to make real and meaningful change in your life. The first step is recognizing the stories that are shaping your life. Let's start to do that.

> *All that we achieve and all that we fail to achieve is the direct result of our own thoughts. You are today where your thoughts have brought you; you will be tomorrow where your thoughts take you.*
>
> James Allen

> *Until you make the unconscious conscious, it will direct your life and you will call it fate.*
>
> C.G. Jung

1.2   Our Stories Matter

We may not be aware of the fact that we've crafted these storiess and as a result may not even know the content of the story. None the less, they are there, just below the surface and they prompt us to take certain actions (or inactions) – which then lead to a result. A reinforcing loop then comes into play – as the results typically reinforce the story – which leads to more actions that support the story – which leads to the results that reinforce the story.

Let's take a simple example about Joe.

Joe grew up in a family where accomplishment was valued. A's on report cards were celebrated. Parents worked hard. Getting into a prestigious college was important. Joe's story goes like this: "Being the best is something I strive for. It's not okay to come in second. It may take hard work and extra effort, but it is worth it." Joe gets into the top tier college, lands the job with the best firm, and rises through the ranks quickly.

The story Joe tells about his life is focused on success and accomplishment. The right college leads to the good company leads to promotion after promotion. Greater accomplishment spills into his personal life – big house, the right neighborhood, and the most prestigious social circles. Joe's story about accomplishment continues to push him higher and higher into his job and community. Not only does this become Joe's story about himself, but it becomes the story others tell about Joe.

He who rules his spirit has won a greater victory than the taking of a city.

Jesus

In which areas of my life is it clear that I cannot achieve my goals with the story I've got?

Jim Loehr

1.3   Unexamined Stories

Joe's accomplishments are shaped by his story – and also continue to shape his story. This is fine, as long as this is the story, and consequently, the life that Joe really desires. The reality for Joe is that he always feels pressured to do more, to take on the next challenge. By any standard, he has accomplished much. Yet he enjoys little. His job is demanding and stressful. His social commitments seem hollow and more about what one "should do" than what he "wants to do". His large home and all the trappings consume his scarce free time and keep him captive in his high paying job in order to pay all the bills.

Our stories, in and of themselves, are benign. No matter what, as humans, we will have them. The heart of the question is: "Is the story about my life the story I want to live out?" In the light of day, many of our unexamined stories would be found to be either fundamentally untrue, unhelpful or off course.

Uncovering and examining your personal story provides you the opportunity to challenge the underlying assumptions that frame your story. In the previous example, Joe might challenge his assumption that he should strive to be the best at anything he attempts. He might reexamine his definition of success. He may be able to better define what is important to him versus what was important to his parents.

> *Only with self-awareness can we begin self-improvement.*
>
> Frank Moran

1.4   Rewriting Your Story

Once you've discerned and evaluated the story that you are seeking for yourself, you have the opportunity to rewrite the story into one that is aligned with your purpose, vision and goals. You can craft a story that propels you toward the future you would like to create. You can create a story that is healthy and life affirming.

Re-scripting your story requires that you know where you want to head and what you want your story to be. It requires a longer term view of the future and your ultimate purpose. It requires suspending doubt,

> *At the center of your being you have the answer; you know who you are and you know what you want.*
>
> Lao Tzu

fear and insecurity and silencing some of the voices of the past.

Rewriting your personal story is a deeply reflective and highly personal exercise. It is not easy; but it is worthwhile.

There are many reasons we begin with our personal story. First is that leadership is an inside out effort. Understanding yourself is job one. Secondly, while your personal story is complex, it is not nearly as complex as the story of your team, division or organization. Doing this work first enables you to then move to rewriting the story of your team or organization.

> *There are voices we hear in solitude, but they grow faint and inaudible as we enter into the world.*
>
> Ralph Waldo Emerson

2   Surfacing Themes

What do you believe about you?

The first step in this process is determining the story (or stories) you have about your life. Sometimes this can feel like searching for something in a dark basement without any illumination. At first, some shadowy shapes may emerge and over time, your story will be clearer and crisper.

Many people have multiple stories about their lives, but in general they tend to be about 5 key themes: Work, Family, Health, Happiness and Friendships. We will use these as a starting point. You may be a person who has an important part of their story in another theme, perhaps money, death, sex/intimacy, trust/integrity, parents, religion or spirituality, etc. If this is the case, write your current story about any additional themes that play a major role in your life.

Following is an exercise that may take several

> *Whatever the reasons, we do not pursue emotional development with the same intensity with which we pursue physical and intellectual development. This is all the more unfortunate because full emotional development offers the greatest degree of leverage in attaining our full potential.*
>
> Bill O'Brien

attempts. Your goal is to identify the story you currently are telling yourself. This exercise is for your eyes only, so give yourself the gift of honesty. Many people experience this process like the peeling of onion. They peel back one layer, revisit it, go deeper and ferret out a deeper insight. With time and effort, they are able to get to the heart of their current story.

Begin by thinking about these questions – and jotting down your thoughts. You need not answer ALL the questions – but read through them and respond to the ones that illicit interest or spark emotion in you.

Here are some questions that can guide you in discerning your current story. Don't feel as though you have to answer each question. Instead, use them as a way to provoke thought and exploration.

Theme	Questions to Ponder
Work	• What role does work play in your life? Is it a necessary evil? Take center stage? Provide joy and fulfillment? • How do you feel about the work you do? • What was the path that led you to the work you are doing? • How does work fit with your larger sense of purpose? • If you had the chance to rewrite your life story, what work would you choose to do? • If you had the financial freedom to work or not to work, what would you do?
Family	• What role does family play in your life? Is it a necessary evil? Take center stage? Provide joy and fulfillment? • How would you describe your relationship with key individuals in your family? Spouse or partner? Children? Parents? Extended family? • How connected do you feel with your family? Are there relationships that require attention or mending? • If you continue down the same path with your family, what is the likely outcome in 10 years? • What is the story you would like to tell about your family? • Is there anything about your current story about family that is not working for you right now?

Health	• How well do you take care of yourself? • What should you tell your doctor about your health? • What role does health play in your life? Is it a taking care of your health necessary evil? Take center stage? Something to worry about in the future? • What is the story you tell yourself about eating well? Exercising? Maintaining an appropriate weight? Taking time to rest and recharge? • If you continue your current story about health, what is likely to be the quality of your life in 10 years? 20 years?
Happiness	• How would you rate your level of happiness in the past six months? • What brings you happiness? • How often do experience happiness in your life? Why? • How do you feel about happiness? Do you see it as necessity, a luxury, self-indulgent or something that will happen later in your life? • If you looked back on your current life 10 years from now, would you be pleased at what you see?
Friendship	• What role do friends play in your life? • How would you describe the quality of your friendships currently? • How are friends important to you? How do you demonstrate to them that they are? • If you found yourself without friends, how would that impact your life? • Look at the patterns of friendships over the past 10 years. Are relationships deepening or declining? How have the types of friends and relationships changed over time? What would you change?

Area	Themes of My Story
Work	
Family	
Health	
Happiness	
Friendship	
Other:	
Other:	

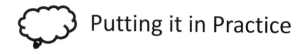 Putting it in Practice

Capturing your Current Story

You now have some beginning thoughts – and some rough notes. For this exercise, you are going to draft a current story about one of the areas you explored. The area that you write your current story about should be one that:

- Is vitally important to you

- Is one in which your current story is not working for you

For example, the previous exercise may have highlighted for you how vitally important your family is to you and at the same time sparked a realization that the way you are currently living your life does not reflect that. Or you may have realized that your story is that health is important to you, but that the hard reality is that you are 25 pounds overweight and can't recall the last time you had a good workout.

Be certain to write this out – there is an aspect to putting something in writing that forces clarity. The writing does not need to be perfect – but does need to be on a paper (or a screen) in some form.

Pick one area from your list. Reviewing the themes you surfaced, write your current story about that theme. Ensure that your story is either written in long hand or captured electronically. Attempt to write at least 3 paragraphs about the area you chose in a journal.

---

3 Fact or Fiction?

Once we begin to surface our stories – we can examine them more objectively. We can ask if they are really true. We can explore if they are helpful or hurtful. We can discern if they are aligned with our inner core and if they are serving us well.

We can use feedback to help us with this step. You can get feedback from a variety of sources: your own observations, from asking others, from reviewing the results you are getting, and from monitoring your own thoughts and emotions. Pay attention. Be aware. Process this feedback from your various sources as interesting and helpful data, providing clues on if your story is accurate or not. And remember that as you ask others for feedback that it is one person's "story" about you – which is infused with their own perceptions, filters and propensity to make meaning of things. Treat their comments as interesting and informative. At the same time keep in mind this is only one data point. However, with multiple data points, you can determine if there are patterns that you need to be aware of.

Review your story in an objective fashion. Often we find our stories are not true reflections of our lives or what we want our life to be.

A Real Life Example: A coaching client of mine, who is unhappy in his executive role, has a story about how he cannot do something different as he needs the income. When examined, his truth is that he has substantial savings, more than adequate savings for retirement and lives well below his means. Now his story is: "I have adequate financial resources, for now and the future. I can choose to do this job, as it adds substantially to my financial security. I can also choose to do something different and my family will still be adequately provided for."

Stories that are no longer serving you well can fall into several categories:

- **Pure Fiction**: Stories that either untrue now or have been untrue all along. They can be false negatives (I can't do anything right. I don't have time to exercise.) or false positives (I can't fail. I am the center of the universe. I'm the smartest person in the room.).

We search for happiness everywhere, but we are like Tolstoy's fabled beggar who spent his life sitting on a pot of gold, under him the whole time. Your treasure--your perfection--is within you already. But to claim it, you must leave the buy commotion of the mind and abandon the desires of the ego and enter into the silence of the heart.

Elizabeth Gilbert

- **Someone Else's Story:** You may be living out a story shaped by someone else. That someone else might be your parents or family, your religion, your teachers, your culture. These stories may have a "should" story line – "I should take the promotion even if it means relocating my family."

- **A Horror Story:** You may be trapped in a story that takes the reinforcing loop into a downward spiral. You have one set back, which changes your story to one of ill luck and incompetence. This leads to another failure and the story begins to define you.

> *It takes courage...to endure the sharp pains of self-discovery rather than choose to take the dull pain of unconsciousness that would last the rest of our lives.*
>
> Marianne Williamson

Review your story. How accurate is it? Are there parts of your story that are not true, or parts that no longer serve you well? Strike out parts that are not accurate. Highlight areas that you would like to craft a different story.

 ## Putting it in Practice

Rewriting Our Story

Now we are ready to rewrite our story – so that it encompasses our purpose, is more reflective of our current reality and leads us to actions that propel us toward that purpose. Our goal is to write personal stories that are true and also free us to be our best, that don't limit or keep us trapped in beliefs that don't serve us well. Remember, you can review and rewrite this story as often as needed.

Again, put pen to paper or fingers to keyboard and write a new story about the area you've chosen. As you write:

- Write in the first person (I have a wonderful family that I cherish.)

- Write in the present tense (My job is challenging and I love it.)

- State your truth, no matter if it is difficult to own. (I feel overwhelmed at work by the pace and demands by customers and my boss.)

- Write it in a way that is truthful, but frees you be be your best. (The amount of change at work is currently overwelming to me and my team. I know that we have the ability to find ways to manage things better, my role as leader is to help us do just that.)

Bonus Exercise: If you'd like to learn more about story and truth seeking, we recommend the book:

The Power of Story: Rewrite your Destiny in Business and in Life by Jim Loehr. Published by Free Press, 2007.

3.1   Thinking about Our Thinking

I suspect that the work on your story (or stories) has prompted many insights. I hope that one of those insights is beginning to see how much your story has shaped your current reality. And I hope you are beginning to see how much of that influence comes from your thought patterns (in this case your story) – most of which operate in your subconscious.

One of the most powerful concepts I've learned about creating positive change is that the fastest and most lasting path is to make a change happens when one starts on the inside. Once I am able to sharpen, shift, broaden or change my thinking about a situation, magic begins to happen. My actions change, my approach shifts and I get different results. Just the act of thinking about something in a new way propels me forward into the future I want to create. Changing behaviors, rather than thoughts, is the more arduous path, as my thinking continually gets in the way, sometimes sabotaging and a minimum getting in the way of sustained forward progress. It is a difficult concept to understand, but once you do, your life will never be the same.

It's a bit of a foreign concept to ask people to "think about their thinking". The world is busy, we

> *He who knows others is wise. He who knows himself is enlightened.*
>
> Lao-Tzu

have things to do. We are on the run and barely have time to breathe, let alone to slow down and think about our inner most thoughts. We believe it is doing that matters – and that reflecting, thinking and observing our inner state is frivolous, inconsequential and slows us down. Nothing could be farther from the truth.

Throughout the course of this book, I encourage you to do the counterintuitive. To slow down in order that you can go faster. To examine your inner thoughts so that you might realize better outer results. The exercises throughout the book will help you do that. You might also find ways to slow things down and create space for introspection. Perhaps it is a run or a hike in the woods or a quiet evening without the TV in the background. You might give Yoga or mediation a try. I just encourage you to put yourself in situations in which you have quiet, solitude and the ability to "hear yourself think". And then to keenly observe, without judgment what you discover.

First ponder, then dare.

Helmuth Von Moltke

 ## Putting it in Practice

In the next week, take a time out for reflection. For at least 30 minutes, spend some time alone doing something that calms and centers you. Breathe deeply. Quiet your mind. Just observe, without judgment. Notice what happens.

Some options include:

- A walk alone in a beautiful location (park, woods, lakeside)
- Sitting quietly in a spot that inspires you (park, museum, place of worship, gallery)
- A slower, more meditative yoga class
- Journaling
- Meditation

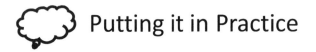 Putting it in Practice

Additional Exercises

Here are three additional ways which I encourage you to experiment with (and hopefully adopt) as you begin to go deeper into this work.

1. **AM pages**.

This practice comes from a The Artist's Way by Julie Cameron and goes like this. Every morning go to a quiet place with a basic no frills notebook and write three pages of "mind dump". Your goal is to capture what you are thinking, no matter how ugly, absurd, unspeakable, convoluted, jumbled or nonsensical. Just sit and capture, in writing, what is swirling inside your head. Do not organize. Do not censor. Continue on until you fill three full pages. Do this the next day and the next day and the next day. Always strive to fill 3 pages, as often the richest material comes just as you think you having nothing else to write. This is not an exercise in writing well. It is an exercise that allows you making your thinking visible. It will be chaotic, wandering, and include things that you would not share with others or aloud. As such, your notebook is for you and you alone. In fact, as a notebook gets filled – I typically shred it – and in the process let go of my old thinking and prepare for the new.

This exercise does many wonderful things for me. It enables me to be more conscious of my thinking. It allows me to get things out that have been swirling around. It allows me to acknowledge the difficult things in my life. It enables me to see patterns and themes. It lightens me. It provides perspective and grounding. It always provides clarity when I most need it. All this for an investment of 15 minutes.

2. **Meditation or Yoga Practice**

Finding a way to incorporate meditation or yoga into your daily or weekly routine is another great way to build the habit of mindfulness and presence into our lives. You may find yoga or meditation classes or groups in your local community. Many of them will have options for beginners. I find that learning something new is better with a teacher. If you enjoy learning alone or don't have access to a class, you'll find many books, videos and audio recordings that can help guide you.

3. Slow the S-R Chain

Slowing the **S-R** chain is a simple and powerful habit you can learn and use to both uncover your thinking and also to immediately gain better long-term outcomes. As a child, your parents may have taught you to count to 10 when you were angered –and that is this concept in a nutshell. In this model the "S" stands for stimulus, the "R" for response.

We all are triggered by a multitude of events daily (the **S**). The stimuli may be positive, negative or neutral. For this exercise we will ignore the more neutral (such as minor annoyances or a pleasant moment) and focus on stimuli that provoke more intense emotion within you. It may be a troublesome email, a driver that cuts us off on the freeway, a team member that disappoints you. It also might be a friend sharing deeply about an emotional topic, being profoundly struck a thing of beauty or something unexpected that tickles your funny bone.

When you encounter a **s**timuli that triggers a more intense emotional **R**esponse, simply lengthen the time between the event and your reaction to that event. While your parents said to count to 10 in the hopes you wouldn't hammer on your sibling, in adult life you choose the amount of time. For some situations, it may be milliseconds, just enough time to squelch that flash of anger and to avoid saying something regrettable. Or you may ask for time to consider something overnight. Other tougher situations may require longer.

In that time breathe, consider your ultimate best outcome and respond with thoughtful actions grounded in your highest intentions. The key here is to pause rather than plow through and then to ask yourself these questions: "What is my highest intention in this situation?" followed by "How might the actions I take most likely make that happen?"

In the next week, begin to notice your emotional reactions. They may range from anger to delight, from dismay to joy, from confusion to clarity. When you feel that emotional tug in your stomach, stop, notice and determine the next best step. Do this with both positive and negative emotional reactions. At the end of your weeklong experiment, journal about your insights.

Suspending Disbelief

If you are anything at all like me, if this is the first time you are thinking about your thinking – you are skeptical. Perhaps deeply skeptical. I understand. I was too. In fact, as I was introduced to these concepts over

15 years ago, I had a difficult time even being able to conceptualize them. Over time, I've worked with them and believe I am only barely tapping into the power of my stories, my thoughts and my beliefs. So I encourage you to suspend disbelief and do the exercises. Observe. Notice. See what you discover. You may have a shift in thinking – and then belief and find the results you get are dramatically altered.

> *The curious paradox is that when I accept myself just as I am, then I can change.*
>
> Carl Rogers

3.2   Better Leadership

One of the paradoxes of leadership is that most often others know you better than you know yourself. Others see where you shine and where you struggle. They quickly learn your idiosyncrasies and hot buttons.

Leaders that are self-aware have conquered job one. A quote that I like states: "I've met the person that is the most difficult to lead, and it is me." Until you have the skill and discipline to know yourself deeply, understand what moves you and have the ability to move yourself to a better place, you are ill equipped to do that for a group.

Leaders that are self-aware are comfortable with both their strengths and their challenge areas. They know what motivates them. They garner trust because they show up, day in and day out, in ways that authentic and credible.

> *The most influential person who will talk to you all day Is you. You should be very careful what you say to you.*
>
> Zig Ziglar

I encourage never to stop on your quest to know yourself deeply and meaningfully. Self-awareness is a skill, so like other skills it takes time and practice to develop. Pause and reflect regularly. Build a daily practice of journaling, quietude or meditation in which you explore your beliefs, thoughts, feelings, actions and results – and in that order. Find ways to get feedback from others as tool to help you see things that you currently cannot. Watch for trends and patterns. Overtime you develop both knowledge and acceptance, and the strength that comes from a rock solid assessment of who you are and who you are not. And remember that you are a living, breathing, growing, adaptive organism. You are dynamic and as such, there is never an "answer", there is only the best observation you can make in the current time. Enjoy the journey inward and marvel at how that journey changes your outer world in ways that are wonderful and unimaginable.

● ● ●

Watch your thoughts, they become your words.
Watch your words, they become your actions.
Watch your actions, they become your habits.
Watch your habits, they become your destiny.

-Lao Tzu

● ● ●

Additional Resources:

Bryan, Mark A., Julia Cameron, and Catherine A. Allen. *The artist's way at work: riding the dragon*. New York: William Morrow, 1998.

Delaney, Senn. *The human operating system: an owner's manual*. 4th ed. Long Beach, CA: Senn-Delaney Leadership Consulting Group, 2008.

Gardner, Andrea. *Change your words, change your world*. London: Hay House, 2012.

Loehr, James E.. *The power of story: change your story, change your destiny in business and in life*. New York: Free Press, 2008.

Lore, Mary J. *Managing thought think differently. think powerfully. achieve new levels of success*. New York: McGraw-Hill, 2010.

CHAPTER 3

We Not Me

Moving from Me to We

As you have followed this guide, you have spent much time focused inwardly. Now is the time we take that knowledge and self-awareness and turn it outward. What you have learned about yourself is invaluable – but the ultimate task is to use that knowledge to achieve something of value for and with others. And as a leader, achieving something of value, by design, means moving from a focus on "me" to "we".

1   Defining Leadership

Pat Murray has the best definition of leadership that I've found:
"Leading is mobilizing the energy and talents of others in pursuit of a worthwhile cause."
There are several reasons I like this definition:

- The focus on a worthwhile cause. By definition, this precludes those who use charisma or force to achieve nefarious outcomes or outcomes that are self-serving.

- The idea of mobilizing – rather than demanding, dictating, forcing, or coercing. This implies that followers follow willingly and is the mark of a true leader.

Many people listen, but never hear, some hear only what they want to hear. A few people but listen, because they want to hear, and then they understand, they needed to listen.

Norbert Harms

- Mobalizing energy indicates that people have a reason to follow. There is little energy if individuals do not feel purpose, possibility and potential in a direction.

- Mobilizing talents implies that individuals are using their skills and abilities, in a cooperative way, toward that better future.

Many people confuse power with leadership. And leadership certainly depends on a powerful skill: to help others see a better future (the worthwhile end) and then desire to personally engage in creating that future. Leadership is not conferred by title, position or force – it is given to those whom others believe are worth following.

"As for the best leaders, the people do not notice their existence. The next best, the people honor and praise. The next, the people fear; the next, the people hate."
- Lao Tse, 604-531 B.C., Chinese philosopher and founder of Taoism from the Tao Te Ching

I learned early (and painfully) in my work with facilitating groups that my results were extraordinarily better when I was able to let go of "me" and focus on the "we". It was easy to focus on "me" – were we following "my" agenda, were they listening to "me", learning from "me". My best sessions are those in which I and able to flip it – and see myself as merely a conduit to help the group do what it needs to do. I can move managing to leading, from pontificating to listening, from directing to guiding, from pretense to authenticity, from telling to exploring, and from a pre-defined outcome to a place of infinite and

It's not about how smart you are—it's about capturing minds.

Richie Norton

Think twice before you speak, because your words and influence will plant the seed of either success or failure in the mind of another.

Napoleon Hill

unexpected possibility more fluidly in this state. The group is more engaged and then the work is theirs. We get better results – all because I move from focusing on "me" to focusing on "we". The same is true with leadership.

You may be saying, if that is true, why have we spent so much time on self-awareness? Here's why:

- **Conscious and aware leaders operate from a more grounded space.** You've most likely worked with or for a leader whose perception of themselves was nowhere near the true reality. If so, you know that these leaders are less credible, less effective and often create unintended negative consequences as a result of their lack of awareness. Hopefully you've worked with leaders who were deeply conscious and aware of who they were, how they showed up and were conscious of their leadership footprint. Operating with a keen knowledge of the current reality is a position of strength – and knowing yourself well provides you the internal guidance to navigate better. Think of the metaphor of driving on a clear sunny day with great visibility contrasted with a drive in dense fog. Clear sunny days are always better.

- **Being aware of your strengths enables you to use them to good advantage as you lead a group forward.** Good at planning – then plan away. Good at motivating – use it. Good at diffusing conflict – step in when relationships fray. This is not the time to downplay your strengths. With deep self-awareness, you know where you shine and can use those skills and abilities for a good end.

A leader has no ego, but is followed by many egos, who get smaller, and smaller, and disappear.

Norbert Harms

Every leader needs to look back once in a while to make sure he has followers.

Unknown

- **Being aware of your challenge areas enables you to find ways to mitigate them.** Bad at planning- delegate it. Horrible at motivating – find ways that you can do this in your own style. Awful in conflict situations – unearth your trigger points and develop strategies around them. Being aware that you have blind spots and trouble areas helps you to navigate the times that require them more skillfully.

- **The process of becoming aware causes you to seek feedback.** As you get more comfortable with both your strengths and challenge areas, you'll most likely find that you are much more open to having others provide you candid and helpful feedback. That feedback is clearly a gift, a way to see yourself through other's eyes. A way to better understand how you impact others. A way to see what you need to do more of, what you need to do less of and what is just fine exactly the way it is.

Remember that self-awareness does not mean self-focused. Our goal here is not self-absorption or narcissism – it is being about know yourself well so that you can, almost effortlessly, use that self-awareness in pursuit of the group goal. An apt metaphor is that of the dance, who diligently trains and is deeply conscious of her body and abilities – so that she can use that knowledge in service of the art. She has spent much time practicing in front of the mirror, her instructors have helped her see how to hold her arms and move her legs, she knows exactly what her leaps and turns feel like, inside and out. Yet as the best dancers step on the

What first separates a leader from a normal human being? A leader knows who they are as a human being.

Stan Slap

If you wish a general to be beaten, send him a ream full of instructions; if you wish him to succeed, give him a destination, and bid him conquer.

Augustus William Hare
&
Julius Charles Hare

stage, all that deep self-awareness underpins, but does not dominate the performance, for the focus of the performance is the audience.

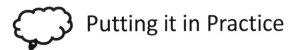 ## Putting it in Practice

Focusing Outward

In the next week, consciously seek to let go of focusing on yourself as you participate in or lead meetings. To do this, take a few moments before the meeting to visualize the outcome you would like to enable. During the meeting, let go of thoughts that are self-centered, such as: "I wonder what they are thinking about me." Or "I need to win this point." When you find yourself wandering back into a focus on you, gently push your attention outward to the group. Ask things like: "I wonder what other people think about this." Or "What do I notice about this discussion." Take a few minutes after each meeting to jot down your observations and thoughts.

2   Spotlight on You

Leaders need to recognize that merely by the act of stepping up or by being put in a position of leadership, ripple effects immediately occur. People watch you closely for cues and clues. As such, they react to what you do and say, and what you don't do and say. They try to guess what your motives are, what pleases you, where your hot buttons are. It is this reason that "role modeling" is so important.

When I worked for many years in a manufacturing plant, I became amused to see how quickly, tangibly and naturally this occurred. Over that time I saw several plant directors come and

> *Remember the difference between a boss and a leader; a boss says "Go!" - A leader says "Let's go!*
>
> E.M. Kelly

go. It was a fascinating exercise to see what the plant managers and supervisors did when a new one arrived. If the new director wore polo shirts, within a week all the plant leaders did the same. As a new director arrived that wore ties, magically ties reappeared into wardrobes. Note that there was not a directive. The new leaders did not ask others to dress like him. Instead, people watched and mirrored.

As a leader, it is important to remember that "every action is a speech". You are the ultimate role model and your words, actions, body language and decisions are scrutinized for clues and cues relentlessly. This quotes sums it up nicely:

People hear what you say.
People see what you do.
Seeing is believing.

When your words and actions are congruent and when you consciously choose to role model what you want mirrored in the organization people are more likely to move forward in the way you intend. When you recognize that those you lead are scrutinizing your actions – and will take action as a result of what they interpret – you choose words and actions carefully and consider the formal and informal, verbal and nonverbal messages you are sending.

And remember – it is what is done as well as not done. What you don't ask about, don't focus on, fail to mention sends the signal that this is not important. People listen for what is said and what is unsaid. The watch for what is focused on and what is ignored. Don't fall into the trap of delegating something important without following up, as this signals disinterest. Avoid unstated

A leader leads by example, whether he intends to or not.

Unknown

The key to successful leadership today is influence, not authority.

Ken Blanchard

assumptions; far better to be clear about your expectations than to let others guess and make things up. Because, by their nature, they will indeed make things up.

This all becomes much easier with deep self-awareness. Good Leaders are authentic – there is no pretense – but there is choice. They ask: What action can I take, in alignment with my values that helps the group I am leading move forward in a positive way?

 # Putting it in Practice

Exercise: Your Leadership Inner Core

Review your inner core from Chapter One. Look at it through a leadership lens. Distill your inner core into your leadership core. What values do you embrace in your work? What strengths do you bring to the task at hand? What are you passionate about in your work?

My Leadership Values	My Leadership Strengths	My Leadership Passions

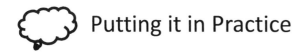 Putting it in Practice

What is your leadership story?

Find some quiet time to reflect on your leadership. Write it out then review it. Is it true? Is it helpful? Is it who you want to be?

Now craft a story of the leader you aspire to be. Write it in the present tense, even though this is a future vision.

 Putting it in Practice

Ask at least three people for their candid feedback about your leadership strengths and challenges. I'd suggest asking a customer, a direct report and a peer. If you want to ask more consider asking your boss (or a previous boss), a fan (someone who really likes you and your work) and an advisory (someone who you've disagreements and differences with). Ask them:

- How they would describe your leadership style

- What they see as your strengths

- Where they see you challenged

- One suggestion on a way you could grow your leadership ability

As you review the feedback, look for common themes and trends. Review this feedback with your description of your leadership. How self-aware are you? What did they see that you were unable to? How can this feedback make you a better leader?

3   Lead? Manage? Both?

People take great pains to differentiate between leading and managing. In this section, we will explore the differences. But before we do, I want to be clear about my beliefs about this distinction:

- This is not an either / or discussion. Leaders must manage and managers must lead. The proportion of time engaged in either may vary according to responsibilities, current demands or personal makeup of the individual.

- One is not better than the other. There are times leadership is called for and other times when management is needed. Discerning what is needed when though and moving into that mode though, is the hallmark of good leadership.

> *Leading is mobilizing the energy and talents of others in pursuit of a worthwhile cause.*
>
> Pat Murray

- There is a fine line between them both. We paint these two approaches as black and white, when in reality they are shades of grey. It is easier to see the differences in the extremes; yet most days leaders are in the middle, doing a bit of each.

So what is the difference between managing and leading? The following chart sums it up quite nicely.

Manage	Lead
Improves existing ways	Finds new ways
Maintains	Innovates
Focus on process	Focus on people
Eye on bottom line	Eye on the horizon
Optimizes resources within the current way	Unleashes energy for the new way
Does things right	Does the right thing
Technical or process focus	Conceptual focus

As a general rule of thumb, in our traditional, hierarchally organized institutions, one manages more in the lower level roles (team leader, supervisor, manager) and leads more as they progress though the organization (director, vice president, executive). Very often, you see this as the depiction of that transition.

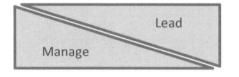

(lower level) Position (higher level)

Each move upward then, challenges those in the new role to give up what they did best in the previous role. Some can do this, others cannot. And those that cannot earn the term "micromanagers", for instead of unleashing the talent and energy of others, they stifle it by their desire to control all aspect of the outcome. Those that excelled at technical and process capabilities find that as their breadth of responsibility increases, their technical depth, quite naturally, does not extend that far. This forces a reliance on leadership skills, and for too many, this is the first true test of these capabilities.

I see a different picture today – one in which the shift between leading and managing is more seamless, which is driven by the situation and not by the position. Where people at all levels can lead, when needed, and where leaders at the highest level develop a comfort with that. And the paradox is that this inversion, or pushing down of leadership, will require the top leaders to not only lead better, but also to manage better. For this calls for an organization and optimization of resources – exactly what managers do well.

Authority without wisdom is like a heavy axe without an edge, fitter to bruise than polish.

Anne Bradstreet

Situations

Manage

(lower level) Position (higher level)

Example is not the main thing in influencing others. It is the only thing.

Albert Schweitzer

Today's environment calls for much more leadership at lower and lower levels of the organization. There are several reasons for this, all compelling. The world is so dynamic and fast paced that what we do know (and hence manage) is diminishing quickly. When the life cycle of products was measured in decades, organizations could become a well-oiled "machine", pumping out goods and services faster and cheaper, with a great need for managers that ensured that the process operated as smoothly as possible. Today, products and services generally have a shorter shelf life – and innovation, reinvention and adapting are the norm. Stability is hard to find.

 # Putting it in Practice

Where do you spend your time?

In the next two weeks, keep an accounting of where you spend your time. Jot down the activity you are engaged in and the percentage of the time that was spent leading and managing. Once you have two weeks' worth of data, step back and not the patterns you see. Do you rely on one more than the other? Were there times you failed to lead but should have? Are there situations in which you are providing leadership, but that require a bit more structure and "management"? What would the ideal balance be for you? What steps might you take to move that way? I've included a few examples to guide you.

Date	Activity	Leadership Actions	Management Actions	Percentage Breakdown of Lead to Manage	Observations
Monday, July 18	Planning meeting for Project XYZ	Focused the group on the larger vision	Ran through the project plan and next week's deliverables	50/50	Vision discussion helped with focus.
Monday, July 18	One on one session with direct report	Listened to career goals.	Explained my expectations for the negotiation they are responsible for.	25/75	Was able to find ways to use this assignment to develop needed skills.

Monday, July 18	Status Update meeting with my Boss	Asked clarifying questions around external events	Reviewed my team's work plan for the next 6 months.	75/25	Boss was more open to questions than I anticipated.
Monday, July 18	Team meeting	Surfaced team frustration with client ABC.	Put in place a plan to deal with client ABC.	60/40	Once we talked about it, the plan became evident.

Date	Activity	Leadership Actions	Management Actions	Percentage Breakdown of Lead to Manage	Observations

4   Your Final Challenge

You Must Remember that Me is not We

There is one final thought I want to leave with you as you make the transition from "me to we". That is this notion that no one else looks at the world just like you do, thinks just like you do, or has experienced the world just as you have. It is easy to fall into thinking that what we experience, see, hear, or interpret is universal. I can assure you that it is not.

We all fall prey to this phenomena; some more so than others. I am struck by the many times as we do assessment work with teams that people are awestruck by this sudden realization. They see the world as black and white; others see a rainbow. They process information in a linear fashion; others more circuitously. They are focused on tasks; others on people. They process information slowly and methodically; others in a flash. All the ways in which we vary presents the leader with a multitude of thinking styles, cultural traditions, worldviews and values.

There are several implications of these multiple realities that are important for leaders to understand. First, you must understand that there is no ONE single way of thinking, no one right answer, no one single perception. The sooner you reconcile yourself to the fact that the world looks very different, all according to your perspective, the better. As such, the second implication is the better you can understand those varying perceptions of your key stakeholders, the better. You have stakeholders up, down, in, out and across

You do not lead by hitting people over the head. That's assault, not leadership.

Dwight D. Eisenhower

The quality of a leader is reflected in the standards they set for themselves.

Ray Kroc

your organization. As a leader, your job is not to agree or disagree with these perceptions, but to understand them enough to guide your decision making.

In fact, you'll come to realize the fact that no one else thinks like you or sees the world like you do and that this is a good thing. There have been two people with whom I've had amazing work experiences with – and they are both very different than I am. In both instances we have created amazing results, but we've done so because together we were more whole than separate. It is easy to, when working with someone with different mindsets, approaches or ways of thinking, become annoyed, frustrated and conflicted. If your mindset is that Different = Bad, you are destined to be mired in conflict and constrained by your own limitations. If your mindset is Different = Better, you can leverage those differences into something of value. Someone said it well when they said: "Together we have a whole brain."

> *Nothing so conclusively proves a man's ability to lead others as what he does from day to day to lead himself.*
>
> Thomas J. Watson

 Putting it in Practice

Valuing Diversity

Name thee people you work with regularly that are "different" than you.

1.

2.

3.

Can you quantify the ways in which they are different?

What do they bring that you lack?

Do you see this as an annoyance or hindrance or as a source of energy and wholeness?

5 Diversity is the Norm

Leading people in past decades has been easier. Not only was the pace of change slower, but chances are you would be leading individuals who were more like you than not. They most likely grew up in the same country you did, maybe even the same area. Their values most likely were congruent with yours. In some industries, you may have shared gender (most likely male), religion (most likely Christian) and age (most likely born in a similar era).

Today you are more likely to have a team that is more dissimilar than similar. You most likely face:

- Up to four generations
- Men and women
- A rainbow of races, countries of origin, languages and upbringings

Those are the things on the surface. Under all that, you'll have a rich variety of thinking styles, worldviews, beliefs and experiences. Those who fail to be able to understand, honor, respect and leverage those differences most have increasingly limited potential. There are few places on this globe that are homogeneous. Those that have a "one size fits all" mentality that implies you must be like me to succeed will be faced with a severely constrained talent pool, disimpassioned workers and continual frustration with others. Those that are open, respectful and honor those differences have the opportunity to create teams that work well across the globe, who can tackle big challenges and who use those differing perspectives to shape their products and services. My money is on them.

> *A good leader is a person who takes a little more than his share of the blame and a little less than his share of the credit.*
>
> John C. Maxwell

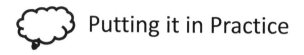 # Putting it in Practice

Find a way to immerse yourself in another culture (see possible options below). As you do, go into the experience with openness and not judging. Reflect on what you've experienced, seen and learned. Asses your level of comfort with people who are different than you. What can you do to continue to learn and grow in this area?

Possible options:

- Travel to a different country or region and experience it like a "local"
    - Rent an apartment or bed & breakfast, rather than a hotel, when you travel.
    - Use public transportation. As appropriate, strike up conversations.
    - Walk and wander. Observe. Get off the beaten path and "tourist" venues.

- Attend a church or religious service that is different than yours. Read or research it before you go.

- Volunteer to teach English to someone for whom English is a second language.

- Make friends with folks from different cultures. Have them share stories and traditions.

- Spend time in an environment that is very different than yours and pushes you to the edge of your comfort zone.

Additional Resources:

Bennis, Warren G., and Joan Goldsmith. Learning to lead: a workbook on becoming a leader. 3rd ed. New York: Basic Books, 2003.

Cashman, Kevin. Leadership from the inside out becoming a leader for life. 2nd ed. San Francisco, CA: Berrett-Koehler Publishers, 2008.

Depree, Max. Leadership is an art. New York: Doubleday, 1989.

Eblin, Scott. The next level what insiders know about executive success. Mountain View, Calif.: Davies-Black Pub., 2006.

Greenleaf, Robert K. Servant leadership: a journey into the nature of legitimate power and greatness. New York: Paulist Press, 1977.

Kouzes, James M., and Barry Z. Posner. The leadership challenge: how to get extraordinary things done in organizations. San Francisco: Jossey-Bass, 1987.

CHAPTER 4
Clarity: Envisioning a Better Future

1   Clarity is Important

As a leader, you are faced with the most
dynamic, changing world history. The number of
options and choices you can make is virtually
unlimited. You have access to more information and
more markets – all within relatively easy reach. There
is great opportunity, but there is also confusion,
complexity and ambiguity. The path forward is not
likely to be well marked.

The good news is that everything is more fluid
today – so taking advantage of opportunities and
charting a new path has never been more needed or
expected. Leaders who can find ways to capitalize on
these factors and who are willing to chart new territory
will thrive.

The bad news is that setting direction is harder
than ever. Long-term planning has been replaced by
scenario planning with a 3 year time horizon. Charting
a course for 10 or 15 years is impossible, given the
amount and pace of change. And the more uncertain
the environment, the more the people you lead look to
you for reassurance and direction.

In this chapter, you'll begin the work that will
enable you to manage both the opportunity and the
challenge. You'll explore how to define the future you
want to create – first for yourself and then for your

> *To the person who does
> not know where he wants
> to go there is no favorable
> wind.*
>
> Seneca

team or organization. In later chapters, you will learn how to create fluid plans so that you and those you lead can begin to make progress. Your outcome is NOT a 10 year plan. Instead it is envisioning the desired state, charting the direction you want to take and defining the next steps that move you forward.

2   A New Way of Thinking

Many people in many organizations across many industries are waiting, and waiting and waiting some more. They are waiting for definitive direction from the top. The want the big plan; the one that is both brilliant and crystal clear. They desire leaders who have all the answers and who make all the right calls. What they really want is someone who creates a safe and known world for them. They are relying on others to show them the way; to save them.

I've yet to see either an organization or a leader that was able to deliver on that expectation. And the chances of that occurring are getting slimmer every day. As the world becomes more dynamic, more ambiguous, and more complex, the reality is that there is no one person who is going to have all the answers and be able to create a sound 10 year plan.

There is another way. A way in which you ask what you would like to create and then get clarity on the few next steps it takes to move in that direction. You are not able to map the entire journey, but you trust that once you know where you are headed, you will be able to find the way, adjust course as needed and continue to make progress.

A leader's role is to raise people's aspirations for what they can become and to release their energies so they will try to get there.

David Gergen

The beauty is that through disappointment you can gain clarity, and with clarity comes conviction and true originality.

Conan O'Brien

2.1   Everyone Can Dream

Let's clear up two things: everyone can dream; having a "vision" is not just for the top brass or the futurists. And secondly, that vision does not have to be huge or world changing – it can be something meaningful to you and the individuals you lead.

It's easy to lose sight of this when we live in a society that places much value on "doing" rather than "dreaming." I recall being chastised as a child for daydreaming too much. I'm certain that I am not alone. Remember those childhood days, when imagination ran rampant? It was fun and it was easy.

As adults, we tend to look outside ourselves for direction. There is great hope that the top leader(s) of the country or company or non-profit will have the "vision." And not only the vision – but a BHAG – a big hairy audacious goal.

Relinquishing vision setting to others means others are framing your life and your future. I believe everyone can create clarity about their future and the future of the group they lead – and with practice, we get better at both dreaming and then making that dream a reality.

> *If you can dream it, you can do it.*
>
> Walt Disney

2.2   Creating is more than the Arts

We see music, art and sculpture as the traditional providence of creating. Creating is much broader than the arts though. Entrepreneurship is a supreme act of creating, as is intrepreneurship. You can create amazing customer service, an innovative product, a breakthrough process, a high performing team, a new service or business offering. On a personal level, you might create rich relationships, a living space with your special touch or a meaningful career.

> *That inner voice has both gentleness and clarity. So to get to authenticity, you really keep going down to the bone, to the honesty, and the inevitability of something.*
>
> Meredith Monk

Without a doubt, we create our lives, one day at a time. The life we create can be one that we truly want, our own unique, one of a kind, only for us type of life. Or it can be a "me too" life, one in which our focus is on doing the "should" and fitting the mold we believe others have shaped for us.

When we come to believe that everyone can envision something worth bringing into the world and that we have the ability to create that which we have envisioned – we open a world of possibility.

3 Step 1: Envisioning

The very first step of the creative process is "seeing" it – no matter what "it" is. Once you begin to see it, you can create it. This is where we need to tap into the imagination we had as children. In this part of the creative process, you do not need to know the "how." Trust that you will be able to figure that out. Getting too practical in this initial phase only leads us to recreating the current reality or dismissing your vision as unreachable. This is a position of resignation and of defeat. Trusting that if you can "see it" you can then "do it" is a leap of faith. Yet we can find example after example of those who have done just that. We suffer much more from cynical realists than from inspired dreamers.

Many great inventors and innovators like Steve Jobs, Thomas Edison, Henry Ford, and Walt Disney had the ability to envision. They did not allow themselves of being limited by the possible. While these examples represent individuals who were extraordinary at creating new possibilities – I suspect that you can name many others that you know personally, who

> *Destiny is not a matter of chance, but of choice. Not something to wish for, but to attain.*
>
> William Jennings Bryan

> *I continue to be drawn to clarity and simplicity. 'Less is more' remains my mantra.*
>
> Stephane Rolland

have envisioned and created something special. It may be a teacher that manages to create a classroom environment that excites students about learning. It may be someone in your organization that has created a new product or service and made it a reality. It may be someone at the gym that far surpasses what they "should" be able to do based on their age or ability. It may be a neighbor who has created a business or a non-profit for a cause they hold dear.

For right now, we are going to operate in a space of possibility. We are going to focus on what could be rather than what is. This is the space for visioning. Once you have a vision, plans will come. Trust that this will happen. Just not at this stage.

In this chapter, you'll learn some basic principles about creating clarity. The exercises will walk you through a step by step process. Know that you will get better with the creative process over time. As such, get comfortable with the doubt and uncertainty you will encounter and the awkwardness of your initial attempts.

The empires of the future are empires of the mind.

Winston Churchill

3.1   Seek Inspiration

Clarity is the counterbalance of profound thoughts.

Luc de Clapiers

Crafting your own script rather than playing out someone else's, creating amazing outcomes at work, bringing that new venture to life – all require inspiration. Creative people are always scanning, always questioning, always exploring. Find ways to actively seek the inspiration you need. If you are launching a new company or product, observe what others are doing. Look across industries for ideas that could be adapted. If you are creating better ways to do things at work, take lessons from disparate places. What happens in a fast food chain? A pit crew? A supermarket?

In addition to scanning the environment and nurturing an insatiably curious mind, seek out others who inspire you. Surround yourself with people who are positive and who understand your desire to stretch yourself. They will not only encourage you, they will be role models and roadblock removers.

Finally, the creative mind works best at play and when rested. Ensure you take some downtime. Find things you love to do, outside of your professional life and pursue them with zest. Find time to laugh, relax, swing in the hammock, or play games with a 3 year old. It seems a paradox, but taking time out to do these things can make our work ultimately speed up.

> *A leader has the vision and conviction that a dream can be achieved. He inspires the power and energy to get it done.*
>
> Ralph Lauren

3.2   Build on your Inner Core

As the vision of what it is that you want to create begins to take form, remind yourself of your inner core. What do you value? Where are your passions? What are your strengths? Use your inner core to shape your vision and how to bring it into being.

Let's take an example of two people who have a vision of helping the homeless in their mid-sized community. Both share similar values of compassion, sharing and helping others. Yet differences in their strengths and passions can take this very similar desire into two different directions.

Sue's strengths are in writing, organizing and planning. She has a passion for connecting people. Sam, on the other hand, has strengths in public speaking, creativity and building relationships, He has a passion for theater and the arts.

Sue found a perfect way to help the homeless (for her) by writing a grant that enabled several, already existing community groups to join forces and offer a comprehensive suite of services to those who

> *And how is clarity to be achieved? Mainly by taking trouble and by writing to serve people rather than to impress them.*
>
> F.L. Lucas

are homeless. Sam, on the other hand, created a small acting troupe consisting of people who have experienced homelessness. He helps them tell their stories in the context of a traveling production – to raise awareness of the problem and to also raise much needed funding.

Both Sue and Sam had the same vision of helping the homeless, but took very different paths due to their inner core. When you find a way to achieve your vision using your inner core, all sorts of good things happen. The work seems easy, you learn quickly, you are motivated and have great energy. When you ignore your inner core, you may achieve your vision, but it will be at a cost.

Had Sam, in our example above, decided to take the grant writing approach, he may have had the persistence to see it through. But rest assured, it would not nearly been as successful, as personally rewarding or as inspired as when he played to his strengths and passions.

The future belongs to those who believe in the beauty of their dreams.

Elanor Roosevelt

3.3　Begin with a Powerful Why

Examples abound of normal, everyday people who create something of value in your community fueled by a powerful why. This is the story of Candy Lightner who founded Mothers Against Drunk Driving (MADD) after she lost her 18 year old daughter, Cari, to a drunk driver. This is the story of Wilbur Wright who was the first to fly in spite of very little money and a rag tag team to support him. Gandhi, Lincoln, Jefferson, Jobs – all had different, but similarly compelling whys. And this is the story of millions of others whose names are not in the history books who find a way to create something important to them in spite of formidable obstacles.

No one is less ready for tomorrow than the person who holds the most rigid beliefs about what tomorrow will contain.

Watts Wacker

Finding the "why" behind your vision provides energy. It invites others to join you. It sustains you in the tough times. It makes the journey to creation worth the effort. As your vision begins to take shape, identify WHY this is important for you personally. You inner motivation will motivate others as well as yourself.

3.4 Suspend Doubt

There are many things that restrain us from creating something big and bold. We can't imagine it in full detail. We are not sure how to make it happen. We question our ability, our resources or our willingness. We get fearful of making a mistake. We ask, "Who am I to do something so daring?"

We also find reasons every day to defer dreaming and then doing. We are too busy, too distracted, too old, too young, too invested in our status quo. This list grows longer. So as you begin to dream and your vision begins to take shape, suspend doubt. Trust that if you don't know exactly how, that you have the ability to figure that out. Know that if your vision is big enough that time and energy and money will be found. Know that you ARE exactly the person that can make this real.

The best way I've found to quell the inner voices of doubt and resistance is to notice them, acknowledge them and immediately dismiss them. Here is a peek inside my head when doubt creeps in:

- Be aware of the doubtful thought: "I will never find enough time to make that happen."

- Acknowledge the thought. For example: My inner voice says, "Time is a concern. It is good to keep that in mind."

> *Dream lofty dreams, and as you dream, so shall you become. Your vision is the promise of what you shall one day be. Your ideal is the prophecy of what you shall at last unveil.*
>
> James Allen

> *The future depends on what you do today.*
>
> Mahotma Gandhi

- Transform the thought. For example, I say to myself: "This is important. I am busy, so I need to find creative ways to make time for this."

- Acknowledge past successes. For example, I say to myself: "There have been many times in my life where I also was very busy and still managed to do (fill in the blank). I know I can do this."

Suspending doubt does not mean that we are blind to obstacles or the difficulty of achieving something great. It does mean that we proceed in spite of the certain knowledge that this will not be easy, that it will require much. But as we do so, we trust that a way will be found.

> *Study the past if you would define the future.*
>
> Confucius

3.5   Quiet is a Must

I've yet to have a great idea or burst of inspiration when I was in a busy, chaotic environment. I have had great ideas when I remove myself from those environments and find quiet. It may be outside in a peaceful place, in a favorite spot in my home, in public space that inspires me. Sometimes the quiet comes in the form of a shower, a drive in the car with the radio off or working outside in my garden.

As you work to create and sharpen your vision, go to that quiet spot that calls you. Take a notebook, be prepared to sit and think. Ensure you are not time bound, but have the time to muse, to mull and to relax. Make it a habit to return again and again. Very few visions are clear immediately – they take shape over time and careful nurturing. And the nurturing requires a quiet space which fosters a quiet and focused mind.

> *Big thinking precedes great achievement.*
>
> Wilfered Peterson

3.6   Use Images and Emotions

As you play around with possibility, include images, metaphors and feeling words. What does your desired future look like? What does it feel like? What will you be doing? What will others do and feel? How do others feel about the result? The root of the word "vision" is visual – to see. As we are able to see a picture of what we want to create, we are granted the ability to convey that – to ourselves and others in a way that creates a desire to move into that picture. The adage is that data tells and emotion sells. Make your vision one that evokes emotion – in yourself and others. The project plan can come later – the vision must precede it.

> *Create your future from your future, not your past.*
>
> Werner Erhard

3.7   Positive, Not the Negative

Naming what we don't want is easy. We don't want to be stuck in our career, we don't want disengaged and disheartened team members, we don't want upset customers or unhappy bosses, we don't want to always worry about money. We don't want our business to lose money or customers or valued employees. These are not visions – these are restrictions that hinder our ability to create.

The challenge is to describe what we do want – really want. Leaders can bemoan all the organizational problems they face, but often cannot articulate what could replace this. Many people can list all the reasons they are miserable in their job, but when asked what they would rather do, are clueless.

So, as we go through this exercise, ensure that you stay state in positive language what you want.

3.8   Make it Tangible

Too often dreams remain heady things. We dream, we think about what could be, but we never get it on paper. As long as your vision is only in your head, you will never have personal clarity, nor will you be able to adequately convey your vision to others.

The tangible form can vary, according to your personal style and those that need to be involved in bringing your creation to life. For some, images on a poster suffice. Others will create words that describe their vision. I encourage you to do both, as images create an emotional and creative response. Words cause you to get even more detail around your creation. For example, perhaps your vision is to create an organization that helps adults learn basic skills which enables them to gain employment. Putting images of the adults you will serve in a prominent place is a strong emotional cue that operates on a sub-conscious level. Putting words around the vision enables you to concisely describe, for yourself and others, the possibility you see. Words alone seldom evoke the emotion that pictures or visuals do. Pictures or visuals create emotional energy, but lack the direction, focus and clarity that words bring. Doing both is the answer.

Don't part with your illusions. When they are gone, you may still exist, but you have ceased to live.

Mark Twain

3.9   This is an Iterative Process

You've heard that creation is 1% inspiration and 99% perspiration. True, but also true that the 1% inspiration precedes and fires the desire to put in the work. As such, don't get bamboozled if your vision is not as clear as you would like. Don't be deterred by a fear of the unknown. You can work through the lack of clarity and the reality of the many unknowns if you

No one saves us but ourselves. No one can and no one may. We ourselves must walk the path.

Gautama Buddha

approach this journey as an iterative one. One in which you take a few steps forward, review, learn, readjust and move forward. In this process, your "why" is the constant, how you get there is fluid.

3.10 Work from the Inside Out

In this work, we'll begin on the inside again by helping you get a clear vision of the type of leader you strive to be. Then we will make the transition to an outside view and create a vision of something you would like to create with the team or organization you lead.

In subsequent chapters, you can take this "outside" vision, the thing that you'd like to create with your team, through the process of becoming a reality. But don't lose sight that this notion of envisioning and then creating a new reality works for individuals, for families, for teams, for departments, and for entire organizations.

Keep your eyes on the stars and your feet on the ground.

Franklin D. Roosevelt

 Putting it in Practice

Your Personal Leadership Vision

For this assignment, you'll take time to envision a picture or vision of the leader you would like to be one year from today. Once you have that firmly in your mind, you will have two choices on ways to solidify that personal leadership vision: a vision board or a future narrative. Select the one that appeals to you most to begin with. I'd encourage you to do both to get the experience of each method and to gain additional clarity. For this exercise, set aside an hour of time.

Find a quiet place where you will not be interrupted. If possible, find a place that provides a sense of wonder and inspiration. For some, that might be by a lake or pond or in a wooded setting or park. For others, it may be in great indoor space – perhaps a quiet corner in the library or a museum or a church. For others, you may have a favorite spot in your house where you relax and think. If quiet music allows you to relax and focus, you may want to play this music quietly in the background.

Take along this workbook and a pen. Take some time to quiet your busy mind by breathing and relaxing. Once you find yourself relaxing and in a reflective space, create a picture of yourself one year from today in your leadership role. Ensure that this picture is one of the "best possible" leader you can be.

Based on your previous work, you've defined your "Unchanging Core," your unique passions, values and strengths. Keep this question in the forefront:

"What type of leader do I want to be one year from today?"

Take most of your time in this exercise to get a clear, mental vision of what this looks and feels like. Make it as concrete as possible – or perhaps even create a story about what you see.

Only after you have a good picture of yourself a year from today, capture your thoughts on paper. As you capture your thoughts, it is more important to get the essence, so use bulleted lists and short sentences. You'll have the opportunity in the next part of the exercise to further define your thoughts.

Option 1: Create a Vision Board

For this option, you will create a visual board or poster that conveys the essence of your vision of yourself as a leader a year from now. Allow yourself the freedom to have fun with this work and to be creative. There is no set format or outcome, only the creation of a visual that helps you "see" your personal vision.

1. Assemble these materials:
    a. Gather up a stack of magazines or publications that are rich with images (not all text) and that you are willing to cut up.
    b. A poster board (size in up to you, but should be bigger than a typical 8 ½ X 11 sheet of paper
    c. Glue
    d. Scissors
    e. Music (optional)
    f. PC & Printer to find great graphics / images to print (optional)
    g. Your notes from the prior exercise
2. Find a quiet place where you can spread out and work without interruptions.
3. Review your notes from the prior exercise. Recreate, in your mind, that picture of yourself a year from today.

4. Flip through your magazines to find pictures, images and words that convey the essence of how you see yourself in a year from now. Find images that appeal emotionally to you. You may find images that inspire you, but that were not in your original vision. It is fine to add onto your vision.

5. Do your best to great a visual representation of you as a leader a year from now; however don't make it an intellectual pursuit to create a one to one match with your list and the images. Stay in a place of flow and possibility.

6. Create a big stack of possible words, images and graphics – then cull your stack to the ones that mean the most to you. Once you've narrowed your selection, assemble them on your board and glue them in place.

Now that you've created a vision board, you'll need to decide what to do with it. I keep mine posted in my office, where I see it daily. Others put theirs in a place where they may look at it more infrequently and others just file it away. No matter what your choice, the task of taking your words into a physical and visual representation is an important step in solidifying your vision. Many folks who have created vision boards and tucked them away out of view for years report that they are stunned when they find them again when they see the degree to which their vision, as represented on the board, has been realized.

As you envision what that is, some of the following questions may help you get more clarity:

- What does it look like? Feel like?
- Where are you spending your time and energy?
- How is your work aligned with your values?
- How do those that you are leading describe you?
- How do others in your organization describe you?
- What do your customers (internal or external) experience?
- How do you feel about the work you are doing?
- What does a typical day look like?
- How do you feel at the end of the day?
- What results is your team/department/organization realizing?
- What amazes you about the progress you've made in the last year?

Option 2: Create a Future Narrative

For this option, you will write a narrative, or story, about yourself, describing your vision as if it is realized.

1. Assemble your notes from the first exercise, a note book and writing utensil. I strongly encourage you to write this narrative in long hand, rather than typing on a keyboard.
2. Find a quiet place where you can work without interruptions for at least 45 minutes. Music is optional.
3. Review your notes from the first exercise. Bring to mind the vision that you had created about the leader you are one year from now.
4. Write a story that takes place one year from now **in the present tense.** You are writing a story that assumes you have already achieved your vision.
    a. For example, you might start with: It is (insert the date a year from now) and I am (insert your leadership role and the work you are doing).
    b. Stay in the present tense. Write as if all that you envision is actually occurring.
    c. Do not constrain yourself to what you believe is possible, based on today. Write about what you would like to have happen, even though you cannot see today how that might happen.
    d. Stay in the realm of possibility and positivity.
5. The goal is to create a future story that is real to you. Spend your time dreaming, describing, and capturing. Spend no time editing or improving your writing – this is for your eyes only.
6. Try to get at least 2 full pages of narrative.
7. When you are done, read through it. Then put it in a place where you can read through it every few months.

Here is a short sample, so that you can see how to write about the future in the present tense:

It is <future year>. Our team is doing amazing work. Our customer satisfaction numbers are the best in the company. I spend my time now on working to develop the team, which I can do now that I'm not spending hours each day dealing with customer complaints. My team is working exceptionally. I've helped them work through some tough issues, and we are much better at getting problems identified earlier and resolving them faster. I look forward to coming to work and leave feeling energized and with a sense of fulfillment.

A Note about This Methodology

Vision board and future narratives are powerful ways to help you get clarity about your future direction. These are not plans (that will come later), but conceptual images about direction. I encourage you to use either one, or both of these techniques in other areas of your life. Use them for your personal life, your family, or other areas that are important to you.

Repeat as needed. I personally do future narratives at least once a year and more often if I am feeling "stuck" in a bad place. It is amazing to look back at 10 years of future narratives. I find that I will write about a future for which I have no idea how it may materialize and then within the year, realize that much of what I've imagined has appeared in my life.

Once you create your vision board or future narrative, be prepared for something called synchronicity. I can't explain why it works, but I can attest to the fact that it does work. Once you get clarity on what you want your future to be and declare it, either by the vision board or the narrative, you'll notice that unexpected and unplanned people, events and things come into your life that help lead you to where you want to be. I wrote a future narrative about doing amazing work with a great team and being able to travel broadly. When I wrote it, I had no idea how that might happen, but six months later, an opportunity came forward in my work that afforded just that. Once you have done the work of creating clarity about your future, be open to the idea that some amazing things may happen that help you get where you want to go.

Your Outer Vision

We've been working from the inside out. You've defined your inner core, explored and rewritten your story and gotten clarity on who you want to be as a leader. Now the time has come to turn our focus outward – to the team, company or organization you lead. From this point on, you'll deepen your skills and insights about leadership through work that you do with the people you lead in your organization. For this work, I encourage you to find something that is important for your team to accomplish, that is significant and challenging, yet could be accomplished in six to nine months.

To begin, select a team that you lead. It might be the team of leaders that report directly to you or it may be an ad-hoc or project team that have been assembled to achieve a specific result and you are in a leadership role for them.

Now we will go through a similar process to the one that you did, as you identified your Unchanging Core and individual story. You may find this easier than your personal work. That often happens for several reasons. First, you most likely spend more time, energy and focus on your team, rather than yourself. Secondly, it is often easier to see clearly about others, than about ourselves.

Your team will also benefit from identifying and getting grounded in its unchanging core. Let's start there.

Team Values

What are the values that guide your team? If your organization has a list of stated values, begin there. Then ask yourself if there are any of those values that have a heightened level of importance for your team. It may be that the list of espoused organizational values are not ones that are "lived" day to day – and that other values are more descriptive. It may be that values have not been defined for your organization or for your team and you'll need to define them.

No matter what the situation, for this exercise create a list of values that:

- Guides the way decisions get made and resources are allocated for your team

- Inspires you and your team

- Are congruent with the work of your team and the direction the organization is headed

- Have real meaning – and will not be "words on a wall"

Remember that values can be aspirational. You might list customer focus as a value, even if you know there is much work to be done to have customers experience this value.

Here are some companies that have core values you might use for inspiration. You will see that there was care and thought put into these AND that they truly do describe what each company strives to do.

<u>Google</u> | <u>Southwest</u> | <u>Apple</u> | <u>Zappos</u> | <u>Amazon</u>

Note that for individual values, a word may suffice. For team values, you'll want some more description so that there is a shared understanding. Even better if your team helps to create the values or discusses how those values relate to their day to day work.

Team Values

Agility	Faith	Diversity
Customer Focus	Family	Eco Friendly
Collaboration	Flexibility	Quality
Community Minded	Focus	Performance
Growth	Freedom	Developing People
Being the Best at...	Financial Stability	Perseverance
Great Design	Fun	Philanthropy
Creativity	Imagination	Passion
Curiosity	Influence	Resilience
Discipline	Knowledge	Respect
Diversity	Leadership	Security
Execution	Learning	Strength
Innovation	Excellence	Teamwork
Environmentalism	Inclusion	Trust
	Making a Difference	Uniqueness

Team Values

1.

2.

3.

4.

5.

Team Strengths

Next, list the strengths your team possesses. Try to list at least 5 and no more than 10. Look back at the exercise you completed in the first module about yourself to guide you in defining team strengths. Here are some examples:

- Deep expertise about our customer base, or product or our process or our organization
- New team members who are willing to try new approaches
- Continuous improvement mindset
- Skills in some team members in being able to manage projects (or other skills)
- Solid level of funding
- Product or service that is profitable (or sustainable or has high market demand)

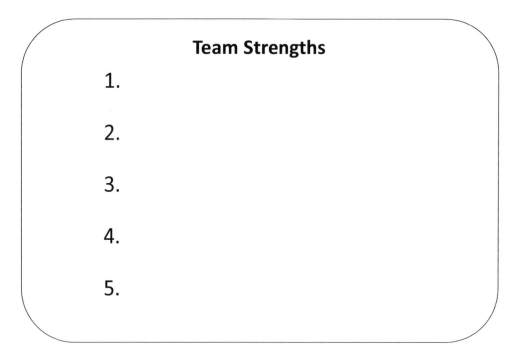

Team Strengths

1.

2.

3.

4.

5.

Passions of the Team

List the things that your team, as a whole, is passionate about. What motives them? When do you see them to most energized and engaged? If you need help, look back and see how you answered this question for yourself.

Compile your notes. Validate that this is a good summary of your team's unchanging core.

Current Reality for the Team

Team Passions

1.

2.

3.

4.

5.

Now, write a paragraph or two about your team's current situation. Write about what is most relevant, however these questions may prompt your thinking and writing:

- What is happening in your organization that impacts your team? Are there strategic or plans that you must respond to?
- What is happening in the larger world that impacts your team? Consider the marketplace, regulatory environment, technology or innovations.
- What is mission critical for you team to deliver on in the next year?
- Where do you see opportunities for your team to be more successful?

- What internal team dynamics impact your team and your ability to deliver results? (Adding or losing talent, morale, growth or decline, skills and abilities, ability to work as a team).

Future for the Team

And finally, summarize your thoughts by responding to this question:
What would it look like if my team was achieving its highest level of potential? What results would we be generating? How would we work as a team? How would our customers respond?

---

4   What You Can Expect

As you learn to define your vision, both for yourself or the group you lead, you'll notice several things that begin to happen. You become more accountable. Over time you'll notice a sense of power that comes from the confidence you gain in your ability to see and shape a desired future. You and your team will have more energy and motivation. And your team, once you have created and communicated your direction, will become more focused, waste less effort, and gain confidence.

You may also surface resistance. It may be internal or external. It may be from your team or your boss. It may be from your family. Surprisingly, it may be from yourself! The clearer your vision and the more important it is to you, the less likely that you will be willing to succumb to this resistance.

Trust that when you encounter resistance, it is a sign that you are working on something really big, something that calls you and something that is worth doing. Resistance rarely surfaces for things of no consequence.

If you find that you are encountering resistance, either your own internal resistance (who am I to do this big thing?) or from others – you may want to read <u>The War of Art: Break through Blocks and Win Your Inner Creative Battles</u> by Steven Pressfield. I find this book to be just what I need when I get stuck or bogged down.

Additional Resources:

Godin, Seth. The Icarus deception: how high will you fly?. New York: Portfo-
      lio/Penguin, 2012.
Haque, Umair. The new capitalist manifesto: building a disruptively better business.
      Boston, Mass.: Harvard Business Press, 2011.
Heath, Chip, and Dan Heath. Made to stick: why some ideas survive and others die.
      New York: Random House, 2007.

CHAPTER 5
Creating a New Reality

Creating Moves You Forward

As a leader, you are charged to make forward progress. You may yearn for stability, for a time or place when things can just move along seamlessly. The hard truth is that there is no steady state, no maintaining the status quo today. For this reason, leaders must be able to motivate their teams to continue to create something new.

1 Moving Forward

Individuals, teams, and organizations are always in a state of flux – and they are either moving toward something that matters to them or moving away from it. In the past, we were more likely to have longer periods that appeared stable, even though in reality they were not. In our old world view, we would maintain for a long period, until something disruptive came along. We would then, after our performance dropped finally take action and begin a long and arduous climb to a new state. The only place we would identify and create dramatically new enhanced value was in the long, hard work of the readjustment, although often even those gains were lost due to resistance and failed efforts.

> *Have no fear of perfection.*
> *You will never reach it.*
>
> Salvador Dali

CHANGE AS AN EVENT

Of course, the periods of stability were not really stable; it was only that the decline was slow enough to barely be discernible. This is like the fact that we age day by day, but don't notice the cumulative effects daily. But on occasion we are startled as we look in the mirror by the changes we see.

In today's world the periods of relative stability are both shorter and less frequent. Some would question if they are more than a nanosecond. This calls for continual adjustment and ongoing creativity.

This is only possible when:

* You have clear line of sight of your goal or what you want to create

* You make regular and continual progress toward that objective

* You maintain stability through a strong inner core (your values, strengths, passions)

* You are able to use the creative process to move you and your team forward

Curiosity about life in all of its aspects, I think, is still the secret of great creative people.

Leo Burnett

 Vision

CHANGE AS A STEADY STATE

1.1 Doing vs. Dreaming

We mistakenly believe that creative people spend most of their time dreaming up novel ideas. This perception could not be further from the truth. Their bright or novel idea is the genesis of their work – but their true work is in bringing their idea to fruition. This takes effort, persistence and diligence. It is the unseen and messy portion of the creative process. It is hard work that takes longer and requires more effort than envisioned at the onset. When we see the outcome, we think of the beginning (idea) and then end (realization) – but make no doubt about it, creating is really about the process in between the two.

> *You can't wait for inspiration, you have to go after it with a club.*
>
> Jack London

1.2 Leaders are Creators

A mistaken belief is that creating is about the arts – music, visual arts, dance, and literature. We typically don't think about leaders as creators, but they are. In fact, in today's world, leaders **must** create. Innovation and creativity are sought after in our world where maintaining the status quo is no longer a choice. Creation is required when we are making our way through situations we have never faced before. Customers demand creativity; the market rewards it.

Creativity is no longer relegated to the Research & Development department. Healthy organizations need a core of creative leaders who can envision and then create. What kinds of things might a leader create? Here is a short list:

> *The best way out is always through.*
>
> Robert Frost

- A new product or service (internal or external)

- A new way to deliver existing products or services (internal or external)
- A new customer experience (internal or external)
- A new market approach
- A fresh approach to reaching new customers
- An internal process that is gets better results
- A high performing team
- A distinctive organizational culture that enables great results
- Increased organizational capability

2 Problem Solve Less

Our western society values, shapes and rewards us to problem solve and to use the analytical left side of our brains. As such, we have deep talent in planning, trouble shooting and problem solving. We reward those that are good "fire fighters", the ultimate imagery of someone responding to an urgent problem. However, in today's world, creating is the more important skill.

There is far less emphasis on using that other side of our brain – the creative, holistic, innovative, integrated side. And as such, we have less talent, focus and training in how to create or innovate. We see art and science as two dramatically different things. We worship creativity in the entertainment industry but dismiss it in business and industry. We covet math and science teachers and cut the arts.

Make no mistake; problem solving has a valuable place in the world. We fall in the trap, however, of not being aware of when problem solving won't solve our problems. And even if we do recognize that we need something different, we are disinclined and ill equipped to move to using that "other side" of our brain and create what is called for.

Problem solving works beautifully if there is a solution and is awesome for technical problems. It is wonderful if what you had before needs a tune up and not an overhaul. However, it does not work for situations which have no immediate fix, for which there is not a known solution and for those that require new fresh thinking.

Problem solving is looking back; creating is looking forward. Problem solving is fixing; creating is building. Problem solving tends to marginally improve the status quo, creating has the potential to create a dramatically new and better reality. Steve Jobs and the Apple products are great examples of not merely improving a known commodity – but of radically creating a new product and experience. Walt Disney did the same with family entertainment.

> If a problem is fixable, if a situation is such that you can do something about it, then there is no need to worry. If it's not fixable, then there is no help in worrying. There is no benefit in worrying whatsoever.
>
> Dalai Lama XIV

2.1 Problem Solve or Create?

The line between problem solving and creativity is thin at times, but in general you can use this as a guide as to when to use either approach:

Problem Solve When	Create When
There are known solutions	You are facing a new or novel situation
The core (process, system, product) is solid and working overall	The core (process, system, product) is no longer relevant or needs a major overhaul
You want to restore or maintain something that serves you well	You want to create something new, fresh and more relevant
You want to replicate or copy	You want something dramatically different from what exists
You experience some type of failure and you want to understand and eliminate that type of failure in the future	You recognize that what you are doing is no longer relevant, no matter how well it is executed
You can isolate a specific problem	The problems are complex and interdependent
You want something to "go away"	You want to bring something new into being

3   The Creative Process

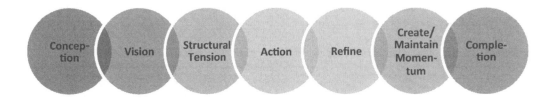

The Process of Creating

Creating is a process that follows a set of steps, beginning with conception and ending with completion. The seven-step process is outlined above and we'll review them one at a time. Although they appear linear in the diagram, very seldom does one walk through the steps one after another. For example, you might have a vision, take some action, and then revisit the vision to shift or sharpen it. The process is iterative in all stages, yet at some point, you will assess progress and determine it complete. This is easier with artistic works and more difficult in organizations, yet at some point you will reach a point of diminishing return. As such, it is helpful to know the steps and follow them in roughly this sequence. At the same time, recognize that the creative path can be irregular and a bit bumpy at times. Just staying with it, remaining open and being willing to do the work will serve you well.

Missing any one of these important elements stalls the creative process.

- Not fully grounding people in the current reality results in a lack of desire to move forward. Individuals may falsely believe it is OK to stay the

Creativity is more than just being different. Anybody can plan weird; that's easy. What's hard is to be as simple as Bach. Making the simple, awesomely simple, that's creativity.

Charles Mingus

same. Some would describe this as a need to create a burning platform. I chose to describe it as an honest assessment of the current state. It is your role to keep your team grounded in the current reality and no false illusions.

- Not describing a compelling future vision results in a lack of direction. Very often we don't like where we currently are, but cannot see where to head. A leader's fundamental role is to create clarity and direction toward a better place.

- Not having a plan results in either no action or misdirected action. The leader's role is to chart a path forward, to ensure their team knows what to do and who is doing it.

In this chapter we are only going to work on creating the structural tension. In earlier chapters you've defined your future vision. In later chapters, we will create the action plans and learn how to engage your team to do the creative work that moves you to your desired state.

1. Conception

In this initial step, you begin to have a notion that something needs to be created. It may be that you are dissatisfied with the current situation or that you have an idea that you think would work. This is an exploratory step, one in which the idea begins to take shape, where you ask many questions and explore many possibilities. The primary issue to resolve in this step is to be very clear about your "WHY", what it is that motivates you to embark on the creative process.

Creativity comes from a conflict of ideas.

Donatella Versace

2. Vision

This step takes you from a general notion to a specific picture of what it is that you wish to create. There is enough specificity in the vision that you can imagine the outcome and the results. While you will not know exactly what the path is to creating the outcome, you have a sense of clarity about the outcome and the results you are wanted to bring into being.

Creativity is contagious, pass it on.

Albert Einstein

3. Creating Structural Tension

In this step, you compare where you want to be with where you are today. By clearly describing your current reality and comparing it to what you want to create, you can begin to craft the plan that will get you there. You will begin solidly grounded in the gap between present and desired future. The juxtaposition of the current reality with the desired future (your creation) creates structural tension – a state of disequilibrium that seeks resolution. This provides energy and direction.

4. Taking Action

This is the step in which your creation begins to take shape. It is also the stage at which many individuals fail to move forward. Whether due to over planning, fear, distractions or inertia, many people just cannot manage to turn their idea into reality. Moving into this step takes courage, discipline and persistence. Taking that first step, even though it may be uncertain or scary, can lead to the next step and then the next step and once again the next step.

Creativity is just connecting things. When you ask creative people how they did something, they feel a little guilty because they didn't really do it, the just saw something. It seemed obvious to them after a while.

Steve Jobs

5. Refining

Many of us suffer from the delusion that great things were done by people who got it right the first time. The creative process is iterative – one of taking a step, evaluating, learning, correcting course and taking another step. And then repeating this process over and over and over again. The mantra is progress, not perfection.

6. Creating and Maintaining Momentum

Make no mistake, the creative path is not an easy one. We get deluded when we see the finished product – without seeing the work, the missteps, the effort and the failed attempts. Finding ways to build energy, celebrating interim progress, setting milestones and deadlines and marking their accomplishment all can provide energy and forward momentum.

You see things; and you say, 'Why?' But I dream things that never were; and I say, 'Why not?'

George Bernard Shaw

7. Completion

At some point, you will want to declare your creation "done". This prevents the tendency to be pulled into long series of continual tweaks that begin to add diminishing value. It allows you to focus on the next creative project. This is an especially important stage for the types of creative project that leaders embark on, as they will require engaging your team in their realization. Declaring a thing "done" and celebrating the progress does many things: frees energy to focus on other important outcomes, creates a sense of pride and accomplishment and reenergizes your team for ever greater accomplishments.

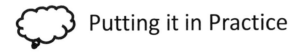 Putting it in Practice

Creating Structural Tension

What is Structural Tension?

Robert Fritz describes structural tension as what occurs when there is a recognized difference between a current state and a desired state that creates momentum toward resolution. A simple example is hunger. When we are hungry (the current state), we want a full stomach (the desired state). The tension between hunger and satiation creates tension – for which we are motivated to take action to reconcile (structural tension). It the tension is large, we might pull into the first fast food joint we see; if less so we might go home and make a nice dinner. No matter, we will take action to resolve the tension and move toward our desired state.

What is true for individuals and for physical needs is also true for organizations and less tangible tensions. As a leader, when you can clearly describe a desired future and help others see the current reality, you've created structural tension that will seek to be resolved.

Here is a simple graphic that illustrates this tension:

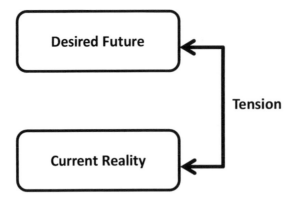

Fritz, R. (1999). *The Path of Least Resistance for Managers*. San Francisco, CA: Berrett-Koehler.

As a leader, there are three actions you do to create a structural tension:

1. Have a clear and vivid description of the desired state

2. Have an honest appraisal of the current state

3. Create and execute an action plan that resolves the tension between the current and the desired or future state

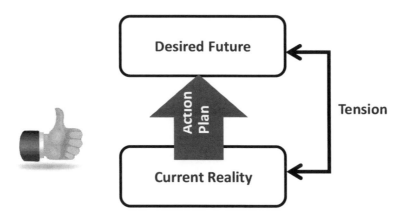

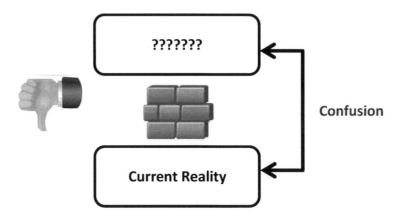

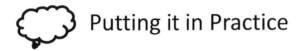 # Putting it in Practice

Defining Your Desired Future

Review your work from the previous chapter. In it, you defined your team's values, passions and strengths (the inner core). You also began to create a vision about a better future by exploring these questions:

- What would it look like if my team was achieving its highest level of potential?
- What results would we be generating?
- How would we work as a team? How would our customers respond?

From this, select one thing you would like to accomplish, hand in hand with your team, which moves you toward your vision of a better future. The goal that you set here is one that you will require ongoing effort, so chose carefully. Here are some criteria that will help you select an appropriate direction.

- Is it tightly aligned with the strategic direction of your organization and fit within your area's responsibility?
- Does it make a difference – to the results your team gets, to your customers and to your team?
- Does it require creativity rather than problem solving? (see the reading for a chart that will help you decide)
- Do you and your team have the resources (time / money) to work on this?
- Does it amplify a passion you and your team share? Does it play to strengths that you and your team have?

Remember that at this point in the creative process, you don't have to know HOW to make this happen – you merely need to describe, with clarity, what you would like to create. So suspend disbelief and skepticism and dream in this step. Here is an example of what it might look like:

What I'd like to create: I'd like our team to create a customer experience that is unparalleled in our industry.

Why it matters: We have one of the best products on the market, yet have not captured a significant market share. Customers like our product but are apathetic about our sales and service process. We are well positioned to grow in market share and profitability if we can leverage referrals and turn existing customer into repeat business.

What it will look and feel like: Our customers love us. They refer us to others. They would not think about doing business with anyone else. They feel valued and important. We get at least 5 emails a week that appreciate our work. My team feels as if their work matters – to the company and to the customers. They have a great sense of personal satisfaction. Our unit profitability has increased by 10%, with repeat business up by 50%. We are getting positive comments on the internet review sites and there is a buzz about our product and service that is making our competitors take notice.

Defining the Future

What I'd like to create:

Why it matters:

What it will look and feel like:

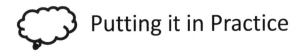 Putting it in Practice

Defining Your Current Reality

Now is the time to take a hard, unvarnished look at the current reality, juxtaposed against your desired future. This is not the time to ignore inconvenient truths, nor is it the time to be modest about what you have that is working well. Describe your current reality as clearly as you can – with no need to justify, blame or rationalize.

Using the past example, here might be what this looks like:

Our current reality: While our product is quite good, our customer service process was cobbled together as an afterthought. Generally, customers don't need to call us, so we are invisible to them. When customers do call, they are served by a team that wants to do well, but are hampered by an inefficient and cumbersome internal system. That results in long phone waits through an automated system. Many times we need to get back to them, rather than provide immediate and timely answers. My team sees customer service as a "nice to do" rather than a "must do". While all are well intentioned, many have never learned solid customer service skills.

Customers generally will need more of our product on an annual basis. While we hope that they reorder from us, we do not proactively ask for their orders. We also cannot track reorders.

Our primary competitor does not have nearly as good a product as ours, but their customer service is far better than ours. Our product is an expensive purchase for them and they do have other options.

Our Current Reality:

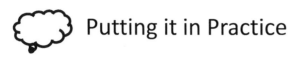 # Putting it in Practice

Putting it Together

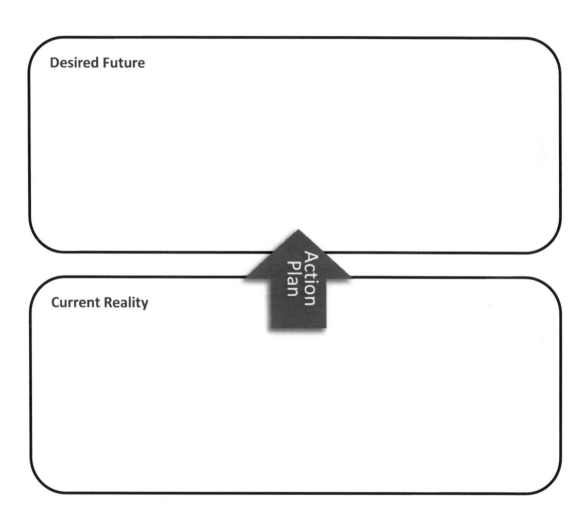

Desired Future

Action Plan

Current Reality

Final Note: Don't Work in a Vacuum

You may be tempted to lock yourself away for several hours to do this. Please don't! As a leader, you are ultimately responsible to create the vision of where you want to lead your team, but you cannot do that in a vacuum. During this process, engage your customers, you team, your peers and your key stakeholders in some discussions. Ask good questions. Listen hard. Share your thoughts. Check for agreement. Look for ways to make your vision more compelling. Ensure that your current reality reflects more than just your vantage point. These discussions can be informal. The key point is to have them.

Having these discussions serves multiple purposes. They broaden your perspective. They ground your views. They provide new ideas and insights. They begin to build interest and curiously about what you want to create.

Here are some questions related to the scenario we used as an example.

Your Team

- How would you describe the service or product we provide our customers?
- What do we do for our customers that they love? They hate?
- What do you think would need to happen for our customers to refer us to others?
- What currently gets in the way of providing great customer service today?

Your Customers

- What is currently working with the service we provide to you?
- How likely are you to refer us to someone else? Why or why not?
- Describe the way in which you use our product or service. What problems or frustrations do you experience?
- What would you like us to do more of? Less of?
- Who do you deal with that provides extraordinary customer service? What is that experience like?

Your Peers / Boss / or Stakeholders

- How would you describe our customer service process?
- What might be the outcomes if our customer service process was exemplary?
- What is the customer experience you would like our customers to have?
- What feedback do you get from our current customers?

Putting it in Practice

Engaging Others

In the table below, make a plan for who you would like to engage in this process and what key questions you will ask them. Jot down what you learned by their response in the Learnings column.

Stakeholder	Question	Learnings

• • •

Thomas Edison, one of the most prolific creators of our time, held 1,093 patents. He is well known for the electric light bulb– and the breakthrough of a filament that was long lasting. To find the right material took a decade of experimentation and a building 2 city blocks that housed over 8,000 various elements that MIGHT be used for this purpose. It was his bamboo fishing pole that ultimately provided the right material—a carbonized bamboo filament that provided long lasting light. These are his words about the creative process:

"Before I got through," he recalled, "I tested no fewer than 6,000 vegetable growths, and ransacked the world for the most suitable filament material."

"The electric light has caused me the greatest amount of study and has required the most elaborate experiments," he wrote. "I was never myself discouraged, or inclined to be hopeless of success. I cannot say the same for all my associates."

"Genius is one percent inspiration and ninety-nine percent perspiration."

• • •

---

4   Progress not Perfection

The creative process is not for wimps. While exciting, it is also arduous. There will be times you will experience the thrill of seeing your creation take shape and form and many more times when you will experience failure and false steps. There are techniques and tactics that are contained in this book that will help you create better, but none can avoid the fact that creating involves risk, hard work and the ability to fail, learn and try again.

When all think alike, ten no one is thinking.

Walter Lippman

Additional Resources

Bryan, Mark A., Julia Cameron, and Catherine A. Allen. *The artist's way at work: riding the dragon*. New York: William Morrow, 1998.

Fritz, Robert. *Creating*. New York, N.Y.: Fawcett Columbine, 1993.

Fritz, Robert. *The path of least resistance for managers designing organizations to succeed*. San Francisco, CA: Berrett-Koehler Publishers, 1999.

Zander, Rosamund Stone, and Benjamin Zander. *The art of possibility*. Boston, Mass.: Harvard Business School Press, 2000.

CHAPTER 6
Moving Forward

1   Moving Forward

You are now at an inflection point in the creative process. You have an idea, a vision, a picture of the future you would like to create. You've gotten solidly grounded in the current reality of the situation – and by juxtaposing that against your desired future, you've created structural tension that has a natural tendency to resolve itself.

So the stage is set, but until some action is taken, nothing changes. This is the step in the creative process that separates the dreamers from the doers. I suspect that like me, you know plenty of people that have big ideas and talk a big game, but never get past the talking. To create something demands an execution mindset, requires action, insists on steady progress toward that which you want to create.

Many others fall into a different trap. They are very busy doing things. They work long hours and put in the effort, but have no clear idea of a vision or goal they are working toward. Working blindly without a goal does nothing more than exhaust you, physically, emotionally and spiritually.

Creating is hard work, often behind the scenes. It requires diligence, persistence and a strong drive to bring into being that which you want to make real. Once something of value is created, others will understimate the effort needed to get to the final point. We may mistakingly believe that creation is about ideas and not hardwilled, strong execution. Not

Derive happiness in oneself from a good day's work, from illuminating the fog that surrounds us.

Henri Matisse

true. Creating something of value requires extreme dilligence that is does not stop until your vision comes into being.

1.1   Structured Iterations

Desired futures that are worthwhile and meaningful are seldom executed in a few weeks or months. They are truly a journey – and a journey into the unknown. As we've noted, the unknowable nature of the journey combined with the turbulence in the external environment precludes detailed project planning. Too often, we default to going by the "seat of our pants," doing nothing or deferring beginning until we know more. Each of these approaches puts us in a reactive mode – rather than an intentional path.

Think of detailed project planning and planning by intention and iteration as two ends of continuum. You might think of them as the difference between a symphony score that is quite detailed, instrument-by-instrument, section by section as opposed to jazz. With a symphony there is no doubt what each person should do and when they should do it. Skill impacts execution and the conductor orchestrates the performance – but every member knows what to do and when to do it. There is a beginning, middle and end – and it is tightly prescribed.

Jazz on the other hand is in the moment – a juxtaposition of several skilled musicians with an ability to listen, react and respond to what they are feeling and what they sense in their musician partners. There is an underlying framework and some fluid "rules" that the musicians know and use. While each jazz performance is unique and different, this art is not produced by unskilled individuals making music by the "seat of their pants." It is the result of highly skilled and practiced musicians who have developed the art of

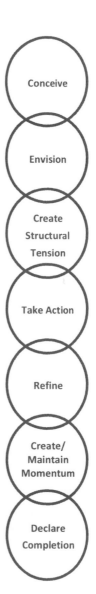

Conceive

Envision

Create Structural Tension

Take Action

Refine

Create/ Maintain Momentum

Declare Completion

being in the moment, working to create something of beauty by a deep collaboration with fellow musicians. It is an apt metaphor for what capable leaders do as they are creating something new.

The steps in the creative process create a framework for leaders to follow– and are the steps you are learning in this book. You've already taken steps to conceptualize your situation, create a vision of your desired future and to create structural tension by contrasting the current reality with the desired future. Most of the heavy work in creating is done in the taking action / refining steps. These are iterative steps – and will be repeated over and over again and each successive iteration will take you closer and closer to your desired future.

> *Writing is like driving at night in a fog. You can only see as far as your headlights, but you can make the whole trip that way.*
>
> E.L. Doctorow

2   Creative Planning

The first step toward execution is taking action – which requires some planning. For the purpose of this work, I am going to assume that you know well the basic planning process of defining tasks, milestones, and dependencies. I'll also assume that you have a fair degree of skill in defining roles and assignments. If this is not the case, I encourage you to develop skills in basic planning or project management.

In this section, I am going to speak to some of the unique aspects of planning for work where you are unable to clearly define each and every step to execution. If you are planning for something that has been done successfully in the past, you will have a blueprint and perhaps best practices for the planning and execution. The planning we will learn to do here is when you are charting new territory and have a vision

> *Dance above the surface of the world. Let your thoughts lift you into creativity that is not hampered by opinion.*
>
> Red Haircrow

of the end state and no experience at all in how to get there. More and more, you are being asked as a leader to do things that have not been done before, to find new ways, to lead forward when you cannot count on your previous technical experience to chart a detailed path.

A great example is the difference between Christopher Columbus's first voyage across the Atlantic and traveling that route today. Columbus had an idea, a fleet and a crew, a new mental model (the world is round), and a sense of adventure. Today's captains have detailed navigational maps, proven routes and navigation instruments that help them know exactly where they are at any given moment. Today's leaders have more in common with Columbus – charting unknown territory with little guidance.

I call this "finding the way" rather than "knowing the way." It is more ambiguous. It is fuzzy, uncertain and unknown. As a leader, it can be frightening to be asked to lead others when you yourself cannot articulate all the precise steps, in sequence, that need to occur. As you lead, you are not certain what you will find. There will be pleasant surprises and unforeseen dangers.

But just like Columbus, with a new mental model, a vision and a team, you too can find the way. Just know that, as the leader, you will need to abandon the role of expert and take on the role of guide.

As I work with leaders in this creative process, they become discouraged when they cannot chart a detailed plan that will get them where they want to go. This is both an internal pressure they put upon themselves and an external pressure from those they lead. Those they are leading desire security and stability – and so the leader must find a way to balance the polarities of known and unknown, stability and change, safety and risk.

> *It is not the clear-sighted who rule the world. Great achievements are accomplished in a great, warm fog.*
>
> Joseph Conrad

> *The creative process is a process of surrender, not control.*
>
> Julia Cameron

To do so, there are several beliefs that must be shed. They include:

- As the leader, I must have all the answers.
- The world is predictable.
- We can't move forward until more is known.
- I expect my leader to define a detailed plan that, if executed, is fail safe.

It is easy at this junction to want to abandon any notion of a plan – and just wing it. Leaders wonder how they can plan the unplanable; they experience distress when they are unable to describe with precision the steps needed or they are unable to predict the time it will take. What needs to happen is to replace your current mental model of a plan with a new one. Traditional project plans with Gantt charts and resource allocations and four levels of tasks are not called for here. Instead, the planning needed when creating is sequential, yet not lock step. It is directional, yet not directive. It is a path and not a formula. As a contrast, think of the difference between building blueprints and a construction project plan and an architect's conceptual sketch and first 3D modeling of the project. The detailed plans depend upon the idea and the initial conceptualization and cannot be drawn up with the more fluid and less precise initial renditions. So it is with what you want to create.

The old saying goes that "Failing to plan is planning to fail." As tempting as it is to go without a plan, doing so results in confusion, wasted effort, frustration, failed efforts and many times creating something that you did not want. Here is a description of the type of plan that can effectively guide you and your team in this creative landscape.

> *Maturity, one discovers, has everything to do with the acceptance of 'not knowing.*
>
> Mark Z. Danielewski

> *When the creative impulse sweeps over you, grab it. You grab it and honor it and use it, because momentum is a rare gift.*
>
> Justina Chen

2.1   Picture the End

If you remember nothing else, remember to do this – the more vividly and specifically you and your team can describe what you want to create, the higher the chances you will be able to create it and the more energy there will be toward creating it. This is more of an emotional description and less of a detailed one. Describe what it is that you want to create and why it matters. Talk about how it feels, for all involved, once you are successful.

There is the story of Steve Jobs, who put a block of wood the size of the iPhone in front of his design team and said that he wanted a phone that size with certain features. Of course, at that time, it seemed virtually impossible to do that – yet the block of wood created a clear, visual picture of the end state everyone was working for. Note in this example, that there was a dramatic, game changing outcome. Far different than if the description of the end state was to "beat the competition" or "reduce the size of current phones."

Do as much as you can to have your team explore, describe and visualize the end state. Keep it alive. I've been on far too many projects where people put in misguided effort toward a future that was not made real for them. When asked why they are doing what they are doing, they are clueless. Leaders are unable to articulate the benefits. Because we need to or because it is a corporate mandate are never good answers.

Be careful to describe the end state as what you want to create vs. what you want to avoid. There is a difference in outcome, energy, engagement and results when you shift from avoiding a negative outcome to achieving a positive one. Try it out – which team working on a new product line would you want to be a part of?

As far as the laws of mathematics refer to reality, they are not certain; and as far as they are certain, they do not refer to reality.

Albert Einstein

Great is the human who has not lost his childlike heart.

Mencius

Team 1: Our new product will solve all the problems our customers experience with our current one. Customer complaints will decrease dramatically.
Team 2: Our new product will provide our clients with a superb experience – so much that they will become loyal customers who refer others with enthusiasm.

2.2   Clearly Define the First Steps

Once you have helped your team understand the future you want to create, the natural reactions will include:

"We don't have (time, money, resources, the right people, or any number of other things)."

"How could we do something that big?"

"We don't know how."

"This is scary….crazy….impo ssible."

In this step, remind yourself of the image of a bridge in fog. You can't see how long the bridge is, but you can see enough to take the first steps. You know enough that you can direct folks to step carefully, to hold on to the ropes. And you trust that as you move along the bridge, each "next step" will become evident. Remember that all you need to know is the destination (your future vision) and the first steps. As reassuring as it would be to have turn-by-turn directions, reconcile yourself and your team to the reality that this is a journey that will not have GPS guidance along the way.

> *If everyone is moving forward together, then success takes care of itself.*
>
> Henry Ford

 ## Putting it in Practice

Create the First Next Step

It's said that a journey of 1000 miles begins with the first step. This is exactly the frame of mind you need to have. Find small, initial steps that take you a fraction of the way toward your desired future and just jump in.

Don't get bogged down in doubt or worry that they are not the right steps or in the right order or that they are too small. Just get started and adjust along the way.

Initial steps are often exploratory, such as research or interviews. They also may involve planning or creating time and place for the work. Here are some examples:

- Create a workspace for the team doing this work.
- Set up a weekly review meeting to assess progress.
- Find 3 other people who have done something similar and interview them.
- Research the topic and summarize key findings.
- Create a list of obstacles that may get in your way – and then plan ways to eliminate, avoid or mitigate them.
- Create a list of success factors – what are the critical elements that define success for your endeavor?
- Define a list of resources you'll need to create your desired future. This can be time, money, people or knowledge (or others).

For your desired future, list 3 to 4 possible logical, next steps. What are they? Who might do them? When would you expect them to be due?

Creating the First Next Steps

Action	Responsible	Due by	Deliverable

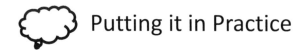 Putting it in Practice

Design a Roadmap with Milestones

There are many reasons to create a visual roadmap for your work. Some of them include helping your team see the path when not every step is known. Roadmaps help team members see some high level sequence and timing – and give them a sense of direction. They help mark progress and enable people to think ahead a few steps at a time.

Roadmaps are NOT detailed project plans. They are typically a graphical (and think poster sized or larger) image of moving from the current state to the desired future state with some key milestones identified.

If you are not so good at creating, Idea Connect (http://store.beideaconnect.com/) has great simple templates that can be ordered at a low cost. Begin by listing major milestones you'll need to accomplish to create your desired future:

What is the best way to graphically show your roadmap and milestones? You may choose to illustrate your roadmap ideas on a whiteboard, PowerPoint, poster or drawing. This is a place to get creative. Engage others is creating a graphic that shows the path you are taking.

Milestone	Approximate Completion Date

2.3   Hold Frequent Checkpoints

Leading forward in today's ambiguous and quick to change environment is very much like walking through fog in other ways. It is extremely easy to lose your bearings, you can't always know what the road ahead brings, and the natural hesitancy is to wait until the fog clears to move forward. You need to understand that the fog is NOT going to lift and instead may get denser. For that reason alone, standing still is not an option.

Once you are moving, even slowly, maintaining your bearings and assessing the next steps are critical. **Holding regular checkpoints is the answer to this dilemma.**

Due to the unknowable nature of the road to the destination, your first role as a leader in the checkpoint is to remind people of the desired future. Describe it again. Help others to see it in their minds eye and experience the feelings that are associated with it. Have others begin to describe it, play with it, imagine it. The more real the desired future becomes in your mind and the minds of others, the greater likelihood you will achieve it, the more momentum you gain and the more energy is created. Helping those you lead see, internalize and then own the desired future makes it real, meaningful, and moves it from a task to a mission.

This is a time for dialogue, not a speech. Having others articulate their vision of the desired future does more than maintain focus, energy and effort toward the goal. Wise leaders seek out the increased richness and depth that others can bring to the future state. They allow others to shape both the end and the means. They know that others can see things they cannot. They know they are not the sole holder of the wisdom contained within the group. They

Even if you fall on your face, you're still moving forward.

Victor Kiam

We demand rigidly defined areas of doubt and uncertainty.

Douglas Adams

are able to shed the notion that it is "their way or no way."

Once you have re-imagined the desired future with the group you lead, you are going to continue the dialogue and exploration by answering these questions:

- What progress have we made?

- What have we learned along the way?

- What is working well?

- What might we shed at this time? (effort, beliefs, ideas, tasks)

- What more do we know than before about the external environment?

- What has changed (or is changing) around us?

- What is then next logical step (or steps)?

We all can bring to mind the image of the artist painting for a bit and then stepping back from the work to examine it in its entirety. That is exactly what you need to ensure happens as you and your team create something new. Do a bit of work, step back, compare the current with the desired, and then determine the next best step.

How often you conduct check points is a function of the size and scope of the work, the maturity of your team and the degree of clarity you are able to develop in the journey. I would suggest the following guidelines:

- Hold them more frequently in the early stages. This helps to reinforce the vision, forces accountability for action, builds momentum and signals importance.

- NEVER go more than a month without a check point.

- Find a balance between quick check points (sometimes daily for 15 minutes) and deeper

Nobody knows how things will turn out, that's why they go ahead and play the game...You give it your all and sometimes amazing things happen, but it's hardly ever what you expect.

Gennifer Choldenko

dive check points. I've seen projects make amazing progress quickly by doing daily 15 minute check points and half day debriefs monthly.

- Create a structure or framework that is used consistently. This begins to shape the thought process needed to create – and will begin to be used daily and not just at check points. It also builds efficiency and a sense of order in the check point process. A simple framework is having everyone one report on what has been accomplished, what has been learned, and what will be done next.

- Insist on truth telling. Listen hard to all voices. Thank others for raising uncomfortable news. Model the way by sharing areas in which you, as the leader, failed or had a misstep.

- Celebrate the progress made, including mistakes. Remember that even a misstep is rich is learning – and has value.

Begin with the strategic (the vision of the desired future) and end with the tactical. Always end with documenting actions to be taken including who is to do them and by when.

Don't dwell on what went wrong. Instead, focus on what to do next. Spend your energies on moving forward toward finding the answer.

Denis Waitley

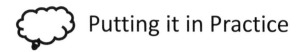 # Putting it in Practice

Design a Review Process

One of the most significant actions a leader can take when creating something new is to maintain focus. And the best way to maintain focus is to hold regular reviews. These reviews serve multiple purposes:

- They signal that you are serious about doing this work
- They drive accountability
- They mark progress
- They maintain momentum
- They allow time for review, reflection and learning
- They provide a space for revised planning

The format of your review process will vary according to your project and your team. No matter how done, I encourage you to include these elements:

- What have we accomplished?
- What barriers have we encountered?
- What is the most appropriate response to these barriers?
- What have we learned?
- What adjustments do we need to make?
- What are the next steps?
- Who is responsible to complete them?

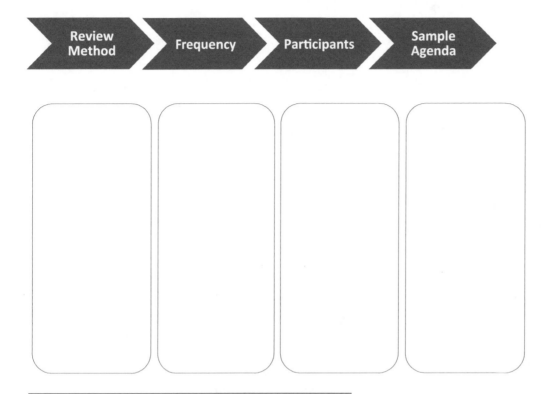

---

3   Avoid a Muddled Mess

There is wisdom in the adage that "too many cooks spoil the stew". It is also true that you cannot create in isolation. As a leader, you will want to carefully manage the dynamic between purposeful and helpful engagement against too many voices and too much input. This section will help you strike that balance.

3.1   Engage with Purpose

Engaging others is a dual edged sword – it can add creativity, energy, motivation and buy in. It can also be burdensome to you and others, can slow you down and can result is cynicism and a sense of abandonment if you are not able to be fully engaged alongside those that you have included in the work. Here is a quick guide about when to (and not to) engage others. As you improve in your skills in this area, you will become masterful at this – just as the jazz master cuing others to come in and out of the work.

Engage More	Engage Less (or not at all)
The work requires creativity and fresh thinking	The outcome is known
Resistance is high and/or buy in is important	The impact is minimal
You need diverse ideas and multiple perspectives	There is little room for creativity
You have time to implement new ideas and fresh thinking	You are in an emergency situation

Engage appropriately

Engagement can vary from a very low level of involvement (give me your opinion) to a very high one (lead a significant portion of this work). Choosing how to engage, who to engage and at what level is a dynamic process in which you pull together your knowledge of your team, their capacity and the work to be done. Give team members a role to play that uses a strength or builds a skill set. Ensure that the work given, no matter how large or small, is needed and heeded. For example, asking for input is a great way to build engagement – however you must be prepared to REALLY listen and to be open to changing your approach based on what you hear. That does not mean that you will incorporate every idea; it does mean that every idea is considered and evaluated.

> *For good ideas and true innovation, you need human interaction, conflict, argument, debate.*
>
> Margaret Heffernan

Set clear short-term expectations

When change is afoot, there is a great propensity for stonewalling, delaying and other forms of passive resistance. Waiting it out is a tactic used successfully in most organizations. To avoid this, divide the work and assignments into smaller, rather than larger pieces, especially in the beginning where you want to build momentum. Set a deadline and hold to it. Check on the work - and hold your team accountable to meeting the deadlines that are set.

The metaphor here is one of a marathon runner. 26.2 miles can be daunting, especially at mile 20. A tactic they use is focusing and completing smaller milestones, one after the other, rather than the finish line. Making it to the next intersection is doable and once there, the next and the next and the next. These smaller milestones keep you moving and motivated – rather than overwhelmed and discouraged.

Capital isn't so important in business. Experience isn't so important. You can get both these things. What is important is ideas. If you have ideas, you have the main asset you need, and there isn't any limit to what you can do with your business and your life.

Harvey Firestone

Keep the end state firmly in mind

This is a repeat, but worth repeating. The more vividly and more often you can help others "see" and "feel" your desired end state, the more aligned their efforts will be. The challenge for you as a leader is twofold – translating your vision into something others can understand and the number of times (and number of ways) you will need to communicate this until others begin to grasp it. Know that you will need to articulate your vision many more times that you ever imagined. The more ways you can find to help your team "see" it – the more they will embrace it. This is not a once and done effort. Repeat and repeat frequently.

Step back and review frequently

Just like the artist who has to step back from their painting to get perspective and see what needs done next, so goes this work. This iterative cycle of planning, execution, review and learning needs to happen in shorter bursts rather than long time frames. This is especially true in the beginning.

You'll want to step back as the leader and assess first – as you have the primary role of leading the work. Then in short order, create time and a process for your team to do the same. This is the time for truth telling, for course correction, for owning and learning from mistakes, and for celebrating progress. Hold a high standard for these reviews – and don't allow them to become just a "check the box" effort. You need to make missteps, solid critique and "do overs" acceptable. To do this, you will need to model the way, challenge your team when they are softening or avoiding difficult topics and reward both failure and success.

> *There are really three parts to the creative process. First there is inspiration, then there is the execution, and finally there is the release.*
>
> Eddie Van Halen

Set the bar high

Over and over again in organizations, I see the tendency for much needed, transformational efforts to get diluted. Important deliverables get "de-scoped" or deferred to Phase Two (which often never happens). Deadlines slip. Hard choices don't get made. The end result is much time, money and energy spent on a lack luster end result.

Set the bar high and know what is non-negotiable. People have an amazing capacity to achieve – when someone asks them to and holds firm on the expectation.

> *The best way to have a good idea is to have a lot of ideas.*
>
> Dr. Linus Pauling

4   A Perilous Path

We live in a world that desires the known, which wants to eliminate risk (or at least manage it), which rewards certainty and short term results. The leader creating a dramatically different and better future operates in direct opposition to all of these. The creative path is unknowable and uncertain. There will be risks and missteps. The view is long term and there will be a short term price to pay for creating something better. Even when the current state may be untenable, people will still cling to it, for it is known. As the old saying goes: "The devil we know is better than the one we don't."

As a leader, you must deeply understand that the more transformative your work, the more you must be prepared for challenges. Be prepared for push back. Fortify yourself for a long and arduous journey. Keep in mind your vision. Know deeply that your work matters and that with perseverance positive change can occur.

I wanted a perfect ending. Now I've learned, the hard way, that some poems don't rhyme, and some stories don't have a clear beginning, middle, and end. Life is about not knowing, having to change, taking the moment and making the best of it, without knowing what's going to happen next. Delicious Ambiguity.

Gilda Radner

The Inner Shift

Our inside out leadership model means that examining your beliefs and "stories" is needed. Review this below and determine if there are some underlying thoughts and beliefs you might shed to help you create.

Shed These Beliefs	Grow These
I should KNOW all the answers in advance	I and those around me have the capacity to find the answers as needed
Mistakes are to be avoided at all costs	Mistakes are a natural outcome of creative work and leadership
Mistakes and failures are sources of embarrassment	Mistakes and failures are sources of great learning
Safety and stability are the goal	Growth and positive forward momentum are the goal
Others will embrace my vision and support my efforts because of my position	Transformative change will be difficult for others to envision, believe in and I'll encounter resistance along the way
I'll be able to create positive results quickly	The work may be long and hard, but is worthwhile

Behaviors speak louder than words and especially for a leader. As such, be very conscious of your actions (and reactions) along the way. What you do will be watched carefully for signals, signs and cues. What you don't do is just as important.

Here are some short examples of actions you can to take foster movement toward your desired future. We'll continue to build your skills in subsequent stages, but use these as starting points.

Be candid about what you don't know – and follow it with a statement of belief in the collective capacity to discover the answer. For example: "I've struggled with that question myself. I must admit, that I don't have the perfect answer. I do know, that by working together, we will be able to find a good answer."

Relinquish tight control over information. Encourage others to seek out information, analyze it and bring it back to the team.

Spend your time and energy LEARNING from mistakes and missteps, rather than assigning blame or deflecting the situation. Conduct a lessons learned session – in which you ask good questions and explore what you now know that you did not in the past.

Be patient. Breathe. Explain. Explain again. Guide. Coach. Explain again.

Find ways to take care of yourself. The work of transformation is difficult physically, emotionally and spiritually. It may be exercise, meditation, eating well, hydrating, being outdoors, reading books that nourish you, or time with a good listener. No matter what works for you – schedule time to do that which replenishes your spirit at least weekly.

My final word of advice to you is to find ways to celebrate along the way. Plan to do a combination of individual celebrations and ones you share with your teams. And then do them. Don't be intimidated by the word "celebration." If it brings to mind something big, time consuming, extravagant, and expensive – substitute another word – such as acknowledgement or recognition or get together to mark progress. The celebrations that are the most meaningful are often personal and sincere acknowledgements of learning, of progress, of effort and of achieving milestones.

It's easy to come up with new ideas; the hard part is letting go of what worked for you two years ago, but will soon be out of date.

Roger von Oech

Innovation distinguishes between a leader and a follower.

Steve Jobs

Here are some idea starters – for both individuals and groups:

Individual	Group
Spend an hour in a favorite quiet place to just think or write	Send handwritten notes of appreciation
Take a day away from work to do something that brings you joy and peace	Designate time in a group meeting to list accomplishments – and then post them.
Do something special at the achievement of milestones – such as a massage, special dinner out, hike in the woods, or something that you really enjoy but rarely do	Give spontaneous applause when team members realize an achievement
Create a list of all that has been accomplished – including how you and team members have grown, what you have learned and what you have accomplished.	Give toasts to progress and to learning – with wine after work or sparkling juice at a team meeting
Treat the special people in your life (spouse, partner, significant other, children, best friend) to time alone just with you – in which you openly appreciate the support they have given you.	Find opportunities to share learnings, failures and progress across the organization (this can be a presentation, in a newsletter or blog or by a special event)
Spend an hour in a favorite quiet place to just think or write	Bring in special coffee or a mid-afternoon snack; cakes and cookies are easy to personalize with a message
Find or purchase something that symbolizes the progress you've made – most of the fun is in the search	Take a few hours away from work to do something fun that builds teamwork and provides a break

5   A Final Note

The actions you will begin as a result of this work (determining the immediate next step, creating a roadmap, and holding regular reviews) are powerful steps that get others engaged and moving on the path to creating your desired future. We would be remiss not to mention that as you begin leading others toward that future – you will begin to discover a range of reactions and emotions. There will be some who are enthusiastically behind you and willing to begin immediately. There will be others who are open, but more cautious. And there are others who are concerned and fearful of the change.

Monitor your group carefully. Talk to them often. Assess their level of understanding, buy in and ability to do what is needed. It will not be uncommon to encounter some of the difficulties listed below. When you do, take immediate action to get back on track and maintain momentum.

> *Ah, the creative process is the same secret in science as it is in art. They are all the same absolutely.*
>
> Josef Albers

5.1   Common Problems Solved

At times, in spite of good efforts taking all the actions we've outlined in this section, you may still encounter obstacles. Below is a quick guide to common challenges leaders encounter and ways to deal with each.

Stonewalling	Create crystal clear short-term actions with firm deadlines that team members are held accountable to hit. Demonstrate that moving forward is absolutely expected.

Misdirection	Very common in the early stages. Often happens with those that are most enthused about the work – as they just jump into it. Provide continual reminder of the end state. Appreciate the effort, even if misdirected, and help people sort out what part of the effort was appropriate and what part was not. Articulate your reasoning, so that others can begin to self-correct without your intervention.
Watered Down Efforts	Halfhearted efforts are often a testing ground (are we really serious) and a way to marginally participate. Reinforce the positive (the effort taken) and be clear about what more is needed. Create a shared agreement on the importance and quality levels – and create an accountability system.
Fear of Failure	The bigger your vision, the higher the fear. As best you can, understand the source of the fear. Know that it may or may not be rational, but it is still real. Have that person(s) begin with very small steps. Celebrate progress. Celebrate learning. Ensure failures are not punished.
Overstating Progress Made	Be suspicious when everything is going smoothly, on time and without problems. Truly transformational change just does not work that way. Listen. Test. Ask for details to really understand. Respond carefully when there are problems and setbacks – so that you demonstrate a zest for solving the problem and not chastising the person who brings forward or creates the problem. Make it the norm to be transparent about the true current state.

Additional Resources:

Bossidy, Larry, Ram Charan, and Charles Burck. *Execution: the discipline of getting things done*. New York: Crown Business, 2002.

Russell, Lou. *10 steps to successful project management*. Alexandria, Va.: ASTD Press, 2007.

Wickman, Gino. *Traction Get a Grip on Your Business*. New York: BenBella Books, Inc., 2012.

CHAPTER 7
Building Engagement

Engagement

Whether you are creating at work, at home or in the community – this is not a solitary journey. There are others that you need to engage, who are needed to help, support, or ultimately be a part of the new creation.

1   Getting Buy In

As you've followed the creative process, you now have a vision, are clear about the difference between where you currently are and where you want to be, and have begun the work of creating, or moving toward that place you want to be. Whether you are creating at work, at home or in the community – this is not a solitary journey. In every change process, there are a variety of stakeholders that may be directly or indirectly impacted. These people are the ones that you need to engage, that need to help or support or ultimately be a part of the new creation. They may be the individuals that are affected or benefit from the changes you are bringing to life. Or, you may need to ensure that they support your efforts rather than block them. There may be others who need to know about your work and as a result, adopt it or use it or appreciate it or buy it.

> *To dare is to lose one's footing momentarily. To not dare is to lose oneself.*
>
> Soren Kierkegaard

The traditional view of the creative is one of creating in some solitary studio and then unveiling their work to the public. The work is seen as solitary, lonely, and done in isolation. When revealed in its final form, it is sometimes a hit and sometimes a miss. In this model one does not know until it is launched.

Creating within an organization, by its nature, cannot follow that path. New businesses, new products or services, new ways of doing things or working together require a group mindset. Creating in isolation and then springing it on your customers, your boss, your co-workers or the larger organization is a recipe for rejection and a quick death. You will face resistance at every step.

Creating within an ecosystem of people (an organization) cannot be done in isolation. You cannot expect people to embrace your new big thing, no matter how needed or wonderful it is, if they are blindsided by it. As such, creating within an organization or existing social system requires bringing people along, engaging them in the process, and helping them see what is being created and why.

At first blush, this sounds like a lot of effort. And it is. In addition to doing the work of creating, you are doing additional work in communicating, engaging, and involving. You may be inclined to skip this work, as it will detract your time and energy from creating, it will be messy, and it will only delay or dilute your work.

The paradox is, that done well, building engagement and buy in can do just the opposite. Proper engagement can:

- Shorten time to adoption – as people embrace what they have had a chance to help create.

- Make your end result richer and more robust, as others can add elements that you alone cannot.

It is easier to resist at the beginning than at the end.

Leonardo da Vinci

Progress always involves risks. You can't steal second base and keep your foot on first.

Frederick B. Wilcox

- Develop positive energy and focus that moves the project along faster.
- Mobilize others to contribute time and resources, so that you are not going it alone.
- Dramatically increase your chances of success.

That being said, doing this and doing it well takes time, effort and skill. As you practice these skills they will get easier, but many of them will be new to you. Allow yourself the latitude to be a learner in this space. Try it, learn from it and do it better the next time. Attempt, reflect and adjust - over and over again until you become proficient.

> *Don't refuse to go on an occasional wild goose chase – that's what wild geese are for.*
>
> Unknown

---

2   Change is Emotional

An underlying concept that is important for you to understand is people's emotional reactions to things that are new. There are some predictable phases that will occur as people move from idea to action to reality. William Bridges describes these stages wonderfully in his book Managing Transitions. As I've helped leaders with hundreds of organizational changes and gone through just as many personal changes, I can attest that Bridges has truly charted the emotional path from introducing a new idea to fully realizing the idea.

The work of Bridges helps us to understand that change is much more than just the physical change itself. Truly changing is an emotional process that occurs over time. Examples abound. We moved to the Midwest in the early '90s. Even though we were settled into the new house, the kids were enrolled in

> *People don't resist change. They resist being changed.*
>
> Peter M. Senge

school, and I had a new job – it took over two years for me to call this home. I started my business in June of 2004, yet for close to 6 months, when asked what I did for a living, I would talk about my previous job and employer. The physical things happened relatively quickly – the move, the new job – but my emotional transition (buy in) took much longer.

As a leader who is creating something new, it is important to understand this dynamic and to work with it. No matter what you do, you cannot avoid this emotional process of transition. You will go through it as well. While you can't avoid it, you can understand it and take certain actions that will decrease the duration and minimize the confusion, angst and distress of transition. The chart on the next page greatly simplifies Bridges' work – but can provide a general overview that can help guide your leadership actions.

> *If you're are paralyzed with fear it's a good sign. It shows you what you have to do.*
>
> Steven Pressfield

Ending → **Transition** → **New Beginning**

Leader Actions during Stages of Change

Stage	Typical Emotions	Questions / Reactions	Leadership Action
Endings (introducing the change)	**Confusion** **Denial** **Excitement**	• What is this? • What does it mean to me? • We don't need to do this. • This too, shall pass. • We are fine the way we are. • I like this idea. • We should have done this sooner.	• Communicate the "Why" – your vision for the future • Paint the Current Reality – why the need for change • Look for the Early Adaptors –enlist them & encourage them
Transitions (the work of moving from the current state to the future state)	**Uncertainty** **Grieving** **Fatigue** **Optimism**	• Tell me more about... • Have you thought about? • I'm not sure this will work • I like the old way. • This is harder than I expected. • I'm tired. • I am afraid of the new way. • I think this will work. • I have an idea. • I like what I see.	• Continue to communicate – repeatedly and in many ways • Be visible • Listen • Take steady action and highlight progress • Involve others • Claim small wins and celebrate them • Voice confidence • Acknowledge fears, frustration and losses
New Beginnings (adopting the new way)	**Caution** **Confidence** **Pride**	• I think I can do this. • This is working. • Will this last? • This is better than I thought.	• Maintain the focus – it is easy to slip back • Celebrate wins • Acknowledge efforts • Support the shift (time, resources, energy)

3   Leaders Go First

Remember that just because this is your vision, your creation and your energy, it does not mean that you will avoid experiencing all the emotions that come with a transition. In fact, as this is important to you, you may experience them even more deeply than those you lead.

The leap between idea and action is a scary one – tantamount to flinging oneself across a wide and deep chasm. There is plenty of personal doubt. Can I do this? What will others think? Do I have all that is needed to make this real? What if it doesn't work? Who am I to do this "big" thing? Why me? Why now? The list of thoughts that will surface in your mind that are have the potential to derail you, slow you down or cause you to abandon or dilute your effort.

Dealing with your own personal resistance is an individual, privately waged battle. Knowing in advance that fear, reluctance and resistance will surface, and that it is a normal part of the creative process, can prepare you for it. Having the discipline to stay the course will help you overcome it. Yet if your desired future is big enough and important enough, most likely you will face your own internal fear and resistance. It is a sign that you are on the right track, that what you have envisioned is big and it matters, that it threatens the status quo and is a meaningful step forward, not just a marginal one.

As a leader, your challenge is first of all yourself – and then those that you lead. Think about it – if you are experiencing some resistance and this is your vision, your idea, your "baby," it is only natural to believe that those who you lead will be even more challenged to put their time, energy and support into

Simplicity is about subtracting the obvious and adding the meaningful.

John Maeda

Electric communication will never be a substitute for the face of someone who with their soul encourages another person to be brave and true

Charles Dickens

creating this new thing. They cannot see the future state as clearly as you can. They may not have such a burning desire to move past the current state. They may not understand the why of what you are doing or how to do it. At best, they may be ambivalent. At the worst, they may be actively resistant.

It may be daunting – but a large part of building your new future involves bringing others along. That is the nature of leadership. So you are both doing the work that creates forward momentum and doing the work that enables others to understand the need, see the path, know what they must do and also desire that which you are working for. This requires not one single act of leadership, but many done in concert and over time.

> *Just because everything is different doesn't mean anything has changed.*
>
> Irene Peter

3.1   Create Shared Purpose

There is a dramatic difference between having those you lead embracing the work that needs done versus only doing it halfheartedly because they must. To the extent that you can create shared purpose the lighter your load will be, the easier the work for all is and the more rewarding it is. Bring to mind the underdog sports team that pulls together with a shared purpose, such as to dedicate their game to someone associated with the team that is facing a personal battle, and you'll know the focus and energy that can result from shared purpose.

Purpose is not about how we do something; it is about WHY we do something. Southwest does what it does so that people have fun. Apple does what it does to bring elegant design and innovation into the world.

> *Why not go out on a limb? Isn't that where the fruit is?*
>
> Frank Scully

148

Ensure that you can clearly and concisely describe your "why." Try it out. Does it inspire you? Will it inspire others?

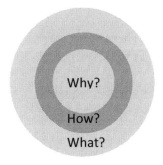

Why = The Purpose

What is your cause? What do you believe?

How = The Process

Specific actions taken to realize the Why

What = The Result

What do you do? The result of Why. Proof.

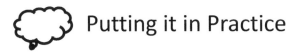 Putting it in Practice

Reinforce, Refine, and Make Real Your Vision

Perhaps the most concise description of the concept of WHY is in a Ted Talk by Simon Sinek called "How Great Leaders Inspire Action". It is why you are doing something that provides focus, energy and sustained effort. Everyone wants to be part of something of value, something that makes a mark and makes a difference. Simon Sinek calls this the Golden Circle, which has Why at the center.

Exercise

Watch Simon Sinek's Ted Talk on the Golden Circle.

Then, create your own Golden Circle. Begin with your "Why" or your purpose. Then summarize the process or how you are going to achieve the purpose. Finally, note the results you will achieve.

Why = The Purpose

How = The Process

What = The Result

3.2 Make It a Shared Journey

Think of leadership as collaborative and shared work to bring something new into the world. There are times where you must direct, but command alone will not get you there. Letting go of absolute control of both the outcome and the work to achieve the outcome can be difficult. It is like seeing your child go out from the safe world you've created in your home. It is scary, and you may feel a sense of loss. You may mourn the belief that you no longer have total control (or the perception of total control). You know that your child will take on a life of his/her own – and that

You'll always miss 100% of the shots you don't take.

Wayne Gretzky

the outcome and the way to realization will be different than you imagined.

In transformational leadership, your role is to envision, to define the purpose, to set the stage and then to unleash the energy. Great things do not happen in isolation. Invite others in. Welcome their help, their energy, and their ideas. Use the words "ours" and" we" more than "mine" and "I."

> *Communication is the real work of leadership.*
>
> Nitin Nohria

3.3 Constant Communication

Now that you have developed creative tension, you've signaled to your team that they are officially "in transition." They see that the current state is not adequate and have a sense of the future you are striving for. It is difficult to know exactly how they will feel about this, except to know that there **will** be feelings and emotions about it. I can guarantee that the emotions will be mixed and are likely to include hope, excitement, fear, anxiety, ambivalence, engagement, concern and anticipation.

Transitory states are emotional times. Always. And in these times, leaders must communicate. I'll share some specifics in this section, but know that communication needs are higher in times of transition than in any other time; people need to hear the details over and over and over again to begin to fully assimilate the meaning. Just as with a child who must hear vocabulary multiple times in various contexts to learn it, so must those around you hear about this work to "get it."

> *Nothing will ever be attempted, if all possible objections must first be overcome.*
>
> Samuel Johnson

Use dialogue, not broadcast

Newsletters, bulletin board postings and emails do not change minds or hearts. Use these forums for sheer information. What does change hearts and minds are face to face, person to person discussions. As the leader, you are the most influential person for your team – and you are the one that needs to be having the dialogue. These are not discussions to demand or force the issue, but to influence. Whether one on one, in team meetings, or in town halls – talk about what you are creating, why it is important, and what others can do to help.

Never be afraid to try something new. Remember amateurs built the ark; professionals built the Titanic.

Unknown

Communicate about the tough stuff

Nothing truly great was created without some sort of pain or sacrifice. Martin Luther King led an effort that resulted in more equality for people of color, yet people who supported the civil rights moment were jailed, beaten and some lost their lives. JFK was a catalyst to propel America to excel in the race to space, but a lot of hard work and taxpayer support was required. Even if your future state is not as grandiose as a man on the moon, it will still come at a price. That price may be additional effort or dealing with uncertainty or learning new skills or a physical move or diverted resources. At times it means old jobs go away. If your change is big enough to get excited about, it will involve loss of the old and effort to create the new.

This is not a secret. People understand this. Yet far too many leaders avoid talking about the cost involved and the pain points. The paradox in this is that the leaders who only paint a "rosy" picture of the work do not make people feel better, even though that may

To listen well is as powerful a means of communication and influence as to talk well.

John Marshall

be their intent. Instead, because people do understand that progress requires a price, they are uneasy with leaders who do not acknowledge it. They wonder if the leader is truly blind to this fact, or is simply reluctant to face the hard questions (i.e. the "elephant in the room"). The leader loses credibility. The paradox is that leaders who acknowledge the pain, the unknown and the uncertainty, gain credibility.

Notice that I said acknowledge. I did not say wallow in it, whine about it, make excuses, or allow it to derail you. I am talking about an honest assessment of the pain, unknown and uncertainty. That makes you real. It sends the message that you understand this will not be easy. Use this statement as a model: "I know this will be hard, but I know that it will be worthwhile and that we are up to it." See how after acknowledging the pain, we were reminded of purpose and confidence was expressed.

Exhibit authenticity and vulnerability

There will be times on this journey to create your new future that you are confused. You may experience doubt or difficulty. You may feel vulnerable because you are out of your comfort zone. There may be difficult things that are hard to discuss. The more aware you are of your inner state, the better able you are to think about the leadership signals that you might be providing and what the team really needs from you. And at times, that may be an acknowledgement that you don't have all the answers. That you have moments of doubt. That you wish this was easier.

This may be difficult to believe. Wouldn't people rather follow someone they saw as invincible or who seemed to know all the answers? Will they want

The most important thing in communication is hearing what isn't said.

Peter Drucker

You might as well fall flat on your face as lean over too far backward.

James Thurber

to follow someone who says they don't know it all, don't have everything figured out?

In times of emergency, leaders who know the way and can command and direct win hands down. Think of Captain Sully Sullenberger, who successfully saved 155 passengers and crew from Flight 1549 when it made an emergency landing in the Hudson River.

Sully could do that because he knew it. He had practiced emergency evacuations over and over and over again. He was prepared to execute the emergency disembarking when it happened.

However, you are most likely leading in a time and place where the way is not known. Where you can't practice because you don't know. Where you know the general direction, but not the specific steps. In these instances, communicating with transparency and vulnerability can actually garner confidence and the willingness to follow.

People can spot a fake a mile away. They see leaders puffing up their chests and proclaiming that they have the answers to the problem at hand – unemployment, stalled economy, education. And they know these problems are complex and that solutions are just as complex. Leaders who operate on bravado and a false illusion of control engender doubt and disbelief.

Authenticity can garner an even greater level of commitment and buy in. Authenticity means that you reveal how much the end state matters. What frustrates you about the current state. And that the future state is important enough and that you have enough confidence in the collective talent that you *will* find the way.

> *He who rejects change is the architect of decay. The only human institution which rejects progress is the cemetery.*
>
> Harold Wilson

> *To effectively communicate, we must realize that we are all different in the way we perceive the world and use this understanding as a guide to our communication with others.*
>
> Tony Robbins

Use stories, images and metaphors

Stories, images and metaphors provide you with short cuts to help you convey your point. Not only can an image communicate quickly – it can communicate deeply and memorably. There are several reasons this is so. Stories build on something we already know – and are grounded in our life experience. It is much easier to relate to and remember, as opposed to isolated concepts and theories. Stories, by their nature evoke emotion – and that also creates a hook. Emotion pulls us in, allows us to relate and helps us care. Finally stories, images and metaphors are highly effective because they use both sides of our brains; we can think and feel, we can analyze and imagine; we can be both objective and subjective.

Aesop knew it. A short story with a powerful punch line creates a memorable and lasting lesson. Who does not remember the story of the ant and the grasshopper or the boy who cried wolf? Artists also know it – hence the popular wisdom that a picture paints a thousand words.

If you can find a powerful metaphor for your change, use it…and use it over and over and over again. Make it a theme. Use the imagery at various places. Typical metaphors often involve journeys, climbing, overcoming a struggle, sports, nature or the seasons.

If you can tell a story – either about why it is important to change or what the future state might look like or feel like – do it!   Your stories may be real or imagined or a combination of both.   You might have a story about your compelling reason to create

> *Take risks: if you win, you will be happy; if you lose, you will be wise.*
>
> Unknown

> *Whatever words we utter should be chosen with care for people will hear them and be influenced by them for good or ill.*
>
> Buddha

something new (why is your innovation needed) or the problem with the status quo. You might begin to use real example stories that highlight progress made or team members that exemplify the right behaviors, attitudes and actions.

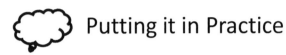 ## Putting it in Practice

Communicate in Ways that Stick

Early in the creative process, your vision is much more real to you than it is to anyone else. Your on-going task will be to help others see your vision, to understand both why it is important to achieve and why staying in the status quo is unacceptable. This is leadership work that you will have to do over and over and over again. You'll have to do it with all your stakeholders – and in different ways. You'll communicate it repeatedly because people need to hear things more than once to truly understand. And you'll communicate it in various ways because people take in information in different ways.

While you will use different communication methods and approaches, you should consistently follow these guidelines:

- Communicate face to face, as much as possible. While email and newsletters and bulletin board notices can support your message, they are NOT the primary means to convey it.

- Communicate honestly and directly. You'll not shirk from difficult information. You'll share what you see that makes the current situation undesirable.

- Encourage two way dialogue and discussion. This aids others' understanding of your message and allows you to assess where your team is relative to the work.

- Remain aware of the other parties' points of view – and communicate with that in mind.

- Recognize that people need both the rational (facts) and the emotional (story). It is the emotional story that really begins to shift understanding and energy.

- Find simple and compelling ways to tell the story.

How you communicate will depend on your own style and the situation. If you've not used some of these ways to communicate with your team in the past, I encourage you to step out of your comfort zone and try them.

For a deeper dive, I would recommend reading Made to Stick by Chip and Dan Heath.

Story

Stories are powerful ways to communicate, especially when you want to be memorable, since they often appeal to our emotional side. As humans, we've used stories to transmit important information through generations and centuries – first with an oral tradition using poetry, song, theater and traveling story tellers. With the advent of printing, stories were captured in books and with the advent of TV and film, we also capture stories in movies, TV and the internet. When you begin to notice, stories are all around us.

Great leaders and coaches are almost always great story tellers. That's because they know that stories can reach deeper, that they create interest, credibility and can create an inner shift in a way that data, facts and reports just can't.

Exercise

Draft a story that embodies the message you want to send. The story steps are:

- What is the one point you want to convey with this story?
- What is the situation? How can you set the scene and create context?
- Who are the characters? How can you help others see them vividly?
- Describe the task. What is this person(s) attempting to accomplish?
- What challenges do they face or obstacles do they encounter?
- How do they resolve the challenge or overcome the obstacle?
- What is the resolution to the story?
- What is the learning or point you want others to take away? Can you summarize it in a memorable short phrase?

Metaphor or Pictures

You've heard that a picture is worth a thousand words. It is true. One of the easiest and most effective ways to evoke pictures to send a message is with the use a metaphor. Think of metaphor as a short cut for communication via the use of a symbol or symbolism. A metaphor takes something that we already know and can envision to describe an attribute of something we don't know as well. This is not a literal description – but one that conveys important attributes that can be difficult to describe. Typically metaphors provide an instant, memorable connection to the message we want to send. For example, perhaps you want to describe the amount of effort it will take to do something. Here are two different metaphors – each one of which provides an instant gauge for just about anyone:

1. This is going to be like scaling Mount Everest in the dead of winter with a strong headwind.
2. This is going to be like going downhill with wheels underneath us and the wind at our back.

These are two different metaphors about effort with two very different messages. But rest assured, these are "stickier" and more compelling than a 500-line project plan. There are times you will want to be more precise with your language, but try to use a metaphor to paint a picture and to communicate quickly, vividly and memorably.

Common metaphors evoke common and shared experiences. Nature, sports, popular culture, animals, and common objects, processes or experiences are all fertile places to find metaphors that you can use to send your message. You may want to listen or read the words of Martin Luther King, Jr. as his work is rich with metaphors and pictures.

Ensure that your metaphor is able to be translated across multiple audiences, especially if your audience is diverse. Once you've found that right metaphor, use the associates' images or pictures as simple reminders.

This is an area where you can ask several creative team members to help craft the metaphor with you. Set aside an hour or so, describe your vision – and then brainstorm away.

Here are some common themes or metaphors:

- A journey
- Climbing a mountain
- Water: stream/lake/river/flood
- Solar system
- Transportation
- Animals

- Body and body parts
- Geography
- Growing
- A community
- Hero's story
- Sports

Experiences

If you can create an experience that helps either paint the possibility of the future or the problem with the current state, you will have gone a long way toward making the emotional shift that is needed. This can be a video or movie, an interview, a field trip or a service project.

For example, when working with an IT team that supported diabetes patients, we toured the diabetes unit of a children's hospital and then heard from a 17 year old patient with diabetes about how her life had changed with her diagnosis. This was a memorable and vivid way to help the team make the shift to be more patient focused in their work – and in an afternoon, we did more to facilitate that shift than all efforts in the past.

Actually experiencing the customer service that your customers receive by "being a customer" can be humbling – and one that can propel work toward creating exceptional customer experiences.

Actions

Finally, actions do speak louder than words. There are no louder words you speak than the actions you take as a leader. As you think through the transformation you want to create, define the actions that are needed. Then think about what you should do as a leader to demonstrate, model and lead the way.

Some examples:

- If you want your team to listen deeply to customers, you begin by listening deeply to them.
- If your vision requires flexibility, you begin by encouraging flexibility in areas of people's work, including your own.
- If your desired future state will need a speedier response to the marketplace, you begin to identify and eliminate barriers that slow the team down in any area.

How can you use these techniques to communicate your message?	
Metaphors	
Pictures	
Experiences	
Actions	

Simplify the complex

Anyone who has created anything at all knows how quickly a simple idea turns into execution complexity. Students in my Entrepreneurship class create (on paper) a simple business – and are always surprised at the complexity. There are work teams to build, products or services to develop and deliver, supply chains to worry about, customers that need found, products to be sold, intellectual property that needs protected and finances to manage.

No matter how complex the situation, your ability to simplify that complexity into something this is understandable, digestible and actionable will separate you from lesser leaders. Jim Collins says it this way: "The essence of profound insight is simplicity."

The simplicity we are talking about here is elegant and clean, not merely stripped down or elementary. Many great quotes are notable for their ability to simply state a profound truth in a pithy and memorable manner. Great design is often a place where simplicity is evident. Michael Graves has mastered the art of simple, yet powerful design with his products. Contrast this to an over engineered car with confusing controls, too many controls, and superfluous accessories.

Once you have your plans or your communication, step back and see the themes that are evident. See where you can simplify. See if you can identify primary elements – that organized your thinking and that you may be able to make evident to others so that they "get it."

If you can't explain it to a six year old, you don't understand it yourself.

Albert Einstein

If you have an important point to make, don't try to be subtle or clever. Use a pile driver. Hit the point once. Then come back and hit it again. Then hit it a third time - a tremendous whack.

Winston Churchill

3.4   Engage the Right People

We've visited this idea earlier, but it bears repeating. When someone is involved in helping to create something, a shift occurs. They become interested. They understand it better. They feel valued. They make it their own.

The key here is to identify the right people, to engage them in meaningful ways and then to be open to their input and ideas. Let's look at each of these.

Identify the right people – Think about what you want to create. Who does it impact? Who needs to buy in? Who might be a show stopper? Is there anyone with disproportionate influence? By this, I mean those people who, if they get behind something can sway many other people. You might call them informal leaders or opinion makers.

Once you've identified your entire list of stakeholders, sort them out. Focus on the people or groups that are both important to your success and influential with those who need to adopt your work. Focus specifically on those individuals, rather than watering down your engagement efforts with everyone. Communicate broadly, but focus selectively on engagement activities – or else you will have far too many tasks and people to manage.

Engage in meaningful ways – Nothing is worse than being asked to do something, especially on a volunteer basis, that is trite or lacking in value. And if you are truly creating something new and something that is needed – there will be no lack of things to do. Here is a starter list of ways you might engage others in the work:

• Thinking partner

• Idea generation sessions

The only difference between a rut and a grave is their dimensions.

Ellen Glasgow

Of all of our inventions for mass communication, pictures still speak the most universally understood language.

Walt Disney

- Feedback on key aspects

- Conducting relevant research

- Identifying questions or concerns others will have

- Helping with the design work

- Reacting to a prototype

- Testing the solution

- Communicating to others

- Becoming an "official" early adopter

- Mentoring you or someone on your team

- Sponsoring your work

As you think of ways to involve people, keep in mind that meaningful does not always mean time intensive. A 30-minute session in which you share your project and a key influencer provides unfiltered feedback can be an amazing contribution. You benefit from their perspective and ideas. They have contributed and feel valued.

Be Open to the Input – Here is the bottom line on engagement and input: If you are not going to do something with the work or the information, don't ask. Think about how frustrating it is to be asked, time and time again, for customer feedback on a process you've provided feedback for in the past and not seen *any* improvement. Or times where you have contributed something to an effort, but it did not get used.

This is all the more reason to be intentional about who you ask (the right people) and what you ask them to do. Your goal is **not** to involve everyone in every aspect, but to ask key influencers or those with a needed skill set to contribute something you really need done.

> *Nothing that is can pause or stay; the moon will wax, the moon will wane, the mist and cloud will turn to rain, the rain to mist and cloud again, tomorrow be today.*
>
> Henry Wadsworth Longfellow

> *The two words 'information' and 'communication' are often used interchangeably, but they signify quite different things. Information is giving out; communication is getting through.*
>
> Sydney J. Harris

A final note: being open to the input does *not* mean that you have to use or adjust to everything that is provided. But you must be open and consider the input. Some you will use. Some you will discard. Some you will adapt. Others will still feel involved, engaged and valued if you listen hard, ask good questions and thank them for their time and effort. If you don't use some of their input, let them know you heard them, you understand their point of view, but are proceeding in a different direction (and include a brief rationale). Artfully executed, this will help you solidify your thinking and earn you the respect of others.

> *Those who expect moments of change to be comfortable and free of conflict have not learned their history.*
>
> Joan Wallach Scott

 ## Putting it in Practice

Engaging Your Influencers

Every creative effort will elicit a reaction. Your will have supporters and detractors. Your job is to identify who you need to be "fans" of the work and thus who you need to engage. There may be many people in your organization or in your potential customer segment. The key here is to focus your time and energy on the ones that really matter. You invariably will have detractors. You will need to determine if they are someone who needs to be converted (by engaging them meaningfully) or who can be silenced by not providing attention or energy to their negativity.

The following chart can help you identify the influencer that you should be communicating with and engaging in your efforts. You can use the chart for groups of people (sales, HR, manufacturing, existing customers) or for individuals. Large efforts will most likely use both some general groups and a few specific names.

The idea is simple – spend the most attention on those that are more influential AND the more important someone is to your effort. Involve them in meaningful ways. Communicate with them frequently. Ensure they know your why and work to convert them into a vocal supporter.

There will be others who are important to your project, but perhaps don't have as much influence as others. Engage them in some way, perhaps not as deeply as your high influencers. There will also be those who are highly influential, but less critical your specific endeavor. It is good to have those individuals on your side, yet they do not need to be deeply involved. You will want to keep them informed, preferably via dialogue and insure that you are "taking their temperature" on occasion. You want to ensure that they never use their influence to derail your efforts, but in general keeping them abreast of your work will suffice.

Finally, there are those folks who are low in influence and are not crucial to your creation. Just because they fall into this category does not mean they are silent, in fact they may be quite vocal or resistant. I've seen leaders make the mistake of spending much time and energy on these groups – to the detriment of the overall effort. Your time is best spent with these groups by amplifying the support of the truly influential – as they will ultimately silence this group. My advice is to "actively ignore" – which means that while you are not interacting directly with them, you do monitor their actions. By doing this, at any time that you feel they have moved up the scale into a position of higher influence, you are able to switch tactics from ignoring into informing, engaging or involving.

Levels of Engagement

The chart below illustrates a model for how to structure your engagement efforts. The next exercise is intended to help you apply this model to your situation.

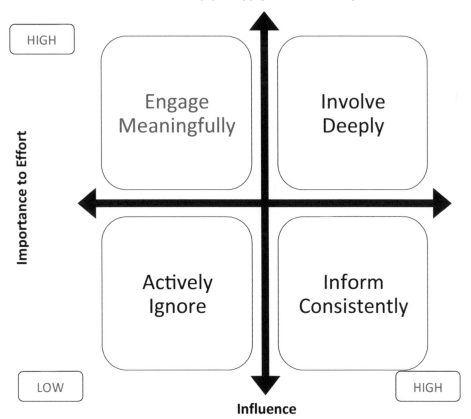

Individual or Group	Category (Engage, Involve, Inform or Ignore)	Actions to Take	Person Responsible

Involve	Engage	Inform	Actively Ignore
• Give them (or someone in their area) a key role • Solicit opinion on a regular basis • Ask them to sponsor your effort • Ask them to mentor a key individual • Have them shape the design • Have them be an early adopter • Be a part of the planning team • Make them a champion of your effort – and enlist them in communicating to others	• Survey for opinions • Schedule regular touch points (meetings, lunch) • Identify concerns or potential obstacles for your effort • Have them test the solution	• Invite to update meetings • Send progress updates • Speak at their meetings	• Assign someone to monitor the group • Provide broadcast updates (newsletters, email blasts)

3.5 Mark Progress / Celebrate Wins

Bridges' work on transition teaches us that on bigger changes that span time, people can easily get discouraged and disheartened. When this happens, it seems much easier to revert to the status quo. As such, it is important as a leader that you help others mark progress and celebrate wins.

Think of this in the same way a long distance runner does. They mark every mile – and celebrate (mentally) having one more mile done. They focus on getting to the next milestone – sometimes a mile marker and sometimes just to the next corner. They focus on and celebrate near term goals, knowing that a singular focus on the finish line seems undoable and is daunting.

Marking progress and celebrating wins sends these leadership messages, in addition to building confidence and momentum:

- I see your effort and I appreciate it

- We are making progress

- This is important and I'm not losing sight of it

- We are really going to do this

- We can do this

Remember that this can be as simple as a handwritten note, food in the break room (with an explanation) or a high five. Bigger milestones may merit more, but focus on more frequent mini celebrations to ramp up engagement, energy and confidence.

> *All changes, even the most longed for, have their melancholy; for what we leave behind us is a part of ourselves; we must die to one life before we can enter another.*
>
> Anatole France

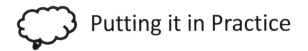 Putting it in Practice

Celebrating Progress

Engaging others is grand. And hopefully, the work itself is rewarding and fun. Even if it is, taking time to celebrate progress is a way to maintain focus, create renewed energy and enhance momentum. And it's fun!

Find something to celebrate this week with your team, family, or work group. Then celebrate!

Here is a list of 50 no or low cost ways you can celebrate. Pick 3 that you will use with those who are helping your vision come to life. You can pick 3 from this list or create your own.

1. Say "Thank you" and mean it. Be specific about what you are thankful for.
2. Ask team members what they need and what you can do for them.
3. Include "kudos" as an agenda item at regular meetings.
4. Arrange for your team to present the results of its efforts to upper management.
5. Acknowledge individual achievements by using team member's names when preparing reports.
6. Write a hand written thank you card.
7. Spend 3 minutes in a team meeting listing all that the team has accomplished. Time the exercise. Record and post.
8. Spend 3 minutes in a team meeting listing what is working well on the project. Time the exercise. Record and post.
9. Go around the table, person by person, and note the positive things that person brings to the team and the effort.
10. Have a potluck lunch.
11. Create a team jingle, cheer or song about the project.
12. Establish a place to display memos, posters, photos, etc. about what you are creating.
13. Establish a "Behind the Scenes/Unsung Hero" award specifically for those whose actions are not usually in the limelight.
14. Coach your team. Positive attention from the leader is a reward in itself.
15. Give special assignments to people who show initiative.
16. Include a team member in a "special" meeting that has high significance.

17. Give team members an extra-long lunch break on occasion.

18. Write a letter of praise recognizing specific contributions and accomplishments. Send a copy to senior management and the team member's personnel file.

19. When you hear a positive remark about someone, repeat it to that person as soon as possible (face-to-face is best, e-mail or voice mail are good in a pinch).

20. Call a team member to your work space to thank them (don't discuss any other issue).

21. Post a large "celebration calendar" in your work area. Tack on notes of recognition to milestone dates.

22. Practice positive nonverbal behaviors that demonstrate appreciation.

23. Support "flex-friendly" schedules.

24. Keep a supply of appropriately funny notes that can be given as immediate rewards. Keep the supply visible – in a basket or box in your office. Encourage everyone to use them.

25. Widely publicize suggestions used and their positive impact on your work.

26. When someone has spent long hours at work, send a letter of thanks to his/her home and include a gift card for a favorite restaurant.

27. Allow a team member to choose his/her next assignment.

28. Share what you are doing and what you have learned with others outside your team. Designate team members to carry the message.

29. Smile. It's contagious.

30. Make a photo collage about your work that shows the people that worked on it, its stage of development and its completion and presentation.

31. Treat team members to bagged lunches/breakfast for a week.

32. Cover a person's desk with balloons for special recognition.

33. Design a "Stress Support Kit" that includes aspirin, a comedy CD, wind-up toys and a stress ball – or design your own.

34. Set up a miniature golf course in your office, using whatever materials you have on hand. Set aside an afternoon or evening to hold a mini golf tournament. Have each area design a "hole" and give a prize.

35. Give a framed poem (poster or card) as a thank you.

36. Acknowledge and celebrate birthdays.

37. Give a note reading, "Thank you. You are a _____!" Attach a roll of Lifesavers.

38. Give a puzzle as an award to a problem solver.

39. Give out (fake) gold coins/stars for a job well done.

40. Bake a gift (cookies, bread, etc.) for an outstanding team performance.

41. Plan a surprise picnic/luncheon/breakfast.
42. Have an ice cream sundae bar. Put out several types of ice cream, toppings and bowls.
43. Purchase a unique pin to serve as a memento for work well done.
44. Take half a day at the park, art gallery or other quiet spot outside your work area to hold informal retreats to foster communication, set goals, and mark progress.
45. Give a personalized coffee cup with an image that conveys what you are creating.
46. Design and give magnets with appropriate messages.
47. Video remarks from happy customers.
48. Pay it forward. Do something nice for someone on the team. Have this start a chain of "pay it forward" events.
49. Watch a funny video or movie together.
50. Invite family / friends in to an event in which you showcase what you are creating.

Additional Resources:

Berger, Jonah. Contagious. London: Simon & Schuster, 2013

Boylan, Bob. Get everyone in your boat rowing in the same direction: 5 leadership principles to follow so others will follow you. Holbrook, Mass.: Adams Pub., 1995.

Bridges, William. Managing transitions: making the most of change. Reading, Mass.: Addison-Wesley, 1991.

Heath, Chip, and Dan Heath. Switch: how to change things when change is hard. New York: Broadway Books, 2010.

Patterson, Kerry. Influencer: the power to change anything. New York: McGraw-Hill, 2008.

CHAPTER 8
A Guide to Polarities

In our increasing challenging and diverse world, we often find we are up against problems that seen to have no answer. We seem to fix one thing, but it creates a problem somewhere else. It may be due to the fact that we are treating these situations as problems rather than polarities. In this chapter, I'll introduce you to the concept of polarities and you'll begin to better sort out if, as a leader, you should be solving a problem or managing a polarity. For many, the concept of polarity may well be something new. If that is the case for you, treat this chapter as a very basic introduction. Then observe, reflect and see if you can find those areas in your life where using this lens may enable you to get much better and sustainable results.

> *Animals are something invented by plants to move seeds around. An extremely yang solution to a peculiar problem which they faced.*
>
> Terence McKenna

1   What is a Polarity?

We deal with them all the time. They drive us mad. They continually frustrate us. They have the ability to divide teams, families, political groups and nations into factious frays.

Yet they are the essence of our existence. Without them, things would be static and lifeless.

A polarity, or paradox, is an intricately entwined state of being – in which seeming opposites get their shape, definition and energy. One without the other is hollow, rigid, unsustainable. Together, the shape of one gives form and definition to the other. When in

dynamic balance, there is a positive tension and a sense of wholeness and health.

From the dictionary we learn that a polarity is defined as the presence or manifestation of two opposite or contrasting principles or tendencies. The Chinese have the concept of Yin and Yang to describe this relationship. From Wikipedia, we learn:

Yin and yang can be thought of as complementary (instead of opposing) forces interacting to form a dynamic system in which the whole is greater than the parts. Everything has both yin and yang aspects, (for instance shadow cannot exist without light). Either of the two major aspects may manifest more strongly in a particular object, depending on the criterion of the observation.

> *Happiness is not a matter of intensity but of balance, order, rhythm and harmony.*
>
> Thomas Merton

1.1   Examples from Nature

Practical examples may help. Nature is abundant with ones to explore – such as light and dark, growth and decline, masculine and feminine, or the positive and negative poles of a magnetic field. An example that you can experience is the process of inhaling and exhaling.

Take a moment to observe your breathing. The two distinct parts, inhalation and exhalation are different – serving different functions and feeling different. Yet, one without the other cannot work. If you try to inhale without exhaling, you soon experience the need to forcefully exhale, just like a balloon overfilled with air. Attempt to forego inhaling and within 20 to 30 seconds, you find yourself gasping for air. It is the delicate dance of inhaling and exhaling that is life giving and sustainable. The two opposite actions act in perfect harmony – one complimenting the other and allowing the other to function perfectly.

There are times we slightly alter the ratio. For example, when I am running I inhale more deeply and exhale more shallowly. When I am tired or frustrated, I exhale (or sigh) more frequently in an attempt to rid myself of tension or pent up energy. Yet even when the balance is slightly altered, I must inhale in order to sigh and exhale in order to take another big gulp of air.

Inhaling and exhaling form a dynamic equilibrium. One exists in support of the other. Inhaling is not good and exhaling bad – they are both fundamentally opposite, but integral parts of the same process. Try not to exhale; you can't. Try not to inhale; you won't last very long.

Another polarity in nature is the visible and invisible portions of a tree. In this image, we see that balance of the below the surface (roots) with the above the surface (trunk and branches). Too few roots, and the tree topples. Too little above the surface, the tree dies.

Other natural examples are that in order for some things to live, others must die. In order for there to be light, there must be darkness. Our human species depends on the masculine and the feminine, the egg and the sperm. We must both rest (or sleep) and be active (or be awake). With too much rest we are lethargic. With too much activity, we are weary. Both states are ineffective and detrimental. Balancing both states creates a "sweet spot" – with enough rest to sustain our activity and enough activity to induce our need to rest.

> *There is no decision that we can make that doesn't come with some sort of balance or sacrifice.*
>
> Simon Sinek

> *It is incorrect to assume that you cannot find any good in the point of view directly opposite yours.*
>
> Daniel Willey

2   Organizational Polarities

Organizations are also rich with polarities that must be dynamically balanced. Here are just a few and there is an extensive list at the end of this chapter.

- Centralized / Decentralized
- Group / Individual
- Short term / Long term
- Controlled/ Flexible
- Fast / Slow

It not just organizations, although that is our focus here. Polarities abound in your personal life, in government, in the natural world. They are everywhere.

2.1   Problem or Polarity?

As a leader, you face both problems and polarities – and plenty of them. One of the key reasons we put people in leadership roles is to solve problems and to make the thorny decisions that come with balancing polarities. I suspect you are well versed in how to solve problems. And I also suspect that no one has even explained the nature of polarities, let alone shown you how to approach them.

There are fundamental differences between problems and polarities. Problems have an answer, an end point, something that can resolved and fixed. With time, energy, money and brainpower, problems can go away. You can find an answer; even though there may be tradeoffs. But no matter how much time, energy, money or brainpower you throw at a polarity, it will

> *Women need real moments of solitude and self-reflection to balance out how much of ourselves we give away.*
>
> Barbara de Angelis

never be solved. Things may appear to get better for a period of time, but sooner or later issues reappear. Perhaps in a different form, but they reappear none the less.

Does that mean you don't address polarities? NO – that is one of the primary functions of leadership. Just know that polarities are not solvable and that treating it like a problem will be ineffective. Let's learn how to tell the difference between a problem and polarity – and later in this chapter you'll learn what to do to tackle polarities.

Here are some examples of both problems and polarities that might help you discern the difference:

Situation	Problem because…	Polarity element….	Polarity defined
Your staff had doubled. You've run out of space and will hire 20 more people in the next 6 months.	There are finite options: build, expand, or move into larger existing space.	Train or hire needed Skills?	After the analysis, you might struggle with these two polarities: "Inside / Outside" and "Short term / Long term" as you weigh the pros and cons of training existing workers or hiring new workers who have the needed skills.
Your competitor has cut their price for a product similar to yours.	There is a clear decision required in how you will respond. Ignore? Match? Change your marketing strategy?	Continue with the existing product or introduce a new one?	The polarity is new / old. Here the dynamic balance is on timing (when to introduce the new) and frequency (how often), rather than always sticking with the old or continually introducing the new.
A new competitor is offering a competing product or service.	Your will rely on analysis and decisions about how to respond.	Compete or collaborate?	Compete / collaborate is the polarity. You might compete head on or find ways to collaborate with this new market entrant.

You've just added new technical capability to your manufacturing process. You existing workforce lacking requisite skills.	You will do analysis (what is the skill gap) and remediation (how do we close the gap).	Invest in new technology or provide stockholder returns?	The polarity is spend / invest. A business must dynamically balance both; it is not an either or.

Putting it in Practice

Over the next week, note some of the polarities that you encounter at work, in your personal life and in the larger culture. Don't worry if your words are not perfect, just note the places where there seem to be two opposing positions that require some sort of dynamic balance, rather than "either/or". A few examples are provided to guide you. You might also review the list of polarities at the end of the chapter for thought starters.

	Work	Personal	Society
Polarity Noted	Candor & Diplomacy	Self & Others	Stability & Change

2.2   Polarities not Problems

Anyone who has spent any amount of time in an organization has felt the pain of polarities being treated like problems. Keep in mind that polarities are states of dynamic balance and not either/or situations. As such, when polarities are treated as problems, organizations tend to swing from one extreme to other. We are all about teamwork and joint effort – for a few years. And once some of the downsides of teamwork begin to appear, there is a big push for personal accountability and individual rewards. The organization shifts, only to find that a few years later, there is angst over the lack of collaboration and the downsides of all this rugged individualism. And the shift begins anew – to teambuilding and teamwork and another "flavor of the month". Any wonder the longest tenured employees in those organizations advise "This too shall pass." As it will.

Another indication of inappropriately dealing with polarities is seen when leaders are locked in endless debate. Coalitions have formed, each one advocating one position, and only one position. There can be no better example of this than the current gridlock in Washington, DC, where nothing gets done due to the inability to move into possibilities that can incorporate a bit of this and a bit of that.

> *There's no such thing as work-life balance. There are work-life choices, and you make them, and they have consequences.*
>
> Jack Welch

 Putting it in Practice

Make a list of times you've experienced (or are experiencing) treating polarities like problems. What do you notice about the situation? What actions did people take? What were the results?

3 Managing Polarities

The time has come to roll up our sleeves and, through an example, illustrate how a leader might help their organization work through a situation that is a polarity and not a problem. Let's use an example of a consumer goods company who is dealing with the polarity between standardization and customization.

There are heated debates about the direction. One camp is advocating for standardization. They argue for the higher productivity, the greater efficiency, the simplified operating systems, and rail against the challenges of customization. The other camp is advocating for customer delight, the higher margins from a higher price point, the customer loyalty and repeat business that will ensue. They eschew any talk of inefficiency or complexity. Who is right? They both are. They are dealing with a polarity – and I'll show you a way to work though this issue.

Here are the steps that we will walk through:

1. Identify that it is a polarity and not a problem
2. Define the higher purpose you are wanting to achieve
3. Name the specific polarity
4. Name the negative and positive outcomes of each pole, in the order prescribed
5. Identify early warning signs of too much focus on either pole

To work with polarities, we will use a simple tool illustrated below. I'll walk you through the steps using this dilemma, but before I do, here are a few step by step instructions. Each portion of the tool is numbered for a purpose. Follow the steps in the order prescribed – and as you work through them a few times, you'll see why. Secondly, know that you may need to draft and

Design is a constant challenge to balance comfort with luxe, the practical with the desirable.

Donna Karan

You couldn't have strength without weakness, you couldn't have light without dark, you couldn't have love without loss.

Jodi Picoult

then revisit your work. There are often immediate insights and breakthroughs. But as these are often thorny issues, they will get clearer the more you work with them, discuss them and think them through.

This tool can be used individually or with a group. I've seen this tool used with over 100 people in the room with great success. As a leader, you most likely will want to use this tool to guide your team through the process of defining and managing polarities.

As contraries are known by contraries, so is the delights of presence best known by the torments of absence.

Alcibiades

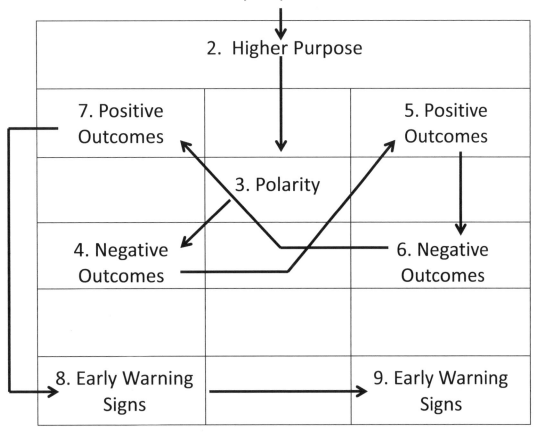

Step 1: Identify that it is a polarity and not a problem

The first step is to know you are dealing with a polarity and not a problem. In this case, the on-going and resolved conflict is a great indicator. Both sides have valid points; yet a path forward is not forthcoming. Over the past 15 years, the company has swung between the two orientations, leaving customers confused and employees bewildered.

Step 2: Define the higher purpose you want to achieve

The first action you will take with this tool is to set an overarching intention or higher purpose statement. The key here is to describe the higher purpose clearly and in the positive. This is more difficult than it might seem. All too often we can describe what we DON'T want; describing what we want is a challenge.

In our consumer group example, after a great many discussions, the following Higher Purpose was defined.

1. Polarity or problem?

2. Higher Purpose To provide a product that enhances the lives of our customers in ways that others cannot, resulting in loyal lifetime customers		
7. Positive Outcomes		5. Positive Outcomes
	3. Polarity	
4. Negative Outcomes		6. Negative Outcomes
8. Early Warning Signs		9. Early Warning Signs

Step 3: Name the specific polarity

Once you have agreement on your higher purpose, the next step is to identify the associated polarity. The key here is to name the polarity using value free language. The list in the back of this chapter will help you do this. List the two descriptions on the chart, one on each side. This team determined the polarity they were struggling with was customize / standardize.

1. Polarity or problem?

2. Higher Purpose		
To provide a product that enhances the lives of our customers in ways that others cannot, resulting in loyal lifetime customers		
7. Positive Outcomes		**5. Positive Outcomes**
Customize	**3. Polarity**	Standardize
4. Negative Outcomes		**6. Negative Outcomes**
8. Early Warning Signs		**9. Early Warning Signs**

Step 4 & 5: Name the negative and positive outcomes of each pole, in the order prescribed

Now you are ready to list the upsides and downsides of each pole. Again, note that there is a specific order to do this, starting with the negatives outcomes of the first pole, moving to the positive outcomes of the second, then the negative outcomes of the second and ending with the positive outcomes of the first pole. Using this order, you'll see how the reinforcing loop works – as well as building a more balanced view of each pole.

1. Polarity or problem?

2. Higher Purpose To provide a product that enhances the lives of our customers in ways that others cannot, resulting in loyal lifetime customers		
7. Positive Outcomes • Unique value proposition difficult to duplicate by competitors • Higher customer satisfaction • Ability to differentiate in the market • Adaptability to future trends • Visibility in what customers value • Ability to command higher prices		**5. Positive Outcomes** • Ease of manufacturing • Greater efficiencies in all areas of the business • Ability to automate all processes • Lower cost to customer • Easier decision making for all (sourcing, mfg., distribution, sales, customers)
Customize	**3. Polarity**	Standardize
4. Negative Outcomes • Higher costs to produce and deliver • Manufacturing inefficiencies • Larger margin for errors in mfg. and distribution • Complexity throughout the system		**6. Negative Outcomes** • Vanilla solution that may not delight customers • Easy to replicate by competitors • More difficult to demand a higher price point • May get really good at producing something that customers no longer value
8. Early Warning Signs		**9. Early Warning Signs**

Now that you have a more complete picture of both the upsides and downsides, you are well positioned to target a position, one whose goal is to capture the upsides of both poles. This is **the** key point. The goal is not and either/or decision. The goal is how to maximize both sides of the polarity and to find ways for them to work in concert. You may **not** be equally balanced, but you still consider and act on both sides.

For example, this company decided that they would offer a basic version of their product at a lower price point, providing manufacturing and process efficiencies. They would offer only five different ways to customize the product, each of which were priced accordingly. The five ways could shift depending on requests from customers; but if a new customization was added, an existing way had to be dropped.

Step 6: Identify early warning signs of too much focus on either pole

An important step in managing polarities is to identify early warning signs that you are in a dangerous spot.

1. Polarity or problem?

2. Higher Purpose

To provide a product that enhances the lives of our customers in ways that others cannot, resulting in loyal lifetime customers

7. Positive Outcomes		5. Positive Outcomes
• Unique value proposition difficult to duplicate by competitors • Higher customer satisfaction • Ability to differentiate in the market • Adaptability to future trends • Visibility in what customers value • Ability to command higher prices		• Ease of manufacturing • Greater efficiencies in all areas of the business • Ability to automate all processes • Lower cost to customer • Easier decision making for all (sourcing, mfg., distribution, sales, customers)
Customize	3. Polarity	Standardize
4. Negative Outcomes • Higher costs to produce and deliver • Manufacturing inefficiencies • Larger margin for errors in mfg. and distribution • Complexity throughout the system		**6. Negative Outcomes** • Vanilla solution that may not delight customers • Easy to replicate by competitors • More difficult to demand a higher price point • May get really good at producing something that customers no longer value
8. Early Warning Signs • More than 5 customized products in the portfolio • Cost per unit to manufacture exceeds $X • Customer complaints increase by X%		**9. Early Warning Signs** • Competitor's products imitating our customized ones • Sales of standard product drop • Repeat orders drop • Retail price for standard product rises in relation to the custom product

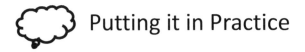 Putting it in Practice

Managing Your Polarities

Now the time has come to more successfully manage the polarities in your world. Select one that you are dealing with, in either your personal or professional life. Use the polarity worksheet to work through the situation.

1. Polarity or problem?

2. Higher Purpose		
7. Positive Outcomes		**5. Positive Outcomes**
	3. Polarity	
4. Negative Outcomes		**6. Negative Outcomes**
8. Early Warning Signs		**9. Early Warning Signs**

4 Optimizing Each Pole

One might think that the goal is to create balance. And indeed, the first step may be to create a better balance, especially if you've been focused only on one pole or have been swinging wildly between the two. However, your ultimate goal is to find ways to optimize BOTH poles, creating a dynamic balance that enables a tension that calls forth the best of both poles. This can lead to many good outcomes including:

- Innovation
- Engagement
- Optimized results
- Focus
- Less wild swings in approach
- Less drama and angst
- Less confusion

Don't give up! It's not over. The universe is balanced. Every set-back bears with it the seeds of a comeback.

Steve Maraboli

5 Slight Adjustments

Those who manage polarities well do this by design. They know the early warning signs and shift SLIGHTLY toward the other polarity when downsides of one polarity appear. These small incremental shifts maintain balance and momentum and prevent the need to swing wildly from one pole to the other. This is a proactive rather than reactive stance. It is one grounded in planning and provides ongoing efficiency and focus. It prevents overcorrection and the dramatic wild swings often experienced in organizations.

This approach is also more prone to success. A dramatic shift from one pole to the other is disruptive and requires major changes within and without. Those changes consume time, energy and resources. They

Some people always tend to clamor for a final solution, as in life there ever could be a final solution other than death. For constructive work, the principle task is always the restoration of some kind of balance.

E.F. Schumacher

create confusion. They require people (employees and customers) to do things dramatically different, to learn new skills, to adopt new beliefs and to approach their work in a whole different way.

Let's use our previous example. If, the strategy of only standardization was failing, the shift to customization would require changes, at a minimum, in:

- Product design
- Manufacturing
- Distribution
- Pricing
- Marketing
- Sales
- Finances
- Human Resources

On the other hand, slight shifts can be done with relative agility and speed. For example, if after a year, it is determined that sales are flat on the standardized products and increasing on the customized product line, there are a number of adjustments that can be made to maintain a dynamic balance, including:

- Adding a sought after feature from the customized product to the standardized one
- Adding one more customized SKU; going from 5 to 6
- Seeking market feedback to understand the shift

If we can stay with the tension of opposites long enough —sustain it, be true to it—we can sometimes become vessels within which the divine opposites come together and give birth to a new reality.

Marie-Louise von Franz

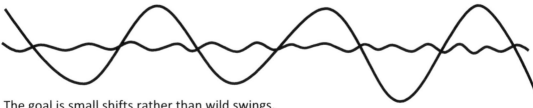

The goal is small shifts rather than wild swings.

6 Summary

I'll be the first to admit that the notion of polarities is a difficult one. It has taken me several years, much observation, reading and thought to get to a level of comfort with the notion. I've had to give up on the perspective of either / or and, when faced with a polarity, find that optimal point of balancing both.

So I encourage you to stay with this work. Continue to sharpen your eye in search of polarities. After a while, you'll find they abound in the places where you face the thorniest, most unrelenting challenges. When you do, see if you can find the underlying polarity contained within. And once you've named the polarity, use the simple tool in this chapter to work through deepening your understanding of each pole, discerning the balance point and then monitoring the early warning signs that signal a need to slightly adjust.

> *The test of a first class mind is to hold two opposing ideas in the head and still retain the ability to function.*
>
> F. Scott Fitzgerald

Additional Resources:

Handy, Charles B. *The age of paradox*. Boston, Mass.: Harvard Business School Press, 1994.

Johnson, Barry. *Polarity management: identifying and managing unsolvable problems*. Amherst, Mass: HRD Press, 1992.

Seidler, Margaret. *Power Surge a Conduit for Enlightened Leadership.* Amherst: HRD Press, 2008.

Common Polarities

- Market Driven vs. Product Driven
- Centralized vs. Decentralized
- Standardized vs. Customized
- Hierarchy vs. Distributed
- Planning vs. Action
- Spontaneous vs. Disciplined
- Reflective vs. Active
- Grounded vs. Visionary
- Task vs. Relationship
- Candor cs. Diplomacy
- Confidence vs. Humility
- Responsibility vs. Freedom
- Group vs. Individual
- Control vs. Empowerment
- Structure vs. Flexibility
- Logic vs. Creativity
- Planning vs. Implementation
- Reduce Cost vs. Improve Quality
- Compete vs. Collaborate
- Stability vs. Change
- Individualism vs. Community
- Differences vs. Commonalities
- Part vs. Whole
- Work vs. Home
- Inner Organization vs. Outer Environment
- Hard Minds vs. Soft Hearts
- Profitability vs. Growth
- Short Term vs. Long Term
- Whole vs. Parts
- Present vs. Future
- Compliance vs. Choice
- Globalization vs. Localization
- Profitability vs. Responsibility
- Control vs. Chaos
- Masculinity vs. Femininity

CHAPTER 9
Team Dynamics

Change and Team Dynamics

Creating change within an organization or group can have far reaching implications. Even when the shift is for all the right reasons and the future state is highly desired, there will be ripple effects and people and groups will react in very predictable ways.

1   You Can't Go Alone

As you create a new future, you are also creating change. By its very nature, there can be no other way. To create a future that is different than today means that something must change. There is no avoiding involving others. Even if it is a solely personal change, those closest to you are affected.

Creating change within an organization or group can have far reaching implications. Even when the shift is for all the right reasons and the future state is highly desired, there will be ripple effects and people and groups will react in very predictable ways.

These are reasons enough for you to build your understanding of how groups operate. The other reason to understand team dynamics is that creating change will almost always require a team. How you lead the team will, in a large part, determine your overall success. Your leadership can

The greater the loyalty of a group toward the group, the greater is the motivation among the members to achieve the goals of the group, and the greater the probability that the group will achieve its goals.

Rensis Likert

shape a team that performs at the highest level and propels you even faster to what you want to create. Your leadership can also result in a dysfunctional team that diverts your focus, consumes your energy, and mitigates any attempt to move forward. The extent to which you understand basic team dynamics and then can lead teams will determine which of these paths becomes your reality.

Alone we can do so little, together we can do so much.

Helen Keller

1.1   We All Need to Belong

The first thing you must understand is that each of us brings a genetically hardwired need to belong. It is deep and mostly subconscious, but there none the less. Infants who only have their physical needs met, but are not held and given personal attention, fail to thrive and often die. Adults in situations in which they are denied connection with others (think prisoners of war or inmates in solitary confinement) also are at risk of dying – an emotional death that brings on a physical one.

As humans, we banded together to survive the elements, to protect ourselves against intruders and to divide the work of day to day living to ensure survival. A simple way to state this is that we are all herd animals. Being separated from the herd creates great and deep seated fear, the fear of perishing. This threat of separation builds anxiety and dysfunctional behavior.

As such, we form groups. If you list the groups you belong to, the list will be long. There are family, work groups, neighborhood groups, social groups, sports or recreational groups, professional groups, religious groups, educational groups, to name a few. And you most likely belong, in some shape or

Winning teams have the least amount of distractions. They have a really tight group of people working towards the same common goal.

Larry Dixon

form, to multiples of them. The take away is this: as humans, we form groups naturally and widely. And belonging to groups is psychologically, albeit unconsciously, linked to our survival as individuals.

The threat of not fitting in or not belonging is ever present, even if it may not be conscious. I suspect that, like me, you can recall a time that you did not "fit in" or were asked to leave a group. For me, I have vivid recollection of those times and the associated emotions of fear, shame and anxiety.

One of the greatest punishments in society that is used is isolation. It begins with time out in a corner as toddlers. Being jailed isolates us from the herd and solitary confinement is the greatest degree of punishment within the prison system. Certain religious orders will use shunning as the ultimate punishment – total isolation from the primary group.

Talent wins games, but teamwork and intelligence wins championships.

Michael Jordan

1.2   Leaders Connect

One of the roles you play as a leader, given people's underlying need to be a part of a group, is to create connection – to the work that you are doing, to the team that is doing the work and to the organization that supports you. Very seldom do we think of this as a primary role. Yet if you think about any great leader, I believe you will find that they created connections between people and also connected those people to a cause greater than themselves individually.

In earlier chapters we have talked extensively about how to connect people to your vision, your purpose, your "Why." In this chapter, we will focus on how to create connection within your team – so that they can focus on the work to be done to achieve the "Why."

Creating connection is important at all times, but is critical when you are introducing change. Change, by its nature, creates uncertainty. Uncertainty breeds anxiety – and anxiety fosters worries about belonging. When you reflect on your own concerns during a time of change, especially one that was driven outside of yourself, you know the questions that you struggle with:

Trust is knowing that when a team member does push you, they're doing it because they care about the team.

Patrick Lencioni

- Will I be a part of this "new thing"?
- Can I learn to do things in a new way?
- What does this mean to me?
- Who will I be working with?
- Will I be able to fit in to the new way of doing things?

If you look closely at most of the fears and anxieties that individuals have in times of change, you'll find most of them rooted in belonging and connection. As a leader, you can help the team overcome these challenges by aligning and encouraging the team's purpose, investment, and performance.

Putting it in Practice

Ways to Create Connection

Belonging is important to everyone on your team. Isolation and disenfranchisement guarantee poor results, turnover, low productivity and a host of other non-desirable consequences. As a leader, you want to create connection – first of all to your purpose and then to your team and organization.

You need to create connection in three areas:
1. Vision – connecting team members to the vision of what you are creating together
2. Values – connecting team members to your "ground" and how you do your work
3. Voice – ensuring each person is valued, can contribute and is heard

Exercise

List below some ways you plan to create connection in each of the 3 areas (Vision, Values, and Voice):

	What	When	How	Responsible
Vision				
Values				
Voice				

2   The 3 Team Issues

There are three foundational issues that teams must resolve to perform well. They are:

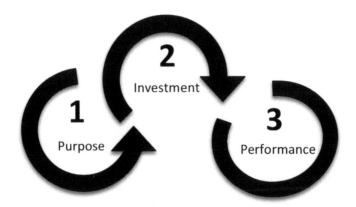

Purpose

Purpose provides direction and energy. The more that you can create a shared fate, the more that you can connect people to purpose, the more likely your team will perform well and achieve what you are setting out to do. A team with a deep commitment to a shared purpose can be an unstoppable force.

Investment

Investment is how much of myself do I need to put toward the effort. We can easily see the outward investment of time and effort. Even more important is the inner risks of self-disclosure and confronting. Sharing how you really feel about something or confronting the team with an issue can be an undertaking that requires much more

Remember teamwork begins by building trust. And the only way to do that is to overcome our need for invulnerability.

Patrick Lencioni

than putting in 10 hour days. Teams that can be straight with each other, that can have "real" dialogues about things that matter and can surface and deal with problems can overcome just about anything. Those that can't, may be stymied by the first problem they encounter.

Performance

Teams that can honestly assess both individual and team performance within the group have an edge. This is where true accountability resides. When teams can discuss, in a spirit of candor, good and poor performance – and how to get better – amazing things begin to happen. In these teams, achieving the purpose has become the goal. Commitments to the team, if not honored, are then enforced. Team members hold each other accountable – and individual performance aligns.

If two men on the same job agree all the time, then one is useless. If they disagree all the time, both are useless.

Darryl F. Zanuck

3   Setting Ground

When joining a group, people very quickly scan the environment for clues about how to fit in. They want to know how to behave, to dress, to talk, to do their work. As a newcomer, your cultural perception is heightened so that you can quickly learn the norms and assimilate as soon as possible. Once you are immersed in an organization or group, the norms become almost invisible, yet continue to exert a powerful tug. You begin to seamlessly adapt your behavior, your dress, your language from situation to situation, so that the "work" you may

The team architecture means setting up an organization that helps people produce that great work in teams.

Jay Chiat

look different than the "church" you or the "family" you.

As a leader, you have a powerful opportunity to shape future behavior by being overt about your expectations and the norms you want your team to practice. The more you do this with intention, directness and clarity, the more likely you are to shape the desired behaviors. Of course, stating expectations is only step one. Modeling them is critical, and the self-awareness you are gaining in this work allows you to continually assess the degree to which your actions reinforce your words and the degree to which you are doing that which you desire others to do. An additional leadership action is monitoring performance so that you can redirect actions that don't match the behaviors you want to see in the group.

Naming, clarifying, modeling and reinforcing the behaviors you want to see is called "setting ground." Think of it this way. People do best when the ground they stand on is solid and easy to see. It is much easier to make progress on a well-lit, smoothly paved road free of obstructions than it is on a slippery, muddy, uneven path in the dark. As a leader, you want to create that firm foundation so that your team members know what it means to belong to your team and what they need to do to "belong." With that firm footing, your team can proceed forward at great speed. Without it, uncertainty, ambiguity and fear take hold.

Here are the elements you'll want to define as you set ground:

- What is our common and overarching purpose?
- Why does it matter?
- How do we do our work?

It takes two flints to make a fire.

Lousia May Alcott

Tell me what you expect from me. Winning team members need to know five things:
1. Tell me what you expect from me.
2. Give me an opportunity to perform.
3. Let me know how I'm getting along.
4. Give me guidance where I need it.
5. Reward me according to my contribution.

Paul "Bear" Bryant

- What controls/rules need to be in place?

- What do we do to honor and respect all?

- How do issues that affect the group get surfaced?

- How do we have real conversations about the things that matter as a team?

- How do we measure our performance as a team? Individually?

- How do people enter the group? Leave the group?

Setting ground is an on-going process, even once you have already established solid ground. Your world is not static and there are many things that can create unsettled ground – and produce anxiety in the team. It can be the addition of a new member, the loss of a member, a new work process, different space, or changed expectations, to name a few. These are relatively common, yet create the need for the group to establish new ground. When these things happen, you'll notice that productivity drops, stress increases and there may be atypical behavior – posturing, questioning, withdrawing, or one-upmanship.

Even more disruptive events cause even more angst and repositioning. Events like a restructuring, sudden loss of a team member, merger or acquisition or catastrophic external event (think 911) are times when almost everyone feels they are on unsteady ground – almost like ice skating on ice that on a pond which is beginning to crack apart. What was known is no longer valid. People ask themselves what it means to belong in the new way of being and question if they belong. The team becomes uncertain and insular. It is not uncommon for productivity to plummet, for people to leave the

Sticks in a bundle are unbreakable.

Kenyan Proverb

Great teams do not hold back with one another. They are unafraid to air their dirty laundry. They admit their mistakes, their weaknesses, and their concerns without fear of reprisal.

Patrick Lencioni

team and for most other outcomes (customer satisfaction, quality, teamwork) to drop as well.

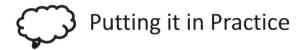 Putting it in Practice

Establishing Ground

Fitting in and belonging is of primary importance to each and every one of us. You help others feel a sense of connectedness to your team by providing them with accurate information on what it means to be a part of the team. We call this creating "ground." These expectations may indeed be ground rules, but the concept of ground rules has gotten so rote and generic that you can go from company to company and see the same ideas that only take space on the wall.

Instead, I encourage you to create expectations that truly reflect the way someone needs to be in this particular team to be fully accepted, valued and contributing. Ground can be aspirational – what you strive to be, but not so stratospheric that they appear to have no grounding in reality. Some examples:

- Bring up issues early. We promise not the kill the messenger.
- We work hard and play hard.
- Solving problems is everyone's job, not just the leaders.
- Respect everyone – even those not in the room.
- We are always looking for a better way.
- We are a part of the community and honor that with service.

If your team has a history, engage your team in documenting your group norms. This can also be a time to examine them and ask if they are serving the team to the degree they need to. As such, some revision may be called for.

If you are forming a new team, you have the opportunity to create "from the ground up" (sorry for the poor pun). You can be clear about your expectations and set the tone from the beginning. A word of warning – ensure that you are willing to do what you expect of others, and you are also willing to correct behavior that is out of bounds. Over time, you will want to create a team dynamic that self corrects so that behavior outside your team norms is noticed and corrected by anyone on the team – and behavior that exemplifies the team norms is noticed and celebrated.

3.1   Team and Non-Work

For the sake of simplicity, let's divide team function into two states: work and non-work. In work mode, the right things are getting done. People are on task, working well together, productive and relatively happy. In non-work, people are distracted, unproductive, fearful, and generally dysfunctional. I suspect that you have worked with teams in both states. And I suspect that you've been a part of a highly functional working team that moved into non-work. Or experienced a non-work team begin to get traction and move into work.

The truth is that no team is in work mode 100% of the time. There are always disruptions, distractions and events that will pull a team into non-work mode. The converse is true as well; there are no teams that exist only in non-work mode, at least over time. If no work gets done for an extended period, the team eventually is disbanded or implodes.

Yet there *are* teams that are in work mode much more often than others. And there are other teams that spend more time in non-work mode. The goal is to stay in work mode as much as possible and to quickly spot when a team begins to enter a non-work state so as to move them back into work mode quickly.

You will know when your team is in non-work, when you see or feel the following:

- There are issues that are real but get avoided
- The conversation in the hallway is different than that in the meeting

None of us is as smart as all of us.

Ken Blanchard

Teamwork: Easier said than done.

Nauman Faridi

- People are guarded and afraid to disclose how they truly feel
- Issues are dumped on the leader; there is no group accountability
- People take sides
- Team members begin to check out
- There is unresolved conflict
- "If only" statements (If only we had more budget, our leaders supported us, the economy was better...) are frequent
- You sense or see tension, fear or discomfort
- Irrational behavior occurs

The better you and your team get at spotting non-work and the more comfortable you become with surfacing and resolving the issues that create the anxiety that created non-work, to higher performing your team, the higher the engagement and the better the results.

> *Teamwork divides the task and multiplies the success.*
>
> Unknown

3.2   Calling Out Non-Work

The very first step, after noticing that the team has moved into non-work, is to call it. And you want to set a ground rule that anyone can call it – not just you. Calling it is a simple observation put forward to the team. Here are several examples:

- I've noticed that we seem to be distracted. I'd like us to take some time to understand what is going on.
- Something feels out of kilter from the way we normally operate. Does anyone else notice that?
- There seems to be tension within the team. Let's take some time now to understand it and deal with whatever the problem is.

> *Cooperation is the thorough conviction that nobody can get there unless everybody gets there.*
>
> Virgina Burden

- We've struggled with this decision for way too long. Why are we stalled?
- I notice more and more conversations happening in the hallway that need to happen with the entire group. Do you see that too?
- Someone brought a concern about the team to me. It is something we need to work through together. Let me tell you what I heard.

At this point, anxiety rises. The person that brings the issue to the team may worry that they will not be heard, that others will disagree, that only they see the issue. They may worry that they will make others unhappy or uncomfortable, and ultimately that they will be ostracized for bringing up the issue.

Once the issue is raised, the group will also become more anxious. This is the "thing" that no one has been willing to discuss. They may worry that the discussion will become emotional or angry. They may worry that the conversation will be heated or will be divisive. They may even worry that their opinion is different than the rest – and it (and by default they) will be rejected.

As such, the more you create expectations that issues must be brought forward and resolved and that this is everyone's job – the more likely that others will take that risk. After time and practice, the team will get better – just know that the first few times will be difficult and awkward.

As much as we would like to believe that there is some "magic formula" or perfect words to say when bringing an issue to the group, the reality is that there is not. As a leader, you must be both straight and sensitive. It's easy to be frank and brutal. It's easy to be sensitive and avoid the real issue. It's tough to do both, but critical to be both

No one can whistle a symphony. It takes a whole orchestra to play it.

H.E. Luccock

It is much more rewarding to get to the top of the mountain and share your experience with others than to show up by yourself, exhausted.

Shandel Slaten

candid and caring if your team is going to deliver good results.

There are 3 factors, if present, that will help you be both straight and sensitive:

- Your intent is **pure**.
- You are **respectful**.
- You are **curious**.

With pure intent, you raise the issue out of a sincere desire for the team to move forward and do good work. You don't have a hidden agenda. You are not out to get someone, to make a point or to drive behavior. A sincere and well-intended attempt, even though awkward or less than perfectly executed, will get far better results than one that is well executed but done for manipulative reasons.

Respecting other points of view does not mean agreement. It means that everyone has a viewpoint and an opinion – and that they all have individual merit. Often the best path combines a variety of viewpoints, ideas and perspectives. Being respectful makes it safe to voice different perspectives and eliminates the anxiety of "not belonging" or being rejected from the group for seeing things in a different way.

Finally, be curious. Ask insightful questions. Listen hard. Being curious means you are open to new ideas or thoughts that challenge your own personally held beliefs. Curiosity is not judgmental. In this state your goal is to be open, to learn, and to understand. Nothing more.

> *Coming together is a beginning. Keeping together is progress Working together is success.*
>
> Henry Ford

> *No member of a crew is praised for the rugged individuality of his rowing.*
>
> Ralph Waldo Emerson

3.3 Discussing Non-Work

Let's learn a simple process you can use when your team is in non-work mode. You've learned how to do the first step, calling it, in the preceding section. The following steps involve facilitating a discussion that explores what is going on, digging deep enough to identify the real issue and then to mutually agree on what needs to happen to resolve the situation.

As noted, putting the "elephant on the table" will create anxiety. Anxiety means that your team is very likely to want to do these things that are counterproductive:

- Minimize the issue (it's not that bad)
- Mask the issue (work on a less difficult issue that is not the real one)
- Hand the work back to you to solve
- Hurry through to move past the discomfort

Your job is to slow the process down enough, make it safe enough and to stay with the discomfort until the real conversation within the team begins and solid progress is made. Ask open-ended questions. Listen hard. Reflect back. State your own feelings and opinions – and name them as yours. Acknowledge your willingness to hear and honor different perspective. Stay calm and focused and trust that the group has the ability to work through this challenge.

> *In union there is strength.*
>
> Aesop

Techniques for Discussing Non-Work

Step	Example
1. Call it.	"Can we take a time out? We seem to be off task."
2. Ask: What are we afraid to talk about?	"Is there something we need to deal with as a group that is not being discussed?"
3. Identify the "real issue" that is being avoided	"What do you think?" "What makes you feel that way?" "How do others feel?" "Are we certain that is accurate?" "What assumptions are we making?"
4. Deal with the "real issue" directly.	"What can we do to resolve this?" "What do we prefer happen?" "What specifically does each one of us need to do?"
When a group is in NON-WORK and someone attempts to get them back to WORK, the initial response will be panic. All that is needed to cope with the PANIC is to OUTLAST it.	

Here are just a few other tips that will help you as you lead your team through dealing with the real issues that provoke angst.

- Avoid surprises. Give your team advance notice that you are going to bring this up. This allows all team members to gather their thoughts and to be prepared for working through this.

- Continue to provide grounding in reminding people of your team agreements or ground rules. These will guide and provide the way for the discussion and the actions that result.

- Speak for yourself and only yourself – in a spirit of curiosity and openness. Use I statements. Ask good questions and then listen.

If you insist that issues get surfaced and provide the space, support and respectful process to explore, listen and learn – the group will resolve the issue. Not only will the issue be resolved, but powerful lessons in how to work together will be internalized – enabling the team to do this as needed. Over time you'll see the team become more candid, more aligned and more galvanized to the team and that which you are creating.

A snowflake is one of God's most fragile creations, but look what they can do when they stick together!

Unknown

Putting it in Practice

Addressing Non-Work in Your Team

Think about a team that you are are leading or a part of that is currently spending time in "non-work." Use the questions below to help you plan how to surface the issue with the team and deal with it.

Issues our team needs to address (they are standing in the way of doing our work):

What I observe	Why it is a problem	Fears I or others may have about discussing it	Questions I can pose to unearth the "real issue"	When I plan to share what I see and feel

4 Teams and Creating

Leaders who are creating positive change in their organizations, communities or the larger world cannot go it alone. Just by the nature of change, someone is impacted. The larger the change the more you will need a team alongside of you who are doing the work, guiding the effort and becoming advocates. The larger the change, the more threatened people will be.

The more you can create a strong sense of connection and of common ground for your team, the more time, effort, energy and thought that will be applied to the work at hand. Without connection and shaky common ground, the team will NOT get the work that is needed done. Not only that, but the more you are forced to deal with dysfunctional team dynamics, the more likely you are to lose focus, grow weary, and succumb to abandoning your vision.

I hope that you have had the opportunity to be a part of a team that had important work to do, a strong sense of connection and clarity about "ground." These are peak experiences, ones that leave an indelible mark on your life. There is energy, a sense of purpose, a deep connection and sense of accomplishment. Those that have had the experience know how difficult it is to fully describe the wonder of it all. Those that have not, I encourage you to find a place where you are likely to work with a team to accomplish something big of value. You will never be the same – and neither will those whose were touched by the work done.

> *It is in the shelter of each other that people live.*
>
> Irish Proverb

*Special appreciation is given to Pat Murray, whose
work this is largely based on and whose insights and
passion into high performance teams is shared here.
He, in turn, would thank Wilfred Bion and Kurt
Lewin for their study, work and thought leadership
in working with groups.*

Additional Resources:

Lencioni, Patrick. *The five dysfunctions of a team: a leadership fable*. San Francisco:
    Jossey-Bass, 2002.
Scholtes, Peter R., Brian L. Joiner, and Barbara J. Streibel. *The team handbook*. 3rd
    ed. Madison, WI: Oriel, 2003.

CHAPTER 10
Productive Conflict

Turbulent Times Foster Conflict

Today's environment is ripe for divergent opinions and conflicting views. We are more diverse than ever. Our work teams most likely have individuals from around the globe rather than down the street. In many occupations, women and men work side by side in relatively equal numbers.

It is the first time we've had four generations in the work place, each with different and at times conflicting expectations, beliefs and worldviews.

That, in and of itself, brings the potential for conflict. Add to that an even increasing pace of change in which what worked yesterday does not work today. Confusion reigns – and with it uncertainty about direction and actions needed. The stakes are high and we feel inadequate. And so the environment fuels conflict as we struggle to know what to do, how to adapt, and how to keep our solid footing on ground that is continually shifting.

Say good bye to the world of homogeneity. To stability. To steadiness. To working side by side with others who looked like you, thought like you, shared your values and past experiences. Know that you are now in a place with a myriad of differences, some small, some big, some inconsequential. Many will create angst and disagreement when a common direction and agreement is what is needed.

> *The harder the conflict, the more glorious the triumph.*
>
> Thomas Paine

1   Reframing Conflict

To lead in today's environment we must, once again, begin with the "inner work". If you believe that conflict is to be avoided you are ultimately faced with a world that appears more bad than good. If you believe that your way is the right way or the only way, you are unlikely to excel in today's environment. If your mindset drives you to prevail in any situation where there are multiple views, you will find yourself in a very vulnerable position, one in which you miss the richness of multiple perspectives that shape good outcomes and viable solutions. If you only see black or white, you miss the rainbow of possibilities that exist.

The belief that conflict is bad drives us to behaviors that undermine our leadership and the work of our teams. This belief compels some to look the other way, to ignore, and to hope the conflict goes away or takes care of itself. For some, the belief that conflict is bad causes us to take actions to flee as fast as we can. Others believing that conflict is bad will do just about anything to bring peace – no matter the consequences to self or others. And others, in an attempt to bring an end to the conflict will unilaterally demand that it cease, most often by forcing their solution onto the situation or hoping that by their dictate to "cease" that it will. It will only cease to exist in open conversations. If not brought to some form of resolution, conflict that is forbidden to have a public face will live on in private places.

I can guarantee that each of us has experienced leaders doing these things. I can also almost guarantee that each of us, as leaders, have used one, two or all of these approaches when conflict appeared in our teams or across our organizations.

> *Peace is not the absence of conflict, it is the ability to handle conflict by peaceful means.*
>
> Ronald Reagan

> *Whenever you are in conflict with someone, there is one factor that can make the difference between damaging your relationship or deepening it. That factor is your attitude.*
>
> William James

Here is the bottom line: the consequences of actions driven by the idea that conflict is bad, may, over time, be far more damaging than the discomfort of dealing with it effectively in the first place. Conflict ignored seldom goes away; it just goes underground and then resurfaces in a new and more virulent form. Conflict that is quelled by concessions at any cost leave those making the concessions bitter and resentful. Conflict resolved by force creates submission, disengagement, a host of passive aggressive counter behaviors and at times sabotage.

In the rest of this chapter, I'll show you how to reframe conflict – so that it is not seen as bad, but as a source of new and different perspectives. You'll learn tactics to better lead in times of conflict. But before we start, I encourage you to do the following exercises to help you lead authentically from the inside out.

> *In dwelling, live close to the ground. In thinking, keep to the simple. In conflict, be fair and generous. In governing, don't try to control. In work, do what you enjoy. In family life, be completely present.*
>
> Lao Tzu

 ## Putting it in Practice

What is Your Personal Leadership Style When Faced with Conflict?

Find a quiet place where you can think and reflect on these questions.

- What are your beliefs about conflict?
- What is their source?
- What did you learn as a child? How did your parents or caregivers handle conflict? What did it teach you to do?
- How does it show up now in your life?

Putting it in Practice

Identify the places in your life that you are currently facing a situation that involves conflict. It may be at work, in your family, in your neighborhood, faith community, community group, or with friends. Try to list at least three, even if you must revert to past conflicts. If you can, see if you can identify the origin or source of the friction. Note your perspective and then what actions you've taken in response. When done, step back and search for patterns or insights. What are things you notice about yourself in situations involving conflict?

Places I currently face conflict	Origin or root cause	My perspective	My actions as a result

2   Is Conflict Bad?

My conflict history is that I came from a family that avoided conflict at all costs. Things always needed to appear "just fine", even when they weren't. Children were told what to do and expected to do it. Push back was not tolerated and if one dared, physical punishment or loss of privileges were the result. The outcome was an extreme discomfort with conflict and a pervasive inability to deal with it in any way other than to "keep the peace" and/or to pretend it didn't exist. Unfortunately that approach took its toll – at work, in my marriage and at times with friends and family.

Over time, and with increasing work responsibility and challenges inside and outside of work, I came to realize that absence of *dealing with* conflict has nothing to do with absence of conflict. Indeed, my artfully dodging conflict drove it deep within, where it grew a life of its own. Not only did it grow bigger and uglier, it would become a burdensome companion – with me all the time, draining energy and focus.

Little by little, I began to experiment with giving voice to that conflict, bringing it into the open, getting to resolution. I began to see what happened when I dealt openly with differences of opinion or when I owned my own voice. To my great surprise, all that had held me back from openly working through conflict did NOT happen. People still liked me. I felt better, not worse. Relationships were stronger and healthier, not torn apart. While I still had some angst about getting issues on the table, once I did confront the issue, things got better. And afterward I was relieved, lighter and less distracted.

For good ideas and true innovation you need human interaction, conflict, argument, debate.

Margaret Hefferman

Mankind must evolve for all human conflict a method which rejects revenge, aggression, and retaliation. The foundation of such a method is love.

Martin Luther King Jr.

2.1   Productive vs. Destructive

Over time I've also learned that conflict can have two faces. One is terribly destructive and hurtful. The other is cleansing, creative and affirming. So, with the knowledge that conflict is inevitable – in every team, every workplace, every family, and every friendship – how might we more often harness the positive power of conflict and avoid the downsides?

When engaged in destructive conflict, there are no winners. One person may prevail, but at the expense of the other and ultimately the relationship. Productive conflict can bring about creative and innovative solutions – ones that neither party could envision on their own. It can bring people together rather than tear them apart. It can heal rather than destroy. It can enable progress on the real issues rather than pouring effort and energy into defending one position and attempting to defeat the other. Here is a chart that describes them both.

Difficulties are meant to rouse, not discourage. The human spirit is to grow strong by conflict.

William Ellery Channing

Productive Conflict	Destructive Conflict
Assumes we <u>both</u> have a valid point of view, even if they are different	Assumes I am right and you are wrong
Is curious and open to exploration	Is dogmatic, closed and rigid
Engages the other in the process of resolution	Shuts out the other. Seeks to impose will rather than resolve the issue
Separates the value of the person from the difference of opinion	Attributes negative personal characteristics to those that disagree
Stays accountable for good results	Blames the other and absolves self of responsibility for a good outcome
Seeks to understand, to explore and then resolve	Seeks to impose their will and force compliance
Sees many solutions; seeks a win-win	Sees their option as the only choice; win-lose mentality
Holds the relationship in high regard during the process	Holds their position as the ultimate and only outcome
Discusses	Debates
Holds firm on predetermined non-negotiable items; willing to yield on less important points	Forceful on the whole; black and white thinking

3   Conflict Triggers Fear

There is nothing like a whiff of conflict to bring out all sorts of unconscious and dysfunctional behaviors. As you've learned in the exercises in this chapter, individual responses to conflict are deep seated, learned early and most of us are not taught ways to deal with conflict in helpful ways. Those that study the brain would tell us that conflict elicits fear, which lights up the more primitive areas of our brain, which then prompts us to flight, flee or freeze. We are either a bear barring our teeth and claws, a gazelle running like the wind, or the infamous opossum, playing dead.

As you learned in the last chapter, one of our deepest fears is not belonging to the group. Conflict screams to us that if we have unreconciled differences we may be disliked, ostracized, made fun of or generally shunned or exiled from the group. Our fears warn us not to bring up divergent points, as we "won't fit in."

We can also get terribly tripped up when the conflict is about values. Your senior team members deeply value hard work, at times over the expense of family. Your younger team members value time outside of work, even if it means that work comes second. Conflict erupts – often about ancillary issues – when the source of friction is over something much deeper and ingrained.

As a leader, you are unlikely to unpack all that deep psychological baggage we carry – be it from our immediate family or our ancestors many years back. However, you can do several things that enable conflict to emerge and be dealt with effectively in your teams. Reframing conflict as helpful rather than hurtful helps. Creating a safe place where differing viewpoints can be examined and insisting that the tough stuff gets discussed opens the door. And modeling ways to have those conversations lights the spark of creativity and improves your team's performance.

> *The number of stressors has multiplied exponentially: traffic, money, success, work/life balance, the economy, the environment, parenting, family conflict, relationships, disease. As the nature of human life has become far more complicated, our ancient stress response hasn't been able to keep up.*
>
> Andrew Bernstein

3.1   The Bright Side of Conflict

So why is being able to deal with conflict effectively so important? We've already discussed some of the downsides of NOT dealing with conflict well, which include:

- Lack of team cohesion
- Formation of competing factions
- Wasted time
- Wasted energy
- Diversion of focus
- Pervasive negative energy
- Discomfort
- Chronic issues that remain unresolved
- Drains health and vitality
- Can create a "toxic" work environment

These terribly hinder a team's ability to perform and to perform well. I'd like you to consider some of the reasons that we don't often discuss, but are very important reasons why dealing effectively with conflict is a vital leadership skill in today's world. If you can do this, you are able to:

- Surface issues so they can be dealt with
- Add richness and variety to possible options
- Build team cohesion
- Ignite creativity
- Avert problems before they occur
- Compete better in a global environment
- Generate new ideas
- Build awareness and understanding
- Have a reliable safety valve
- Enable people to feel valued and be heard

It may be helpful to reframe the metaphors we use for conflict into ones that are more helpful. Our typical framing is one of win/lose – with an array of war metaphors. Win the argument, crush the opposition, shock and awe. It may be more helpful to think of conflict as natural friction – and that you can use that

> *Creativity comes from a conflict of ideas.*
>
> Donatella Versace

> *Conflict is inevitable but combat is optional.*
>
> Max Lucade

friction to spark a fire, to sand wood to a beautiful
finish, to create heat and warmth and light.

 # Putting it in Practice

Contrast a poorly managed conflict in your life with one that had a positive
outcome. What were the differences? In beliefs? In approach? In outcomes?

	Poorly Managed Conflict	Well Managed Conflict
Beliefs		
Approach		
Outcome		

4 Leading the Way

As the leader you send very strong signals, even if you don't intend to, about how the team is going to address differing viewpoints or potential problems. As such, reframing conflict and creating the ability to deal with differences in helpful ways will begin with you. As you've done the exercises, you have started to see how you deal with conflict – and therefore, most likely how your team deals with conflict. If your tendency is to fight, I suspect that you have a team that "walks on eggshells" and does all it can to avoid bringing issues up to you. On occasion, there might be a brave soul who will fight back, but often this is a last resort tactic when pushed to a breaking point. If you are of the "flee" sort – there may be some on your team who know how to advance their own agendas, knowing you will succumb. If you are a "freezer" – your group may be paralyzed as well, feeling stuck and mired in age old situations that never get addressed. They may wonder why you can't see and deal with the things that are so painfully real for them.

As you move from fighting, fleeing or freezing to finessing conflict –you'll want to be clear and straightforward with your team. Let your team (or peers or family know that you are going to approach disagreements differently and that you expect different things from them. Be as specific as possible; here are some thought starters.

- In the past I've been the first to shoot down different ideas. I recognize that is a problem and am making a commitment to you to listen, discuss and consider. I'd like you to begin to bring your ideas forward more often and to let me know if I move into "non-listening" mode.

> *Conflict is the beginning of consciousness.*
>
> M. Esther Harding

> *Conflict builds character.*
> *Crisis defines it.*
>
> Steven V. Thulon

- There are some difficult discussions we are not having as a team. I believe that is holding us back, so I want you to know that I'm going to begin getting them on the table so they can be resolved.

- Several of you have raised this issue in the past and I've not addressed it, hoping it would resolve itself. It has not. As such, we'll take 30 minutes in our next team meeting to discuss different views on the situation.

You may want to explicitly state your expectations around challenging the conventional thinking or raising different points of view. Setting a new norm about raising issues can help others both get comfortable and more skilled at bringing things to the table. Here are a few team ground rules to pick from:

- There is no issue that we can't work through.
- We focus on the position or problem, not the person.
- Absolutely no personal attacks.
- Bring little problems forward quickly before they become big ones.
- Be open to opposing or different ideas.
- Divergent ideas help us create better solutions.
- Have the tough conversations around the table, not in the hallway.
- Everyone has the obligation to bring forward issues or concerns.
- We can disagree, argue and wrestle with things inside the team, but then agree on direction and leave those disagreements in the room.

I think you get the idea, which is to clearly state your expectations about dealing with conflict to your team. Of course, then your role as a leader is to model,

> *Mankind must evolve for all human conflict a method which rejects revenge, aggression and retaliation. The foundation of such a method is love.*
>
> Martin Luther King

> *An eye for an eye will only make the whole world blind.*
>
> Mahatma Gandhi

encourage them and support team members as they
bring uncomfortable conversations to the group.

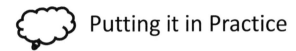 # Putting it in Practice

Take some time to note what you would like your team to do – and what you need
to do as a leader to model the way. Some examples are provided to fuel your
thinking.

Desired Team Behaviors	What I Need to Do
Surface issues quickly	Probe for them Listen carefully when they are brought forward Thank people for surfacing them
Consider new ideas and ways of thinking	Use value free language Insist on respecting other's points of view Be open to new ideas myself
Be open to push back or new ideas.	Listen before I respond Ask open ended questions Remember that I don't have to have all the answers

5   A Five Step Process

You may have noted to date that "conflict" has many sources. It might include differing viewpoints, concerns about an approach or plan, or interpersonal or team dynamic frictions. The common denominator is that as a leader, you will want to surface and deal with them in a timely and helpful manner. Every situation will unfold a bit differently, but in general, these five steps can guide you.

All war is a symptom of man's failure as a thinking animal.

John Steinbeck

Step 1: Notice

At this stage you are sniffing for smoke. Sensing comes first. Being alert to those places where friction begins to show is the work of everyone on the team. Give everyone permission to be watchful for signs or signals that we may need to slow down a bit and explore what is happening. Why is there a lack of energy about the new product? What is stalling the work on this part of the project? Why is a team member unusually quiet or withdrawn? What are others seeing about our plan that causes them angst?

Step 2: Name

Knowing when to fight is just as important as knowing how.

Terry Goodland

Here you are confirming there is something smoldering. When you or a team member senses that there may be concern, frustration, or lack of agreement, give everyone permission to bring it to the team. This is the surfacing and validation step. You've seen some smoke, now is the time to determine if there is a fire (or not). The conversation might get started like this: "I suspect that there are some strong feelings about our plan. Is that the case, and if so, can we discuss them so that I understand?"

Step 3: Ground

This step is containing the fire, so that you benefit from the heat and light but don't allow it to rage out of control. This is an important step and one that is often missed. After you've noticed and named – and before you are ready to jump into the conversation, take a moment to ground people in two things:

1 - The ground rules

2 - The higher purpose

When disagreement is surfaced, anxiety for many (not just the person with the divergent views) will arise. Reminding everyone that they are a valued part of the team that we'll be able to work through these differences openly and respectfully will go a long way to quelling that internal anxiety. Reinforcing the ground rules the team has established will help ensure the process to resolve the conflict will be productive and not destructive.

Reminding others of your higher purpose also grounds the discussion to focus on the desired outcome. The higher purpose is what you are working to achieve – and could be a financial, customer, product, project, process or team outcome. A statement like: "I'm curious to hear and consider other viewpoints on our approach. We can shift our approach but need to remember that our work must be complete by <future date>." grounds and focuses the discussion.

> *Peace is not the absence of conflict but the presence of creative alternatives for responding to conflict – alternatives to passive or aggressive responses, alternatives to violence.*
>
> Dorothy Thompson

Step 4: Explore

Now the energy of the fire is manifested. If set up well, this is the rich part of the process in which ideas and approaches are discussed. There may be healthy, but heated discussions. There may be dreaming. There may be deep dialog. There may be deep division, but if each person in the conversation both contributes and considers, shares and listens, is candid and caring – the conversation will be rich and helpful. New ways can surface. There is energy here born of possibility and potential.

Step 5: Decide

The final step where you extinguish the fire. Bringing closure to this process is important – so make a conscious and verbal statement about what you've learned, where you are and what the next steps are. It may be that just surfacing the issue has been enough (it often is). It may be that the way forward becomes evident during the discussion. Or it may be that there is more to be done before resolution happens. No matter the circumstance, sum up where the group is at, get clear on the next steps, and check for agreement. Leave the room united – even if at times that means there is more work to be done on this topic.

Ten Tips for Successfully Using Conflict to Spark Creativity and High Performance

1. Raise issues as they come up. State them in neutral terms.
2. Be curious and open minded. Explore. Probe. Ask open ended questions. Dive deeper.
3. Define the intention or outcome clearly and check for understanding with your team. Define the litmus test for a solid solution. Be clear about any non-negotiables and decision rights.

Ideas stand in the corner and laugh when we fight over them.

Marty Rubin

When you have a conflict, that means that there are truths that have to be addressed on each side of the conflict. And when you have a conflict, then it's an educational process to try to resolve the conflict. And to resolve that, you have to get people on both sides of the conflict involved so that they can dialogue.

Dolores Huerta

4. Encourage alternative points of view. Seek them out. Ask what is missing. Make having an alternative view something that is valued rather than denigrated. Ask what the situation looks like from multiple viewpoints – customer, owner, peers, co-workers, and our boss.

5. Insist that all voices are heard.

6. Maintain focus on the issue, situation or problem. NEVER let it divulge into personal attacks.

7. Insist that the team work through them to resolution. Hang tight through anxiety and the inclination to avoid or defer – you own discomfort and the teams.

8. List options and their consequences. Step back and examine them as objectively as possible.

9. Pick your timing. If heated, take a break but insist on finishing the work.

10. Let go. Don't sacrifice a good outcome by holding on to your position.

> *Conflict is inevitable, but combat is optional.*
>
> Max Lucade

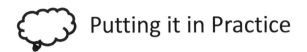 Putting it in Practice

Practice With a Conflict You Are Currently Facing

Look at your list from Exercise 2. Pick one conflict you are currently facing and take steps to resolve it, using what you've learned so far. Plan your approach and then reflect on what you've learned about yourself, others and conflict.

Planning Sheet:

Before the conversation:

- What is the conflict?

- What is your point of view?

- What alternative views do others have?

- Who is involved?

- What is your higher intention?

- Are there any non-negotiables?

- What ground rules are important as you bring this to the table?

- How will you set up a conversation to discuss this?

After the conversation:

- What went well?

- What would you do differently?

- What did you learn that surprised you?

6 Tough Situations

Even as you approach difficult situations more confidently, proactively and with the lens that the conflict can both heal and help your team, you still may encounter tough situations. Here are some common ones and some thoughts on how to move past them.

Disrespectful Dialogue

If you have individuals in the conversation who act disrespectfully, call an immediate time out. Notice what you see, and remind everyone of the need for respect. Note that respect deals with both listening and exchanging. Insist that those that are lobbing personal assaults cease immediately. Challenge those who are not listening with an open mind as well.

Emotional team members

This is the yin and yang of conflict. It tends to surface with things that people really care about and those things elicit emotion. Get comfortable with the fact that this will be an emotional process. Emotions can range from anger to sadness to disbelief to excitement. Strategy one is just to hang in there and wait out the discomfort. It's hard not to jump in and fix it or to divert the attention to a safer emotional space. Just staying with it and giving the emotions some breathing room is a powerful act. If however, the emotions seem too intense or people are ceasing to function very well, simply call a "time out". It might be a quick break to breathe and think. Or it may be that we need 24 hours to collect our thoughts. The key is coming back to it. Do not let a time out turn into a tune out.

Avoidance / Denial

This is a very common response. Teams will go for long periods without surfacing discussions that need to

In dwelling, live close to the ground. In thinking, keep to the simple. In conflict, be fair and generous. In governing, don't try to control. In work, do what you enjoy. In family life, be completely present.

Tao Te Ching

Peace is not absence of conflict, it is the ability to handle conflict by peaceful means.

Ronald Reagan

happen. As a leader, you can name what you are sensing and bring the issue into the daylight. You can also grant permission by asking this question: "What is the one thing we are not discussing, but need to?"

Inability to see other perspectives

Find ways to surface different thinking. The book Six Thinking Hats by Edward DeBono provides a great model, with each person taking on a different way to look at the situation. You can also send folks out to observe or talk with others. Seeing things with different perspectives is a skill. Stay at it, stay OK with it and folks will begin to think bigger and broader.

Inability to value other perspectives

You can't force people to appreciate other points of view. However, you can insist that those thinking differently are not demeaned, shut out or shut down. See the first strategy on disrespectful dialog. Repeat often.

Inability to concede graciously

In grade school we called them sore losers. They hung on to their point till the bitter end, even when they knew they were not going to prevail. At this point it is NOT about the issue. It is about saving face and not giving in. There are a few strategies you can take. You can take all points under consideration and own the decision. You can role model the ability to state your views firmly while still considering others. You can insist on respect, knowing that goes for everyone. Perhaps the best strategy is never framing the discussion as a win/lose proposition – but instead a discuss/decide process.

Group Think

When you get a sense that everyone is either saying what they think is "correct" or that the group is being swayed heavily by one individual, solicit individual thoughts. Go around the room and ask everyone to contribute or to respond to a question. If

When a gifted team dedicates itself to unselfish trust and combines instinct with boldness and effort, it is ready to climb.

Patanjali

Whenever you're in conflict with someone, there is one factor that can make the difference between damaging your relationship and deepening it. That factor is attitude.

William James

the group is really entrenched in group think, have them take on an alternative (but imaginary) position. You might ask: What would our most difficult customer say about this? If you were being the devil's advocate, what would that look like?

Pairing

This is a variation of group think in which coalitions begin to form, groups of 2 or more who organize around a particular position. People will start to use "we" when this happens (or sometimes the nebulous "they"). When this happens, insist that individuals speak for themselves. Find a safe way for each person to contribute individually. Note what you are observing and ask everyone to speak their personal truth.

7   Some Final Notes

A good manager doesn't try to eliminate conflict; he tries to keep it from wasting the energies of his people. If you're the boss and your people fight you openly when they think that you are wrong - that's healthy.

Robert Townsend

It is easy to get overwhelmed on this topic of conflict. On Amazon alone, there are 3,227 books on conflict resolution. I'll leave you with four key beliefs, which if you embrace, will enable you to lead perfectly fine in this area:

1. Conflict can be productive.

    –   If you embrace the idea that out of conflict comes good things, better approaches, richer ideas, stronger relationships, higher performing teams – you'll be willing to do this work.

2. There is no one right answer.

    –   If you let go of one answer or your way and are open to the possibilities in differences, amazing things can unfold.

3. Intention is more important than technique.

    –   Your intention is to foster good outcomes while respecting others is much more important than

Conflict is the beginning of consciousness.

M Esther Harding

five steps or ten tips or following a prescribed process. Be open. Listen. Stay with it. Good things will happen.

4. At the heart of creativity lies conflict.

    − You know you are on to something really important when you illicit emotion. Rest assured that some dissonance, debate and discussion precede alignment, agreement and solid forward progress.

Additional Resources:

Bono, Edward. *Six thinking hats*. Boston: Little, Brown, 1985.

Fisher, Roger, William Ury, and Bruce Patton. *Getting to yes: negotiating agreement without giving in*. 2nd ed. New York, N.Y.: Penguin Books, 1991.

Patterson, Kerry, Joseph Grenny, Al. Switzler, and Ron McMillan. *Crucial conversations: tools for talking when stakes are high*. 2nd ed. New York: McGraw-Hill, 2012.

CHAPTER 11
Growing Others

1   Learning Fast is a Must

I remember, and you may too, when what you learned in high school or college set you up for life. You went to trade school, college, the military or completed an apprenticeship, and learned skills that had a long shelf life......maybe 20 years or longer. In that world, learning new skills was needed on occasion – when a promotion loomed, or when new equipment or technology came around. Learning was seen as a special event, something that primarily happened in your youth. Nothing could be further from the truth now. To be successful today (and maybe even to survive), the need to learn new things is paramount.

The phone is prime example of this acceleration. The first commercially accepted phone was a rotary phone. Then 43 years later came a touch phone. And 17 years later came the first mobile phone, which was not very mobile and was more like a suitcase. Sixteen years later, flip phones made the scene; 6 years later Blackberries; 5 years later, the iPhone. Major technological shifts that used to take decades, now take months or years. And not just in communication technology, but in virtually every aspect of our life.

Today we live in a world where half of what a college engineering student learns will be obsolete before she graduates; where careers are measured in years and not decades; where the hottest new jobs in 5 years do not even exist today.

> *You can teach a student a lesson for a day; but if you can teach him to learn by creating curiosity, he will continue the learning process as long as he lives.*
>
> Clay P. Bedford

This is a world in which learning is a mandate and not a luxury. Turn around twice and your skill set is obsolete. You barely recognize the technology. The market has shifted. The ability to learn and to learn fast may be your biggest competitive edge.

Just as hothouses accelerate a plant's growth, you need to find ways to accelerate your own growth and that of others. Hothouses provide abundant sunshine and warmth for fast growth. They also take much tending. They need continual watering, as the heat dries the soil quickly. Yet plants do accelerate their growth, even when the weather is inclement and inhospitable to the plants left to fend for themselves outdoors.

This is the metaphor for you as a leader. As you create optimum conditions for yourself and your team to grow, they will grow faster and better than average. As you grow yourself and others, you increase your team's capability as they can do much more. You also grow capacity, as you are no longer dependent on just one person to do specific things. But just as with a hot house, accelerating and spreading the learning for your team requires care, time and attention. There are rewards for the effort – for you, for your team, and for your organization. They include:

- Increased performance
- Deeper bench strength
- Less reliance on a single person
- Breathing room for you – it is no longer ALL on your shoulders
- Better engagement (the #1 job criteria for the millennial generation)
- Retention of top talent – these people want to be challenged and be where people invest in them

> *I am learning all the time. The tombstone will be my diploma.*
>
> Eartha Kitt

> *Get over the idea that only children should spend their time in study. Be a student so long as you still have something to learn, and this will mean all your life.*
>
> Henry L. Doherty

2 Real World Learning

I've participated in more than my share of lectures, training sessions, online learning, and courses. I've read countless books and attended numerous conferences. And I've learned something from most of them.

Yet when I list the events that prompted the MOST impactful and relevant learning to me in my career, none of these make the list. All these things can help set the stage for learning, but to truly learn something requires doing it, practicing it, failing at it – over and over and over again.

I've learned best when I've had a big challenge at work that I must solve. When I want to learn to do something that I can't do now and search for individuals to show me how. When I've had someone take an interest in me and show me the way and open me to new possibilities. For me, real world learning, happening real-time is the most lasting and the most relevant. Research shows us that 99% of the population is just like me.

That's good news for you as a leader. It means you don't have to wait until the next time a class is open to help your team members learn. You will never again be hampered by a lack of training budget. You won't have to figure out how to get the day-to-day work done while someone is at a training session.

It does mean that you play a very active role in helping your team gain new skills and improve existing skills. It means that you no longer outsource your personal or team's development to HR or the training area. It means that you will be able to contribute something meaningful and lasting to those you lead and to the organization.

> *It's what you learn after you know it all that counts.*
>
> Harry S. Truman

> *For the things we have to learn before we can do them, we learn by doing them.*
>
> Aristotle

This chapter will provide you with some basic learning principles and then with several low or no cost ways to develop you and your team on the job.

3 Learning Accelerators

Scientists have spent lifetimes deconstructing the human brain and understanding how we learn. It is fascinating, complex and deep. My bookshelves groan with these tomes. For the sake of time, I'm going to distill this knowledge into few basic principles that will guide you well. When you incorporate these principles into your development efforts, learning will be faster, richer and easier. In our hothouse analogy, these accelerators are like fertilizer.

A single conversation with a wise man is better than ten years of study.

Chinese Proverb

3.1 We Learn Best at Our Edge

I'm going to borrow a term from yoga to explain this concept: our edge is that place where a comfortable action just begins to become uncomfortable. It is where you are not straining, but where you a just a smidge past your current range. If you turn your head slowly to the right, you'll find a point at which it is no longer easy, but it is not yet painful. This is your edge. Continue to push on the edge for a period of time, and you'll be able to do more. Force yourself past your edge too quickly and you will inflict injury.

Pushing people too fast and too far is the same as pushing past your physical edge and causing injury. It is ineffective, as a state of anxiety pervades. They are confused and struggle. They have none of the basic skills to build upon. Think about a time where you

I am always doing that which I cannot do, in order that I may learn how to do it.

Pablo Picasso

were in an academic class and failing – and you will know the experience of spending more time in a state of anxiousness about the situation than in a learning state.

On the other hand, there is a danger of aiming too low. Staying in your comfort zone does not promote learning and growth. Instead it breeds complacency and a clinging to the status quo. When you never push against your edge, you become stale and feel "in a rut."

Learning opportunities should challenge us – but not undo us. The best ones are just beyond our grasp – enough so that we must stretch and grow. Too low a challenge and we are bored. Too high a challenge and we are overwhelmed.

Your learning edge will continually move – as you gain skills your edge shifts accordingly. Continually pushing into your learning edge yields steady growth as well as an increased capacity to learn. Depending on the skill, everyone's edge is in different place. As a leader, you can be a keen observer and discover your own edge. You can use both observation and dialogue to discern where the edge is for the individuals on your team.

I never teach my pupils. I only attempt to provide the conditions in which they can learn.

Albert Einstein

3.2 We Learn Best when We Link

Our brain is filled with already existing neural pathways. Think of them as well-worn pathways in which information flows naturally, almost effortlessly. For example, if you were walking down a hillside, you would naturally take the path that has already been cleared. Blazing a new path takes much more time and effort than traversing an existing by-way; so does creating new neural pathways. As such, we can use those paths already ingrained in our brain to our advantage when learning new things.

Learning something totally new, in isolation, is extremely difficult. A shortcut to learn new things or remember new information is to link it to something you already know. If I am learning to code in a new language and can see the similarities to the ones I already know, my learning goes faster, as I already have established mental models and neural pathways. This phenomenon is why learning your third language is much easier than learning the second one. It is the trick that performers who remember 100 names in the room use. They do not attempt to recall every single name in isolation. Instead they use linking to associate your name with something they already know and can recall. Kris Taylor may have had on a crisply (Kris) tailored (Taylor) jacket. While it sounds MORE cumbersome, linking really does help us recall and learn better.

Here are some ways you can link or connect information:

- Use similes to draw parallels between things they already know. This is like an ant colony...a busy highway...a playground...a game of chess. This account is like the one you worked on earlier...

- Cluster information so that you organize it a way that shows connections and linkages.

- Use visuals and diagrams to show linkages. Mind maps are great ways to show how things are connected.

- Images and image rich comparisons help us link a concept to something tangible. Listen until your ears hurt is a rich image. Just telling someone to listen does not nearly have the same impact.

Give me a fruitful error any time, full of seeds, bursting with its own corrections. You can keep your sterile truth for yourself.

Vilfredo Pareto

If you learn only methods, you´ll be tied to your methods but if you learn principles you can devise your own methods.

Ralph Waldo Emerson

- Use memory aids. It may be a rhyme, a catchy phrase or an acronym that helps.

- Help people see the underlying structure of how something is organized.

3.3   Practice Makes Perfect

Learning any new skill takes time and practice. If you can do something well the first time, it means that you already knew how to do it! Many times we are impatient – we want mastery to come immediately after learning. Practice is grunt work but there is no avoiding it. How much practice time does a pro sports player have under their belt before they take the field? An airline pilot? A musician? Why would we think that other skills can avoid the need for practice?

Recent studies of experts across many fields show us that reaching mastery takes 5 to 7 years of steady practice. Yet, my experience in organizations is that expectations are terribly out of synch with this notion. You go to a 3-day class and get certified. You are given one assignment, and if not done to a high enough level, you are seen as incompetent and never given the opportunity again. You are shown once and expected to maintain production standards.

As a leader, managing your expectations about performance levels in a learning stage is key. Expect lower productivity. Expect errors. Expect naive questions. Expect nervousness. Provide multiple opportunities to practice. Allow time. Be patient, but don't confuse patience with low standards. Be patient with honest efforts, with clumsy initial execution, with less than perfect results. But be impatient with complacency, laziness or lack of effort.

> *You learn something every day if you pay attention.*
>
> Ray LeBlond

> *Man's mind, once stretched by a new idea, never regains its original dimensions.*
>
> Oliver Wendell Holmes

3.4   Feedback Required

Extended practice is needed – but that alone is insufficient. Practicing doing something poorly only reinforces bad habits and does not improve performance. A few years ago, I wanted to learn to swim. I took a few initial lesions and then practiced several times a week for many months. Even though I spent time in the pool, my swimming was not getting any better. I was practicing the same poor form, over and over and over again. Once I found an expert swimmer to watch my strokes and tell me what I needed to do differently, I made great strides in a short amount of time.

Dancers, no matter the level, have mirrors and instructors. Sports teams have coaches and game tapes that provide them with information on their level of execution. As a leader, you can provide the source of feedback that helps your team members see what they are doing and learn how to do it better.

Both giving and receiving feedback can make us uncomfortable. We need to get over it if we want to be our best or we want our team to perform at higher levels. Once I began to see feedback as a gift – rather than a threat, I began to seek it out. Feedback has enabled me to be better, to see things more clearly and to stop making mistakes. In reality, NOT getting feedback was the threat!

Immersion in experience is the most fundamental learning mode throughout life.

Guy Claxton

Tell me and I forget. Teach me and I remember. Involve me and I learn.

Benjamin Franklin

3.5   All Feedback is Not Equal

Some feedback both improves performance and increases motivation. Some feedback squelches both.

Avoid providing feedback that is:

- Disrespectful

- Vague
- Threatening
- Untruthful
- Judgmental

Providing feedback that is specific, timely, candid and welcomed is a skill learned over time. When all four of these elements are present, performance will soar. Let's look at each of these:

- Specific – Telling someone they did a "good" job is nice, but not very helpful. The more specific you can be in your feedback, the more actionable it becomes, the more knowledge gets transferred and the more the learner understands about what is important.

- Timely – Real time is best, if appropriate. If not, close in time is the second best alternative. The longer the lag in feedback, the less value it has. Feedback given at an annual performance review about something that happened 8 months ago falls into the utterly useless and totally annoying category.

- Candid – Diffusing, masking, and watering down feedback is confusing and sometimes misleading. I've sat in on feedback sessions in which a leader believes they are warning someone about serious behaviors that need to change and the person walks out thinking things are just fine. Candid does not mean cruel. It does mean straightforward and clear.

- Welcome – Even the best feedback is not helpful if the person on the receiving end is unwilling. Find the right time, the right place – and then ask the person if they would like some feedback. If done in a spirit of helping, most all will say yes. And if they say no, point

> *Learning is a treasure that will follow its owner everywhere.*
>
> Chinese Proverb

> *I don't think much of a man who is not wiser today than he was yesterday.*
>
> Abraham Lincoln

taken. Spend your leadership energies developing those who are willing and open.

4 3 Win-Win Methods

In this section, I'll share with you three proven and highly effective ways to develop yourself and others. In addition to being powerful learning mechanisms, they do not require out of pocket money or out of job time. They do require your time and energy as a leader – as nothing really worthwhile is totally free. You can use these development methods every day.

> *I am always ready to learn although I do not always like being taught.*
>
> Winston Churchill

4.1   A Feedback Rich Environment

Performance does not improve and new skills do not get mastered without feedback. High performing teams know this fact and are "feedback rich," meaning feedback is sought out, welcomed and flows freely; not relegated to formal reviews. It means that feedback is everyone's responsibility and that feedback is provided up, down, and across the team. It means that people are invested in improving their own performance and that of those around them.

The feedback I am referring is informal. It is in the moment. It is brief. It can be delivered many times in the course of a day – spontaneous, helpful and real time.

> *I think it's very important to have a feedback loop, where you're constantly thinking about what you've done and how you could be doing it better.*
>
> Elon Musk

As a leader, others look to you for cues and will follow your lead. Unless you are willing to model the way by both giving and receiving, do not expect that others will follow. If you are not willing to receive feedback, do not assume that your team will relish receiving feedback, no matter how skillfully it is given.

So your first task as a leader is to be open to receiving feedback. In fact, it is to be much more than open: to welcome it; to seek it relentlessly; to be grateful for it; to act upon it.

Modeling the way means both seeking feedback and providing feedback. There are two types of feedback that you can seek or provide. The first is pointing out where there is room for improvement – we'll call this constructive feedback. The second is pointing out what the person is doing well – we will call this appreciative feedback. Appreciative feedback does not need to wait until there is perfect execution. Instead, provide appreciative feedback for efforts that are closer to the desired level, moving in the right direction, showing effort and progress.

Too often we are quick to point out places to improve and lax to point out what is being done correctly. Both are needed, but knowing what is working is far more likely to get faster performance improvements. Think about this example – if you have asked for directions, is it more helpful for someone to tell you the 3 streets you need to take or to tell you all the streets you do NOT want to take.

In learning you will teach, and in teaching you will learn.

Phil Collins

Here is a quick formula to providing **constructive feedback** as you spot opportunities:

> Ask for permission to deliver feedback

- *I have some ideas on ways that you might get better results with that. Would you like to hear them?*

> Describe the behavior you see

- *I noticed that you are very quiet in our team meetings.*

> Describe the effect or results

- *When that happens, we don't get the benefit of your expertise or perspectives.*

> Present an alternative

- *I'd like you to share more in the team meetings, especially when we are discussing XYZ.*

The formula for **appreciative feedback** is very similar:

> Ask for permission to deliver feedback

- *I wanted to provide you some feedback on XYZ? Would you be open to that?*

> Describe the behavior you see

- *Your contribution to our team meeting on Tuesday was very insightful and helpful, especially when you talked about XYZ.*

> Describe the effect or results

- *As a result, I've totally changed my perspective on how to deal with that situation and am going to take the suggestions you outlined.*

> Show gratitude

- *Thanks for having the courage to push the team on that topic. It will really help us do better with XYZ.*

As you provide feedback, stay focused on the situation and avoid judgmental words will avert defensiveness. If your intent is to see someone do better and you offer feedback in a spirit of helping them do that, the chances are that the results will be just fine.

Research has shown that the ratio of appreciative feedback to constructive feedback should be 4 to 1. I believe that every leader needs to find the ratio that works for them and to avoid imbalance. In reality, you and your team do many things well and some things not so well. Even in the things that are done well, chances are there is room for improvement. Feedback can help you do that.

> *Feedback is the breakfast of champions.*
>
> Ken Blanchard

 ## Putting it in Practice

Grow Yourself: Seek Out Feedback

To get comfortable receiving feedback, seek out 3 to 4 people whose opinion you value and who know you well enough to provide feedback. You might solicit feedback about your leadership in general, your performance on a particular project or your service level to customers. I encourage you to ask the people you select to give you feedback face to face. This enables you to ask additional questions for clarification.

Your invitation can be as simple as a note that says:

I would really value and appreciate your feedback on my performance with (subject). If you could make the time, I'd like to have a conversation with you in which you share your thoughts on what I've done well and where I have room for improvement.

When you have your meeting, listen closely to understand their perspective. Do not rationalize, explain, or get defensive. Be certain to thank them for their time and insights.

4 people I would like feedback from:	
The topic I would like feedback on:	
Notes from the feedback I received:	

Grow Others: Spend a Week Providing In-The-Moment Feedback

For one week, focus on providing real time, in-the-moment, feedback. Strive to provide more appreciative than constructive feedback. Remember that these are not formal, sit down sessions, but quick discussions (1 to 2 minutes) as you interact with your team.

MY GOAL FOR FEEDBACK: I will provide feedback to _____ people this week. (Fill in the number of people.)

Notes on your progress:	What you observed as you provided feedback:

4.2   Coaching Conversations

A coach is a person who can guide your thinking, ask insightful questions and listen. They provide candid and helpful feedback. They may or may not be expert in the specifics of your job. You can hire a coach, but know that coaching is a skill that you can develop.

Let me differentiate coaching conversations from feedback. Feedback, as described here, happens frequently, quickly, freely, and in the moment. Coaching conversations are more structured, happen less frequently, and are more in depth conversations. Coaching conversations include feedback, but are not limited to feedback. In our hothouse analogy, feedback is like water, which flows freely and frequently. Coaching conversations are like fertilizer – applied regularly (but not daily) and nourishes at a deeper level.

The number of people you want to engage in coaching conversations may vary, depending on your intentions, the size of your team and your available time. It may be only one person; it may be more. It does not need to be everyone on your team. Reserve coaching conversations for those you lead that are at a point where they are able to benefit from coaching to break through to a higher level of performance.

Coaching conversations are mutually agreed upon sessions with an ultimate purpose or goal. Insist that the purpose or goal is explicit and mutually agreed upon and understood. Here are some common coaching goals:

- To develop more awareness of my leadership style and its impact

- To improve communication skills

- To develop strategic thinking skills

- To improve my sales ability

These are fairly broad – but give you some categories. You'll want to get more specific with the goal of your coaching session. For example, if the broad goal is to improve communication skills, the specific and actionable goal may be "to present effectively in groups of 20 or more" or to "ask more open ended questions to understand a situation before I respond". Getting specific fosters better learning.

The flow of a coaching conversation goes like this:

- A reaffirmation of the goal or focus area

- Affirmation of your commitment (more on that later)

> *The purpose of learning is growth, and our minds, unlike our bodies, can continue growing as we continue to live.*
>
> Mortimer Adler

> *Experience teaches only the teachable.*
>
> Aldous Huxley

- A review of progress made or challenges faced since the last coaching conversation
- The heart of the coaching conversation (see below)
- A capturing of insights and points covered
- An agreement on the next actions to be taken

The Heart of the Coaching Conversation

The heart of the coaching conversation can vary, according to the needs of the people in the conversation. One coaching conversation may move through several of these areas – this is a fluid process and one that you will become more skilled at over time. The coach determines where to lead the conversation, but typically spends time in one of more of these areas:

- Exploring possibilities
- Asking compelling questions
- Providing candid feedback
- Being a thought partner
- Reframing situations, beliefs and attitudes
- Providing alternative ideas and perspectives
- Reflecting back what is seen, heard, and felt
- Teaching and advising
- Synthesizing complex or disjointed situations
- Helping to articulate a plan of action

Make Your Commitment Visible

No doubt, there is great skill and complexity in engaging in coaching. There are many books you can read. You can take classes. You can pay thousands of dollars to become a certified coach. And that is all fine.

> *There are some things you learn best in calm, and some in storm.*
>
> Willa Cather

> *The first rule of management is delegation. Don't try and do everything yourself because you can't.*
>
> Anthea Turner

But don't let that overwhelm you or deter you from having coaching conversations with those around you that you want to invest in. Here is the reason why.

As I think back over my long career, I've been the recipient of many coaching conversations, ranging from ill equipped bosses to highly paid professional coaches. The conversations from which I've grown the most and reaped the greatest benefits were NOT those that were perfectly executed by a highly paid professional. They were with leaders who had these things in common:

- They cared deeply – about me and my success
- I knew they cared because they expressed their commitment in words and deeds
- They were willing to be open and candid – even when it was painful or I might not want to hear it
- The asked great questions
- They listened deeply
- They expressed confidence in my ability to do more, to achieve greater things

As such, find a time early in your coaching conversation to express your commitment. It can be as simple as saying, "You are a person who I can see much possibility. I'd like to help you be able to realize your potential."

If you are willing to show up in those ways with your team members, good results will happen. Guaranteed.

> *If you want one year of prosperity, grow seeds. If you want 10 years of prosperity, grow trees. If you want 100 years of prosperity, grow people.*
>
> Chinese Proverb

4.3   Developmental Delegation

Every organization I've been in over the past 10 years has one thing in common – more work to do than resources to do it. This is a challenge, but also an

> *There are many things which we can afford to forget which it is yet well to learn.*
>
> Oliver Wendell Holmes, Jr.

opportunity. It presents you with numerous ways to delegate tasks, projects and assignments that give someone a chance to develop new skills.

Sometimes we get a bit squeamish about delegation. We might avoid delegating because we want to hold on to something we do well, we don't want to overburden others, it may not get done perfectly, or it may not get done in the way you would do it. If you carry around some of those beliefs, I'd like you to reconsider. Delegating the right tasks to the right person can present them a challenge and an opportunity to grow. When delegated something important, I may feel pride that you had confidence in me rather than resentment for being asked to take on more. I may be excited to learn something new and do something different. And remember, there may be new ways to do things; you may not have the exclusive formula on success at this task.

With developmental delegation, I am NOT talking about dumping the tasks that no one wants to do on some unsuspecting team member. I am NOT talking about abdicating your responsibility to see that things get done correctly. I am NOT talking about sink or swim.

I am presenting the idea that by delegating real and significant work that can help someone develop a needed skill and supporting them along the way can develop your team's capacity and capability.

Perhaps someone on your team would benefit from learning how to collaborate across the organization. The next time YOU are asked to be on a cross organizational team, delegate it to them. Your role will shift from the "doer" (participating on the team) to "developer" (supporting the person from your team who you delegate this to).

I've learned that people will forget what you said, people will forget what you did, but people will never forget how you made them feel.

Maya Angelou

Here are some examples; you could delegate:

- A presentation to someone who needs to develop presentation skills
- Developing a white paper to someone who needs to learn to research, analyze and write
- The design of a new process to someone who needs to develop systems thinking
- The leadership of a volunteer group to someone that needs to learn how to motivate by purpose rather than position power
- Participation in a cross functional project to someone who needs to establish relationships across the organization
- Dealing with a difficult customer or supplier to someone who needs to learn negotiation skills

> *He who would learn to fly one day must first learn to stand and walk and run and climb and dance; one cannot fly into flying.*
>
> Friedrich Nietzsche

Here is a 6-step process you can follow:

1 Create a list of your team members and 1 to 2 areas for development

2 Find delegation opportunities that provide appropriate opportunities

3 Hold a delegation dialog. Be clear about both the task and the developmental opportunities.

4 Monitor progress throughout the assignment.

5 Provide learning support. This can be readings, books, courses, coaching conversations, and real time feedback.

6 Debrief at the conclusion of the assignment (more frequently if a long assignment, a highly visible project or a large stretch for your team member.

Developmental delegation can be one of the most powerful tools you have as a leader to increase others' abilities. Done well, confidence blooms, capacity increases, and your job gets easier. As a quick summary, let's look at each of the elements in developmental delegation:

It is real work that needs done with real consequences. This provides both motivation and focus. We've all been asked to do "made up" work. We know how demeaning and frustrating that is. It can be frightening to delegate important work to someone in a learning mode. There are two ways to overcome this. The first is to provide support and guidance behind the scenes (not micromanagement) so that you reduce the likelihood of failure. The second is to gauge readiness. If the gap between the skill and what is needed is wide, have them shadow first or give them a smaller portion of the task.

You can link a developmental goal to the task. It is helpful to create a list of your team members and the skills you've agreed upon that they would like to develop. Then create a list of developmental

The illiterate of the 21st century will not be those who cannot read and write, but those who cannot learn, unlearn, and relearn.

Alvin Toffler

opportunities. The list can include ad hoc assignments, projects that need more time and attention than you can provide or day to day portions of your job that another person could handle and benefit from doing. Comparing these two lists should enable you to match tasks with developmental opportunities.

Intentions are transparent. Discuss the assignment and the specific skills you want the person to develop. Help them see how they are linked. Not having this discussion greatly diminishes the chances that the person you are delegating to will develop the skills you had in mind. This discussion will provide focus on the learning objective. It can also provide a sense of accomplishment and pride in the task that may not have been present if it was merely something added to their list of tasks.

Learning support is provided. After you've found the right task to develop the desired skills and engaged your team member in the work, you have one more important thing to do – provide support. The amount and type of support you provide will be dependent on the maturity of your team member and the complexities of the assignment. The less mature your team member, the more learning support you'll provide. The more mature, the less. At a minimum you'll want to have regular coaching conversations to assess progress, provide guidance and to make visible the learning. Leverage other options to deepen the learning as well. You can assign a mentor from outside your area, provide readings or learning assignments or provide the opportunity to go to a related course or conference.

Live as if you were to die tomorrow. Learn as if you were to live forever.

Mahatma Gandhi

There is a huge value in learning with instant feedback.

Anant Agarwal

Putting it in Practice

Grow Others: Delegate to Develop

Use this worksheet to help you prepare to delegate an assignment once you have matched a team member's developmental need with a task to delegate.

Team member to develop:

Skill to work on:

Assignment to delegate:

About the Assignment
What are the overall objectives of this assignment? What needs to be accomplished? Why is this important?
What skills and abilities can the employee develop in this assignment?
What deliverables are expected?
What level of quality is expected? What does success look like?

When does this need to be done?
How will we evaluate the results of the assignments?
What non-negotiables do you have about this assignment?
When will check points about the assignment be held?
What support will you provide?
What questions might you ask to check for understanding about the assignment?

5 More No Cost Methods

By our nature, people are natural learners. As such, you can set the stage for learning any number of ways. We've just reviewed three methods in the past section. However, there are MANY no (or low) cost/high impact ways that you can develop yourself and your team. In this section, I'll describe them briefly. There are many resources on the web, in bookstores, and perhaps in your organization that can help you implement them.

Debrief or After Action Review

The military and sports teams have perfected these. The concept is simple – after an "action," taking time to sit down and discuss what went well, what went poorly, and what you will do differently the next time in the same or similar situations. The more you do these, the better you get at them, the more candid the conversations and the likely people are to do them "real time" in many other situations.

Reflection

This resembles a debrief, but on an individual basis. This is quiet time set aside to look back at a set period of time (day, week, month, or year) and think about what has gone well, what has not and what you will do differently. Highly effective leaders make reflection a top priority. Some take half a day a month, others carve out shorter amounts of time daily.

Mentoring

A mentor is a person skilled at what you want to learn. They are experts; they have done this before. A mentor will share knowledge and guide you along the way. Some companies offer formal mentoring programs – although mentoring happens informally in all organizations. Don't hesitate to either be a mentor to someone or to ask someone to mentor you.

> Education is a choice. We don't become educated by watching television, and we don't learn a whole lot having similar conversations with the same, safe people day after day. Our education comes from pushing up against boundaries, from taking risks that may seem at first to be overwhelming, and by persevering past the first disappointments or shortfalls until we reach a point at which actual learning takes place. Determination and perseverance are absolutely vital to developing a true education--rarely, if ever, do we learn the most valuable lessons in the first few steps of the journey..
>
> Tom Walsh

Questioning

If you've ever had the experience of someone asking just the right question at just the right time – you know the power a simple question can have in helping you gain perspective, summarize your thoughts, or create a flash of insight. If you do nothing else than learn to ask powerful and provocative questions – your team will benefit.

 ## Putting it in Practice

Grow Your Leadership Skills with Daily Reflection

Find a place to record your daily reflections. It may be a journal, a notebook, a tablet (paper or electronic, although I prefer paper).

Begin to set aside 10 minutes at the end of each day. Find a quiet place. Turn your PC and phone off. Perhaps turn on some quiet music. Jot down what you have learned from your experiences today. Note that this is not a review of your "to do" list. You may have had a chance encounter, come across a flash of insight or had someone teach you something.

Write today's date and your reflections. Focus on your insights and learnings, and not your accomplishments. Answering any of these questions often helps me formulate my thoughts:

- As I think back over my day, what insights or learnings did I have?
- What patterns or themes do I see?
- What can I learn from what went well today? From what went poorly?
- How will what I learned today going to help me tomorrow?
- What might I want to do differently as a result of what I've learned today?

Be diligent about doing this practice of daily reflection for at least 30 days, due to the importance of practice in cultivating a habit. At the end of 30 days, ask yourself:

- What value has the practice of reflection brought to my life and my leadership?
- Is this something I want to commit to on an on-going basis? Why or why not?

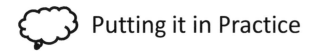 Putting it in Practice

Grow Your Team with Debrief Questions

Find a time in your natural work flow that conducting a debrief session would add value. It could be at a milestone date in a large project, at the completion of a smaller project, at the end of a time period (week, month, quarter), at the delivery of work to a customer, after a major presentation, or when you've experienced a change in work activity.

Ensure there are no surprises. Let your team know your intent (to get better) and your process (to hold a debrief).

When you gather, remind your team of your purpose (to learn and to improve) and set some ground rules. Some ground rules you may want to consider include:

- No subject is off limits.
- Our goal is to get better, not to place blame.
- Discuss what went well and what did not.
- Everyone has a voice.

It is helpful to assign a note taker or scribe. This role can be rotated so it is not a burden to one person. This person is to take notes, record them and distribute them to all participants.

To begin, have a few prepared questions. These questions are typically open-ended and spur discussion. They can be as simple as:

- What did we do especially well?
- What made that happen?
- What do we want to improve in the future?
- What will it take to do that?

You'll want to leave some time for other comments or questions. A great way to set this up is to ask: "What have we not discussed that we really need to?"

As you lead the debrief, you can model the way by sharing candidly and non-judgmentally. You can listen carefully and ask follow-on questions. You can be curious and not defensive. Finally, you will want to thank others for insights and perspectives.

To end your debrief, summarize what was shared. Most likely there will be action items – so make sure the scribe knows what they are, who is responsible for completing them, and when they are due. Use the template on the next page to guide you.

6 Develop Side by Side

Always remember that developing others, by its nature has another person involved. This is not a stealth operation, but a mutually collaborative process where these things are occurring:

- There is candid and on-going dialogue about the person's strengths, skills and challenge areas.

- They are in control of the decisions about their goals – but share them fully so that you can support them and plan for them.

- You are transparent about the skills you want them to develop and how you will support them.

`There are times when we see potential in a team member for more, but they are reluctant to step up or to do more. In those cases, you may need to build their confidence in their ability. Or you may need to back off, because your vision for their development is not what they see. At times it is hard to discern the difference. Open dialogue, the right questions, your support and taking things in smaller steps can help both of you discern if this is a confidence issue, a lack of knowledge issue or truly is a personal life choice situation.

`There is a thin line between supporting and encouraging your team members and forcing your agenda on them. If you find yourself wanting to "fix" someone else, you are most likely over the line. If you continue to push after being told that is not what they want, back off.

Leadership and learning are indispensable to each other.

John F. Kennedy

What is important is to keep learning, to enjoy challenge and to tolerate ambiguity. In the end there are no certain answers.

Martina Homer

7   A Wonderful Gift

Investing in your personal growth and the development of others takes time and effort. It is not always easy relinquish control of a task you do exceptionally well and with minimum effort to someone who struggles with it. It is hard to give candid feedback; to ask probing questions and then just listen; to help someone else do it when they may not do it "your way."

Once you take the time to do this and your team members begin to gain in skill and in confidence, you'll find that your job is easier – as you have more people that can do more things. You'll have fewer crises as you will have multiple eyes averting problems. You and your team will have more flexibility – as others can begin to fill in and cover for each other.

There are benefits for the organization as well. In today's environment, skill and agility are paramount. The higher the capacity and capability of your team, the more likely you are to perform, to adapt and to contribute to the overall organization.

And finally, if you want to truly have an impact and leave a long lasting legacy, developing others is your ticket. I can look back over my career and recall the people who encouraged me, who invested in me, who took a chance on me, who gave me opportunities and then were there to encourage me as I struggled. It may have been only one 3-month assignment, but the lessons learned yield dividends for a lifetime.

I have never in my life learned anything from any man who agreed with me.

Dudley Field Malone

We learn by example and by direct experience because there are real limits to the adequacy of verbal instruction.

Malcolm Gladwell

Additional Resources:

Buckingham, Marcus, and Curt Coffman. First, break all the rules: what the world's greatest managers do differently. New York, NY. Simon & Schuster, 1999.

Lombardo, Michael M., and Robert W. Eichinger. FYI: for your improvement: a guide for development and coaching. 4th ed. Minneapolis, MN: Lominger Ltd., 2004.

CHAPTER 12
Organizational Ecosystems

Our Interconnected World

Most likely you interact with people who live across the globe. Your network, thanks to technology and tools like LinkedIn and Facebook, is large, connected and not geographically or time constrained. As a leader who is creating positive change, these interconnected webs of relationships can either propel you forward or be your undoing. It has never been more important to nurture relationships, understand how complex human systems work, and to know how to work within them to affect change.

> *If you want to go somewhere, it is best to find someone who has already been there.*
>
> Robert Kiyosaki

1   Globally Networked

As humans we are drawn to one another. Even in the most sparsely populated regions, you'll often see clusters of homes. We join groups and draw our identity from them. From prehistoric times onward, this has been the case.

An amazing phenomenon is happening. Our groups are getting larger and larger. They are more diverse, more global. 100 years ago your group may have consisted of 150 people in your community, workplace and church. The numbers were small, the geographic range finite and relative homogeneity was the rule.

Not the case today. Most likely you interact with people who live across the globe. Your network, thanks to the internet, is large, connected and not geographically or time constrained.

Creating positive change cannot be done in a vacuum. Your actions affect and depend on your team, your peers, your division, your organization. And we are increasingly aware of the impact our actions make on our communities, our families, our environment and our fellow humans – across the globe.

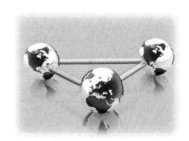

1.1   All Organizations are Unique

The metaphor of ecosystem helps us to think about human organizations. Wikipedia describes an ecosystem as:

*An **ecosystem** is a community of living organisms (plants, animals and microbes) in conjunction with the nonliving components of their environment (things like air, water and mineral soil), interacting as a system. These biotic and abiotic components are regarded as linked together through nutrient cycles and energy flows. As ecosystems are defined by the network of interactions among organisms, and between organisms and their environment, they can come in any size but usually encompass specific, limited spaces (although some scientists say that the entire planet is an ecosystem).*

Organizational ecosystems consist of a network of people inside an organization working together in the larger networks outside of the organization (supply chains, marketplaces, legislative and social networks). These ecosystems are interdependent; what happens with a disruption in your supply chain impacts the inner workings of your organization, and consequently your customers.

The currency of real networking is not greed but generosity

Keith Ferrazzi

Just as no two natural ecosystems are exactly the same, organizational ecosystems are unique and varied. They all have some common elements. There are certain things that both define the organization and give it structure. There must be a purpose for existing. There is work to be done and a way to divide and organize the work. There is a social structure; in some organizations it is a hierarchy and others a matrix (a great example of a more complex, intertwined web). There are rules and policies, rewards and consequences. Just as genes in DNA manifest themselves in different ways even with the same genetic pool, organizations take on their own special way of being.

Culture is perhaps the best way to describe the uniqueness that is evident in every group or organization, in spite of similar structures. As I would travel from manufacturing plant to manufacturing plant when I worked for a larger printer, it was evident that each plant had its own signature culture, even though it was the same company, the same equipment, the same customers and the same products.

In this chapter, we will look at two ways of looking at organizational ecosystems: through the lens of systems thinking and then through organizational culture. Both are deep and complex fields – so our goal in this chapter is to introduce some basic concepts and to create a general awareness. I do hope that you'll be more alert to these dynamics as you lead and also that you become interested in learning more.

It is important to note that due to the complexity and the dynamism of human systems, there is no one who can perfectly predict or effortless manage through them. It is my hope though, that by awareness and a few practices we will share, that you become more

Managers are not confronted with problems that are independent of each other, but with dynamic situations that consist of complex systems of changing problems that interact with each other. I call such situations messes…Managers do not solve problems, they manage messes

Russell Ackoff

aware, observant and better able to exert your leadership to achieve your vision.

1.2   Every Intervention has a Ripple

Given the complexity of human systems, it is naive to think that you can introduce change, of any kind, without the organization reacting. Due to myriad linkages and interdependencies in an organization, every intervention has a ripple effect – up, down and across your organization and then to others in your larger networks. Even actions as seemingly benign as observing a human system changes it. You may recall the Hawthorne effect, based on studies in the 1920s at a Western Electric factory outside of Chicago on productivity. Short-term productivity boosts were documented and attributed to the act of being observed – nothing more.

The larger the change you are affecting, the bigger the ripples. In fact, with really large scale shifts they may seem like tidal waves. Some will be intended. Others will be unintended. Some will be expected. Others will totally blindside you.

There are two messages here that are important for leaders. The first is recognition that there will be ripples and that you need to be prepared for them. Some are very predictable. Some are avoidable. Others are not avoidable and need to be weathered through. If you have a ripple free change, then I can guarantee you have failed to conjure up a big enough vision. The absence of ripples only happens when you are nurturing the status quo.

The second idea is that with some pre-planning you can anticipate and minimize many of the ripples. Knowing how your project impacts others and what they are likely to feel and then do is helpful. It is

> *The richest people in the world look for and build networks, everyone else looks for work.*
>
> Robert Kiyosaki

> *I have yet to see any problem, however complicated, which, when looked at in the right way, did not become still more complicated.*
>
> Poul Anderson

information that can help you help them to be open to the changes, rather than to resist them.

1.3   Basic Systems Thinking

Systems thinking can help you as a leader discern and then leverage underlying principles. From Leverage Networks, an organization that provides resources for systems thinking, comes this description:

Systems thinking offers you a powerful new perspective, a specialized language, and a set of tools that you can use to address the most stubborn problems in your everyday life and work. Systems thinking is a way of understanding reality that emphasizes the relationships among a system's parts, rather than the parts themselves. Based on a field of study known as system dynamics, systems thinking has a practical value that rests on a solid theoretical foundation.

We cannot, in this one chapter, begin to make you a systems thinking expert. We can however, provide an overview of some concepts that will serve you well. We can also hope to whet your appetite for more.

Concept 1: Complex systems, when disrupted, find new patterns

We stated it earlier and will reemphasize it here. All parts of a system are interconnected in some way. These systems, by their nature are adaptive. As such, when a change occurs in one part of the system, disruption occurs across the system. The very interesting thing is that even the most complex and seemingly random systems, after a disruption, settle into a new pattern of being. This phenomenon is true

Placing a system in a straitjacket of constancy can cause fragility to evolve

C.S. Holling

All things appear and disappear because of the concurrence of causes and conditions. Nothing ever exists entirely alone; everything is in relation to everything else.

Buddha

across a range of sizes – from sub-atomic particles to global communities.

Think about a busy traffic area, for either foot or vehicular traffic. There are regular and predictable patterns. You know to avoid this street at this certain time or you will face a long wait. When those regular patterns are disrupted by construction, new patterns emerge and emerge very quickly. Traffic finds a new pattern, and soon has the same predictability and flow (or traffic jams) as before.

There are several reasons that this is important to know as you introduce something new. The first is that no matter how chaotic and uncertain it seems during the transition (the time of disruption) a new normal will emerge. Things will become routine; order will reemerge. Do not despair.

The second is that during this time of disruption, there is an overwhelming tendency of the system to find a new structure, a new pattern. There will be a huge tendency to revert back to the original form; organizations are noted for their ability to ward off intrusions that threaten their stability. The more stable the system and the less dramatic the disruption, the more likely it will return to its original state. The more unstable the system, the more likely a disruption will result in movement to a new and different state. As such, the most difficult changes to make are small ones in stable organizations.

To successfully see your creation come to life, you must be diligent NOT to allow things to slip back to the status quo. Do this by maintaining focus, continuing to review progress and measuring outcomes. Keep the heat on – for longer than you think is needed. Otherwise, old ways reemerge, and all your efforts for change will be lost.

In addition to steady focus over time on the new way of being, you can find some ways to make the new

> *You think that because you understand 'one' that you must therefore understand 'two' because one and one makes two. But you forget that you must also understand 'and'.*
>
> Sufi teaching story

> *No man is an island, entire of itself.*
>
> John Donne

way the path of least resistance. Some simple examples:

- If your change has a technology component, retire the old software or equipment. If you can't pull the plug, at a minimum stop supporting the old system.
- Make it easy to do things the new way. Apple's iPhone is a case study for ease of use – which was followed by broad scale adoption of the new phone and discarding of the old.
- Make the old way socially undesirable. Smoking is a great example. When the campaign to end smoking moved from individual consequences (your own poor health) and to social ones (second hand smoke), significant and real changes began to occur.

> *When we are blind to systemic causes of problems, all the solutions we try will likely make matters worse*
>
> Esther Derby

Concept 2: Unintended consequences

The visions that we are working so diligently to bring into existence have only our highest and best intentions. We desire happy customers, a better community, a stronger business, improved education. Yet due to the fact that your new creation exists within an existing structure (be it your company, your community or your family), it changes the structure. Some of those changes may be anticipated; many others will be unforeseen and unintended. Unfortunately, sometimes the unintended consequences actually run counter to what we are trying to achieve.

Here are a few examples that you may relate to:

- Texting changes the way we communicate. Automobile accidents as a result of texting are an unintended consequence.

> *We must therefore rediscover, after the natural world, the social world, not as an object or sum of objects, but as a permanent field or dimension of existence*
>
> Maurice Merleau-Ponty

- The Internet enables us to have access to more information than ever before. It does many good things – like fostering research, education and collaboration. It also provides terrorists with information that does great harm.

- We erect high rises to house the low income population, in an effort to be more efficient in the delivery of services. They become isolated centers of poverty, inculcating a legacy of poverty and crime.

You may never avoid unintended consequences, but you certainly can reduce the number and severity of them. Taking time, early in your creation, to map out upstream and downstream implications can help you see, and then mitigate unintended outcomes. Listing all stakeholders and the impact of your creation to them can also help. Asking "what if" also helps, as does thinking out 3, 5, or 10 years into the future.

Concept 3: Time delays

It would be wonderful if we could run a quick test and determine the consequences of our actions. Unfortunately, that is not the case. As changes are made to human systems, some impacts are not felt immediately. In fact, some will not be realized for years or even decades. When Alexander Graham Bell invented the telephone or Henry Ford the affordable automobile, there is absolutely no way either gentleman could have predicted the impact of their creation on the world over time.

The fact of time delays when dealing with human ecosystems should not cause you to stop your efforts. But you may be well served to pause and think forward. What might happen over time? How long

> *When we think in terms of systems, we see that a fundamental misconception is embedded in the popular term "side-effects"...This phrase means roughly "effects which I hadn't foreseen or don't want to think about"...Side-effects no more deserve the adjective "side" than does the "principal" effect. It is hard to think in terms of systems, and we eagerly warp our language to protect ourselves from the necessity of doing so.*
>
> Garrett Hardin

might it take for your creation to manifest its consequences?

The principle of time delays always means that you will continue to scan for cause and effect – well past the time you might think is prudent. And you won't be surprised not to understand the full consequences of your work for quite a long time.

Concept 4: Underlying structures

Every structure, either physical or social has an underlying structure that gives it form and shapes how it works. It is your skeleton that enables your body to have stature and movement. It is the keystone that holds the arch together, the pilings that support the bridge. There may be many other structures that are at play in each of these systems, but some have more impact on the integrity of the system than others. Lose a toenail, and it may be painful. Damage your back and many of your essential life functions may be severely compromised over time.

Social systems also have an underlying structure including a few underlying structural elements that exert disproportionate influence. If the change you want to realize competes with the underlying structure, you are doomed from the start. As an example, perhaps you want your team to provide better customer service. You describe, in great detail what that looks like. You ensure your team understands why this is important. You provide training and coaching and support. Yet no matter what you do, phone calls are cut short, team members are curt rather than personable and your customer satisfaction ratings continue to be dismal. If you peel back the organizational structure, you might find that the way pay and performance is measured and rewarded is by call volume, not by caller satisfaction.

All things appear and disappear because of the concurrence of causes and conditions. Nothing ever exists entirely alone; everything is in relation to everything else.

Buddha

Trouble makes us one with every human being in the world - and unless we touch others, we're out of touch with life.

Oliver Wendell Holmes Sr.

No matter how much you exhort your team members to exhibit different behaviors, the underlying structure will always circumvent your efforts.

Your job, as a change leader, is to identify, to the extent possible, the underlying structural elements that can either support your change or get in the way. When you identify those that will be at counter purposes, you can take steps to change them so that they are in alignment and support for what you want to accomplish. Here are some questions you can ask to begin to "see" and understand the underlying structure:

- What work policies and procedures are in place? Which are formally documented and maintained? Which are informally adhered to?

- How are people rewarded?

- How are decisions made? Who holds decision making rights?

- Are there external factors that add structure? (Think laws, agreements, regulations, etc.)

[Language] can serve as a medium through which we create new understandings and new realities as we begin to talk about them. In fact, we don't talk about what we see; we see only what we can talk about.

Fred Kofman

1.4   Use Successive Approximation

At this point, you may well be discouraged. It is hard to anticipate the effect your creation will have on the world. You know there will be unintended consequences, but you don't know what they are or how big they will be. You have enough to be concerned with in just getting your creation launched, without worrying about all the upstream and downstream effects.

Don't despair. There is an approach, mimicked from nature that can help us understand and adapt to the ripples we create in our organizational ecosystems as we bring our creation to life. It is an approach that mirrors evolution. When you consider it, when we are creating something new we are evolving, bringing into being something that did not exist before.

Evolution is a series of successive approximations, one small mutation (or change) after another. Successful ones stick. Unsuccessful ones die. Over time, this series of small, but influential approximations, yield something big, something different. And it happens one step at a time. Evolution also involves shedding, or not carrying forward attributes that are no longer useful. As man began to walk upright, the length of his arms got shorter and shorter – by design.

To use successive approximation with your creation, you create a portion, launch it and test results. You learn what works and what does not. You get ideas for the next generation. You go back to creating and improve the original and discard that which adds little or no value. Once again, you put your creation out there and do a live check. And you do this over and over again.

Entrepreneurs use this approach and call it minimally viable product or MVP. They will launch as quickly as possible with only enough so that a consumer will pay for it. They then see what works, what is missing and what the customer is ambivalent about. They then create a better version and repeat the process. As the second version has more value, the price point reflects that.

Note that successive approximation is in direct opposition to the notion that you build something in the "lab" or in isolation and then do the grand reveal. It flies in the face of the notion that something must be perfect to be released.

Successive approximation is an approach that works well in today's organizations for several reasons. In previous chapters we've discussed that today's environment changes so quickly that the world you

> *We need to work together to optimize the system as a whole, not to seek to optimize separate pieces... Optimizing separate pieces destroys the effectiveness of the whole. For the organization to work well as a whole, the components must work together*
>
> Brian Joiner

> *There (is) order and even great beauty in what looks like total chaos. If we look closely enough at the randomness around us, patterns will start to emerge.*
>
> Aaron Sarkin

began in will not be the one you end in. When you are creating something big, it is difficult to know each step of the way. Successive approximation can help. And given the interconnected and networked world we exist in, there is virtually no way to predict exactly who will be impacted and what the result will be in advance.

2   Culture Wins Always

Now that you have a taste of systems thinking, let's look at one of the most invisible, yet powerful organizational ecosystems you'll face: culture. Organizational culture is roughly described at how "we do things around here" – its foundation is the shared values and norms of the organization. Culture includes how decisions get made, how work gets done, what is deemed important and how relationships work. It is the pattern of collective behaviors and mental models.

Culture is played out and reinforced daily. For example, I worked within a culture where collaborative decision-making was the norm. There were meeting rooms everywhere – and they were full most of the time. Very seldom did people do work alone or make unilateral decisions. Of course, decisions were slow to be made and across the board, leaders were better at facilitation than decisiveness.

A simile I use is that culture is to organizations as water is to a fish. For the most part, the water is as invisible to the fish as air is to us. Unless it becomes fouled or unavailable, the fish exists within the water, almost oblivious to its presence. Yet, it is terribly vital – for food, oxygen and movement.

Organizational culture is almost as invisible. Once you are in the organization and acclimated to the culture, it becomes just "the way things are done." Yet it is a powerful force that shapes most everything that happens within an organization. That is why changing a culture is a long and arduous process that is often unsuccessful. A common phrase proclaims that culture eats strategy and structure for lunch.

As you implement your vision, you need to make the culture "visible" so that you can see where your change may run afoul of the existing culture. Once you can see it, you then must find ways to reshape the culture in ways that support what you are bringing forward.

Culture has also been likened to an iceberg – with only a small tip visible and a great and weighty mass below the surface. Given this, how does one determine what the culture of the organization you are working within is? I'll be the first to say that it is an imprecise art, for many reasons. There are cultures within cultures. There are subtle differences that are hard to describe or define. We don't have wonderful language or tools to define it. It's hard to see it when you are immersed in it.

Even so, having some awareness of the culture you are influencing is far superior to being clueless. Here are a few ways you might get a better understanding of an organization's culture:

- Ask an outsider or a newcomer. Both will have fresh ideas and be able to see things with more clarity. Ask them what strikes them? What seems different? How would they describe the people? The environment? The way work gets done?

- Look to the stated values and norms and do a gut check. You'll either affirm that these are truly day-to-day guiding principles – or you'll

A bad system will beat a good person every time

W. Edwards Demming

be hard pressed to see any way in which they are made evident. Either reaction tells you something.

- Review the stories that are told – about your founding, about organizational wins, about what it is like to be here. What are the jokes told about working here? What do you share in orientation? On your website?

- Ask others how they would describe working here. Ask a wide range of people and questions, listen hard and summarize.

2.1   Defining the Transformation

To understand how what you are creating may either be supported by the existing culture or run afoul of it, it helps to define the new behaviors that will be required and then the inner or mental model that also must shift.

Examples are helpful, so let's use one to illustrate. Your vision is to create an organization that is known for innovating new products and bringing them to market quickly. To do that, you need everyone in the organization bringing forward ideas. The list below shows the behavior you want– and also some of the inner transformations that must occur.

In this example, the more hierarchical and stratified your organization, the more culture will work against you. In addition to the mindset of hierarchy, you will find that there are many policies, processes, structures and rules that reinforce the hierarchy – and these will get in the way of ideas being freely generated, listened to, and acted upon in the organization.

> *Without reflection, we go blindly on our way, creating more unintended consequences, and failing to achieve anything useful.*
>
> Margaret J. Wheatley

Behaviors	Inner Transformation for Employees	Inner Transformation for Leaders
Ideas are surfaced by anyone in the organization – in all roles and in all levels	• I can contribute creative ideas. • It is safe to bring forward those ideas. • My ideas will be listened to.	• I don't own all the good ideas, they can come from anywhere in the organization. • My reactions to the ideas brought forward will either encourage or discourage more ideas in the future. • My role is to listen and make it safe to bring ideas forward, not to judge the idea or the person.

 Putting it in Practice

Defining Vital Behaviors

All change requires different behaviors. You will have to do things differently if you want to get different results than you are currently getting. Most likely, the future you are creating involves others, who will also need to do things differently.

Not all behaviors are equal when it comes to change. Typically there are a few key or vital behaviors that when done and done consistently, yield a high likelihood of success. A great example is with losing weight. You can literally find thousands of behaviors that are advocated. Eat a Mediterranean diet, don't eat after 7:30 at night, eat only protein, eat no protein….the list can go on and on. The reality is that there are only two vital behaviors that you need to do: eat less and move more. If you do those two things, you are likely to successfully drop pounds.

Vital behaviors have these characteristics:

• Leads directly to better results.

• Breaks self-defeating patterns.

• Causes many other positive behaviors to follow naturally.

Think about what you are creating. What are the vital behaviors that you or others need to do to be successful? Again, we've provided a few examples and then space for you to define the vital behaviors that will help with your initiative.

My Intended Result	The Vital Behavior
A bank of ideas for potential new services	Every team member adds ideas to the idea bank weekly
Deliver our new product on time	Anyone on the project team can flag problems that get in the way of schedule attainment
A high performing team	Issues and problems get discussed and resolved when they occur

2.2   Shifting the Culture

I don't believe that you can make a wholesale cultural change. I do believe that you can exert influence in an organization or group to shift or shape the culture. You can't turn the iceberg into a tropical island, but parts of it can melt or get larger or change shape.

There are six levers of influence that you can use as you shape the culture. These levers come from the work of Patterson, Grenny, Maxfield, McMillan and Switzler in the book Influencer: The Power to Change Anything. I'll summarize the levers here – and encourage you to explore their web site, where you will find many free tools and support resources.

The Influencer model is based on the idea that in order for change to occur, individuals must change, teams must change and organizational systems must change. And for change to occur there must be both

> *When we seek for connection, we restore the world to wholeness. Our seemingly separate lives become meaningful as we discover how truly necessary we are to each other.*
>
> Margaret Wheatly

the motivation (the will to change) and ability (the know how to change).

The model states that there are six levers you can use to influence the change you want to create. For example, if you motive individuals to make the change, you'll have pulled one lever. The more levers you pull, the more likely the change you desire will take hold and will be sustained. Again, an example will help you understand. We'll build on the innovation example above.

Your Aim: Innovate new products and bring them to market quickly A Vital Behavior: Everyone in the organization brings forward ideas		
	Motivation	**Ability**
Individual (personal)	• Tell stories of individuals at all levels across the organization who brought forward ideas. Highlight both the internal satisfaction and the positive impact to the organization and your customers.	• Teach the "ideation" process to everyone in the organization and allow ample time to practice the skills.
Team (social)	• Identify people across the organization (at all levels) held in high regard and make them facilitators for ideation sessions.	• Provide these facilitators across the organization for team ideation sessions. Have them model the ideation process and support team in learning how to ideate.
Organization (structural)	• Remove any policies or procedures that get in the way of new ideas flowing upward. (for example – needing a manager's sign off to submit an idea for consideration)	• Put in place systems that make it easy for new ideas to be submitted, recognized and acted upon. Appoint a visible and highly influential leader to implement the system.

To see a simple and fun example of these six levers at work, watch All Washed Up on YouTube, a video that illustrates the six levers to get a group of children to wash their hands before eating some tempting and tasty cupcakes.

Culture is complex. Changing it can be hard. But when you have culture working for you it is like having the wind at your back. Things are easy and happen almost effortlessly. There is sustained effort on the right things. Having the culture work against you is hard work, and many times, a futile effort. In order for you to ensure your vision gets realized, do what you must to get the culture supporting your change rather than working against it.

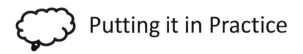 Putting it in Practice

Identifying Levers of Influence

Now that you have identified the vital behaviors, you'll want to find ways to influence others to adopt those behaviors. Refer back to the guide on our discussion of the six levers for more information and an example.

Your Aim:

A Vital Behavior:

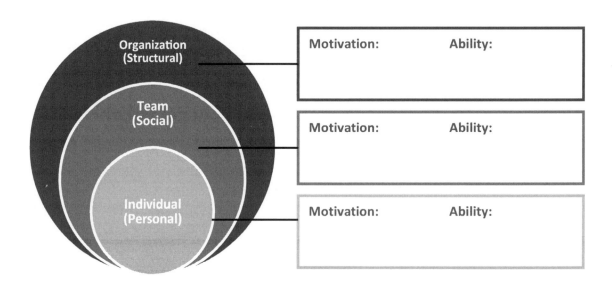

3   Leadership Actions

We've broached some concepts in systems thinking and organizational culture. I suspect, at this point, this chapter feels very theoretical, without a clear line of sight about how you might lead differently so that your creation has a much better chance of being realized. In this section, we'll provide you with some leadership practices that will help you in work better within organizational ecosystems.

3.1   Build Strong Networks

You may see creating something as internal work, often done in relative seclusion. That is the image of the creative artists or writers, who barricade themselves from the outside world to produce their creation. And that may be true for solo endeavors.

Nothing could be further from the truth for those of us who create in organizations. As we create new companies, new processes and approaches, new products and services we must immerse ourselves in our work and in the social settings into which our work will both be created, emerge from and live within. I've yet to see a relevant organizational change that happened in isolation.

As a leader who creates within an organization, your internal and external networks matter. Your external networks provide perspective, ideas and inspiration. Your internal networks provide support, resources, feedback and credibility. Determine who matters in the work you are bringing into being and then develop and nurture your networks with intention.

> *A woodsman was once asked, "What would you do if you had just five minutes to chop down a tree?" He answered, "I would spend the first two and a half minutes sharpening my axe.*
>
> Anonymous

The golden rule of networking and relationships is mutuality. The best networkers are relationship focused. As such, they give freely. They share. They connect. They support. They ask what help they can provide and follow through. They create relational power, which is very different than position power.

Very seldom will you be able to create something new and big organizationally only by position power. Relational power, on the other hand, will serve you well.

If you don't already have a wide and strong network, begin now to create one. If you do, nurture it. And if you don't have any idea of how to go about it, spend some time reading Keith Ferrarzzi's book Never Eat Alone.

> *Reflection and action must never be undertaken independently.*
>
> Paulo Friere

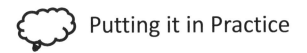 # Putting it in Practice

Building Relationships

Relationships, inside and outside your organization, can contribute greatly to your success in achieving your vision. You'll want to nurture a variety of types of relationships. Each different category will provide something valuable, but different. The more global your work, the more global your network needs to be.

Be intentional about building a variety of relationships. Only having a great network within your line of business is limiting and will not promote your ability to see bigger picture, to understand global trends, or to introduce new or novel ideas and approaches into your work.

Relationships are built a step at a time, over time. Strong and enduring relationships are two way – there are times you take and times you give. The best relationship builders are those that give freely. Make a list of 10 people you would either like to establish a relationship with or strengthen the one that currently exists. It may be that you would like to establish a relationship outside your business and outside your field, but don't have a name yet. If so, just list the category and some action steps you can take to find someone in that category. We've provided a few examples to get you started.

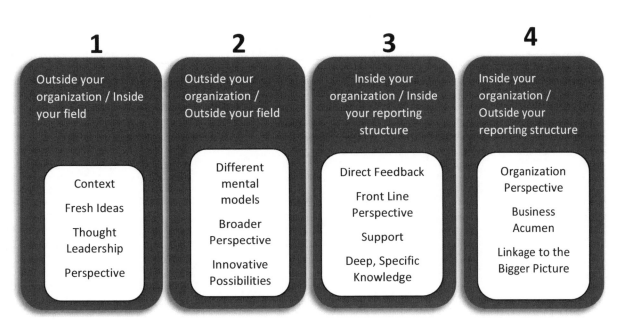

1

Outside your organization / Inside your field

Context

Fresh Ideas

Thought Leadership

Perspective

2

Outside your organization / Outside your field

Different mental models

Broader Perspective

Innovative Possibilities

3

Inside your organization / Inside your reporting structure

Direct Feedback

Front Line Perspective

Support

Deep, Specific Knowledge

4

Inside your organization / Outside your reporting structure

Organization Perspective

Business Acumen

Linkage to the Bigger Picture

Relationship (Name)	Category (from previous page)	Current State	Desired State	Action Steps
Jane Smith	1	See infrequently at professional meetings	More regular contact	Set up a quarterly lunch get together.
????	2	Very few professional contacts outside my field	1 to 2 relationships in different fields that can help me expand my thinking	Look at our church directory to see who might be a good relationship to nurture.
Joe Smith	3	Respected peer, but only interact in meetings	Enlist him as a "go to person" when I need to get feedback on how my initiatives are being received in our business unit	Ask for his feedback directly. Determine if he would be open to regular sessions.
Jenny Smith	4	Does not know me, but is my counterpart in another division	Mutually share information about business trends in our respective areas	Find a time to connect at the next leadership meeting.

3.2   Get On the Balcony

If you remember nothing else about systems thinking, remember that it helps you look at the big picture. And the more you can see the big picture, the more likely you are to create something that is relevant and the more likely it is to be adapted.

I'm going to borrow an image from Leadership on the Line by Heifetz and Linsky – that of "getting on the balcony." They describe the day to day actions going on in an organization as the "dance floor." This is where the action happens, where things are spinning wildly (sometimes a bit out of control). They contend that leaders, at times, need to extract themselves from the dance floor and get on the balcony. Here you can see the dance floor and have a much broader and more holistic view of all the action and how different elements are interacting. You can see who is sitting on the sidelines and who is dancing alone.

Good systems thinkers extract themselves regularly from the day to day and find ways to observe, think about and plan for the big picture view. Then then reenter the day to day, and work side by side, doing the work for a while, only to return to the balcony for a bird's eye view.

The image of the balcony is illustrative only. There is no physical balcony. But you can construct a mental one and develop a practice by which you regularly remove yourself from the day to day to observe and reflect on the big picture. Perhaps you take an hour a week or half a day a month to go somewhere quiet and where you will not be interrupted. That break allows you time to step back and do some "big picture thinking," to determine what needs correction, where you need to exert influence and where things are going

> *Thinking is the place where intelligent actions begin. We pause long enough to look more carefully at a situation, to see more of its character, to think about why it's happening, to notice how it's affecting us and others.*
>
> Margaret J. Wheatley

> *Nothing is purely random, every event is at most chaotic. People have invented the word 'random' for describing the behaviour of things that they simply can't comprehend.*
>
> Leslie Dean Brown

well. You can then jump back in the dance floor again –
until the next time you schedule time to get on the
balcony.

> *A problem never exists in isolation; it is surrounded by other problems in space and time. The more of the context of a problem that a scientist can comprehend, the greater are his chances of finding a truly adequate solution.*
>
> Russell Ackoff

Putting it in Practice

Likely Consequences/Unintended Consequences

No change occurs in isolation. It has ripple effects – and can impact others both upstream and downstream, inside and outside of the organization. Think about the change you are bringing about. Who might be affected? What consequences are likely? How are the implications likely to be received? What can you do in a proactive stance to encourage acceptance and to decrease resistance?

The Change:

Who is affected?	How are they affected?	Likely Reaction	Actions Needed

3.3   A Final Note

It's easy to get overwhelmed in today's highly
connected and interdependent global world. It is a
challenge, but also an opportunity. For those leaders
who are able to create and leverage networks,
understand how systems work, maintain a big picture
view and understand how to effect change, amazing
things can happen. Never could you reach so many
people so easily. Never have more markets been open
for your product or service. Your influence can be
greater today than ever before. Understanding
systems and culture is a critical skill set to make that
happen.

Additional Resources:

Oshry, Barry. *Seeing systems unlocking the mysteries of organizational life*. 2nd ed.
          San Francisco: Berrett-Koehler Publishers, 2007.

Scharmer, Claus Otto. *Theory U learning from the future as it emerges : the social
          technology of presencing*. San Francisco, Calif.: Berrett-Koehler , 2009.

Senge, Peter M. *The fifth discipline: the art and practice of the learning organization*.
          New York: Doubleday/Currency, 1990.

CHAPTER 13
Shedding

1   The Concept

As a leader today, you are faced with a world of complexity. One in which there is more to know, do and react to than ever before in the history of our species. It is estimated that there is more information in one week's edition of the New York Times than people in the 18th century would encounter in their ENTIRE lives.

As leaders, we are always asked to do more and then asking those we lead to do more. To be more productive. To be on solid financial footing. To check more things off the ever growing "to do" list. To grow sales. To add a new product or service. To use this new technology. To react to this new innovation. To do more and more and more and more.

In this chapter, I'm going to encourage you to take a different approach. One that has the ability to take things off your "to do" list, to simplify your life and to create space and breathing room. In our Evergreen Leadership process, we call this shedding. It is based on a simple, natural trait that evergreens possess – and it is one of the traits that make them so resilient and so able to thrive in a multitude of environments – even very hostile ones. Unlike deciduous trees, which experience deep and long cycles of rapid growth, rapid loss of foliage leading to dormancy, evergreens remain in a steady state of "green" by shedding a little of what they no longer need every single day. You'll not see a bare evergreen, but you will see green ones all year

> *Life is really simple, but we insist on making it complicated.*
>
> Confucius

long with a carpet of shed needles – testament to the fact that although virtually invisible, new growth has replaced old growth in a never ending process.

In most organizations, the mental model is not one of shedding continually and incrementally. Instead we continue to pile things on and on and on. And at some point, the market shifts, a competitor upends us or our product/service begins to tank. Then and only then, do we embark on a radical and painful readjustment. We reorganize entire departments, close plants, right-size the organization, attempt a big transformation, and embark on a big change effort. Sometimes it works; sometimes it doesn't. And given the pace of change in today's environment, no organization has the 3 to 5 years it takes to reinvent itself.

The path today is continual evolution, smaller incremental adjustments. Entrepreneurs call these "pivots" – small changes, over time, as you learn and react to customer feedback. Apple intentionally obsoletes its bestselling products with new ones; rather than allowing each product to run its course and waiting until sales dip to determine what's next. No matter whether you call it shedding or pivoting, letting go of what no longer works and adding healthy growth back into your organization day by day enables you to stay fresh, relevant and timely. Our earlier work on visioning has helped you identify what you want to add. This chapter will help you take away things that are distractions, discouragers, and blocks.

We live in a culture that believes more is better. Throughout this chapter I'm going to ask you to examine this belief and see where it shows up in your life and in your work. Is it true that more clients are better – or is it that the "right" clients are what is really better? Is it true that getting more done is the goal, or is it getting the right things done? Is faster always better or is there a more optimal pace?

Organization isn't about perfection; it's about efficiency, reducing stress and clutter, saving time and money and improving your overall quality of life.

Christina Scalise

Simplicity is the ultimate sophistication.

Leonardo da Vinci

In this chapter, I'm going to ask that you entertain a different belief – that more is not better – better is better. And that better might be less of some things and more of others. Along with examining beliefs about more and less and better, I'm going to encourage you to find things in your work and life that you can discard, eliminate, get rid of. To shed so that you can grow. To simplify so that you can amplify. To free so that you can focus. To lighten so that you can think. To unburden so that you can breathe. To live within the paradox of less and more – and to know when less really is more.

As you do this work, I want you to keep in mind the evergreen way of shedding, which is both continual and incremental. This is not about big dramatic changes, but about small steps to remove what is no longer useful or needed. This is about remaining vital by a continual process of regeneration in small increments, rather than a wholesale change. It is almost imperceptible day by day. Yet when you look back you will be amazed at the cumulative effect of those multiple tiny actions of shedding what is no longer needed or not aligned with your higher purpose.

At the heart of the process of shedding our way into transformation is consciousness. When we act with consciousness about our future vision, our guiding values, and our intentions – we can better know what to keep and what to let go of. This consciousness forces upon us the question of what do we want in our lives and our organizations and what don't we want. There is a much different power and energy in choosing to decommission a product line with intention than there is to malinger and have the market, our boss or the board force the issue. Acting with intention to remove something empowers us;

Give me the discipline to get rid of the stuff that's not important, the freedom to savor the stuff that gives me joy, and the patience not to worry about the stuff that's messy but not hurting anybody.

Vinita Hampton Wright

Clutter is the physical manifestation of unmade decisions fueled by procrastination.

Christina Scalise

limping along sub-optimally refusing to end what no longer serves us puts us in a much weaker position.

Too often we only consider shedding negative things. Our attention gets focused on eliminating pain points, dysfunction or things that we would clearly like to be without. And so it should be. Those things that annoy, distract and get in the way should be our first targets for elimination. Yet I encourage you to also consider the relatively neutral things in your life that could also be shed. And the really brave among us will examine and shed negative, neutral and positive things, shedding across all three categories to get to the core.

Apple is a highly visible example of shedding the positive. A part of their strategy is to kill products before the market does. They are continually working to replace their most successful products BEFORE they begin to wither and die. Contrast this with a traditional norm of "milking" the last penny of profitability, without reinvesting, in old product lines. That approach may maximize profitability, but it saps excitement about your offering to customers and drains employee's energy for doing their work.

As you learn to shed, you'll experience something quite marvelous. As you let go, get rid of, eliminate – you will have an experience of being freed. You'll feel lighter. More calm and peaceful. And then the marvelous thing happens - better things begin to appear in your life, your business, and with your team. When you simplify, you can amplify what you truly want. Clean and simple.

Any intelligent fool can make things bigger, more complex, and more violent. It takes a touch of genius — and a lot of courage to move in the opposite direction.

E.F. Schumacher

Out of clutter, find simplicity.

Albert Einstein

You'll learn more about how to shed in this chapter, but here is the short list:

- Identify what is important
- Eliminate everything else

I repeat: Identify what is important and eliminate everything else. Simple to remember; hard to do.

 ## Putting it in Practice

To set up the work of shedding, clearly identify what is most important in your personal life and in your work life. These can either be shorter term goals (spend quality time with my children, get my Master's degree, reach my sales target for the year) or lifelong aspirations (be a good parent, have work that uses my skills for a higher cause, create an organization where people love to work). Some people will create their higher level list first, and then create an aligned list for shorter term goals that support the longer term intentions. Do what feels right to you.

List no more than five, three is optimal. I suspect this will be very difficult, so here is a clue. If you have more than five items in any one category, think about which ones better align with your inner core. The stronger that alignment, the more likely those items should make your "short list".

The Most Important Things to Me		
	Personally	**Professionally**	**For the team or organization I lead**
1			
2			
3			
4			
5			

2   As a Leader You Go First

By this time, you'll not be surprised that as leaders, there is some inner work to do before you begin to work with your team. Shedding is both a way of thinking and a way of doing. Let's look at some ways in which you can begin to learn this process of letting go and lightening before you tackle the work with your team.

The foundational step is to deeply know your overall intention and then hold true to it, in spite of distractions, diversions and the prodding of others around you. This is based on the previous exercise, so if you've not done this work, I strongly encourage you to complete it. Your list becomes the yardstick by which you measure whether to remove, maintain or add new things into your life. It simplifies and clarifies the decision making process.

If a personal intention is getting your Master's degree, then you can shed the things in your life that get in the way of doing that. If your intention is to travel broadly, you may want to eliminate the things in your life that require maintenance when you are away (pets, gardens, your home). A personal example: even though I love teaching at a college level, I stopped teaching for one semester to do three things that were a higher value for me: support my daughter and her newborn twins, complete this book and provide excellent service to my clients.

> *The greatest step towards a life of simplicity is to learn to let go.*
>
> Steve Maraboli

> *There is no greatness where there is not simplicity, goodness, and truth.*
>
> Leo Tolstoy

2.1   Your First Step

Let's begin with a concept I learned from Stephen Covey's book The Seven Habits of Highly Effective People – the Circle of Influence and Control. This is a simple, but powerful concept that puts those things that we have control over in the center, things that we can influence in the next concentric ring and the things we are concerned about, but have no ability to either control or influence on the outer most ring. For example, I am concerned about global warming. Even though I can do very little on the macro problem, I move into my circles of influence and control. I can influence by encouraging legislators to address the problem or by supporting groups that are doing good work in this area or by raising awareness with people I know. Moving even deeper into the circle of control, I can choose to drive a higher mileage vehicle, walk or bike instead of drive, recycle, plant trees, and a host of other actions.

It's far too easy, and compelling, to want to stay in the circle of concern, which is an outward (rather than inward) facing stance in which you abdicate personal responsibility and heap blame on the nameless "them". Spend a day listening to conversations – and where energy is spent. Notice that the least effective people spend most of their time in the outside ring and that the most effective folks ask what they can do. Where do you fall?

> *A simple life is not seeing how little we can get by with—that's poverty—but how efficiently we can put first things first. . . . When you're clear about your purpose and your priorities, you can painlessly discard whatever does not support these, whether it's clutter in your cabinets or commitments on your calendar.*
>
> Victoria Moran

Covey's advice is spot on – to spend your time and energy with those things that you can either control or influence and to let go of those things that you cannot. It is truly amazing when we begin to notice just how much time, energy and emotion we can spend on things that we have absolutely no control over. The weather. The economy. The government. Other people.

Letting go of the emotional energy we spend on things out of our control, like worrying or being frustrated (and that is about all you can do for things in this category) not only improves your mood, it dramatically improves your effectiveness. Every ounce of energy diverted from those things out of our control and reinvested into things we can influence is magnified. The less energy wasted on futile pursuits and instead focused on places we can have an impact – the larger our sphere of individual effectiveness. The key here is to spend your time, energy, emotion and good work on things you can influence. So begin now to shed time, energy and emotion on those things that you either control or influence.

The serenity prayer by Reinhold Niebuhr sums this up quite nicely:

God grant me the serenity to accept the things I cannot change, the courage to change the things I can, and the wisdom to know the difference.

> *Fools ignore complexity. Pragmatists suffer it. Some can avoid it. Geniuses remove it.*
>
> Alan Perlis

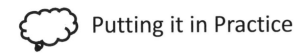 # Putting it in Practice

Spend the next 24 hours listening to conversations, your own and others with an ear to categorizing if the topics discussed are in circles of concern, influence, or control.

Where do others spend most of their time?

Where do you spend most of your time?

Have you discovered anything you want to shed?

---

3   Know Your Intentions

I noted in the early part of this chapter that this work of shedding has two relevant aspects:

1. Identify what is important
2. Eliminate everything else

Seems rather easy. Not the case. Sometimes things simply put are the hardest to do.

Step 1 requires clarity and discernment. I know that I personally struggle with prioritizing – as many things seem important. There is interesting work to do, places to visit, people to meet, valuable work that needs done, compelling causes to support. It's easy to say yes to one thing and then the next and the next and the next. And before I turn around twice, I am overextended, frazzled, running to and fro, both exhausted and not doing anything very well. This is a vicious cycle, rather than a virtuous one.

> *It is not a daily increase, but a daily decrease. Hack away at the inessentials.*
>
> Bruce Lee

Step 2 involves simplifying, reducing, removing. It also means saying no, something I struggle with. And others do too. As funny as this may seem, at times this is hard, even to things I don't want to do. I know that, for me, this is more about not wanting to disappoint others. However, in the long run I disappoint myself and at times the "other" to whom I failed to speak my authentic truth.

So while difficult at times, asking these two questions can help you determine what to shed and what to keep:

- What is most important to me?
- What can I eliminate that is not aligned with that?

> *Good habits are worth being fanatical about.*
>
> John Irving

3.1 Categories to Consider

Most often, when we think of eliminating things, we think in terms of physical things. Clutter. Unneeded material things. Items we own that we either don't use or enjoy any more or whose maintenance cost have started to exceed what is reasonable. And material things provide a wonderful start at shedding. Yet I'm going to encourage you to think much more broadly about shedding – and to include categories like:

- Thoughts & beliefs that no longer serve you well or get in your way
- Relationships that are toxic or at the least non-nurturing
- Routines and habits that you engage in "just because you always have"
- Expectations that are not yours or are unrealistic
- Things, clutter, material possessions

> *Simplicity is about subtracting the obvious and adding the meaningful.*
>
> John Maedo

- Household chores that can be eliminated or simplified
- Social obligations (obligations being the key word)
- Time on social media, email and other electronic communications

 # Putting it in Practice

Believe me, I know how overwhelming cleaning up the clutter can be. So here is a great way to tackle it that I learned from my brother. My parents lived in the same home for over 50 years – and being depression era babies – they had a penchant for saving EVERYTHING. And I do mean everything; they even had a box labeled "String too short to save". Rather than tackle the inevitable "big" clean up, Rich instead would clear out a bag a week, sometimes two. Slowly the piles diminished, bag by bag, so that when it was time to sell the house only the bigger and more important things were left.

Make a list of the things in your life you can shed. If they are material things, physically fill one bag a week and take it to charitable cause or put it out with the trash. If you are shedding non-material things, tackle them one by one, week at a time. Within a few short months, you will find that you've made great progress, almost painlessly.

What I will shed:

My plan for shedding it over time:

3.2 Helping Your Team Shed

There is a wealth of information on simplifying (aka shedding) in your personal and home life. There are books, magazines, articles, personal services, and entire stores devoted to simplifying and organizing your life. Not so much at work. And as a result, at work we tend to be additive rather than subtractive, even though economic pressures have meant that there are smaller numbers of people doing increasingly more work. The mantra is to "do more with less" – and the phrase is not intended to mean doing more of the right things and less of other things. It means do more work with less resources (time, people, and money).

Technology has only exacerbated the problem. People are connected to work literally around the clock, with no periods of respite. What we used to think would simplify and make our work easier has only made it more complex and demanding.

Never has there been a more important time, as a leader, to help your team shed. By enabling them to shed, your focus will sharpen, your productivity will skyrocket and you'll get the "right" results, rather than just lots of work effort.

Just as in your inner work, ask these two questions about the work of your team:

- What is most important to our work?

- What can we eliminate that is not aligned with that?

I do believe in simplicity. It is astonishing as well as sad, how many trivial affairs even the wisest thinks he must attend to in a day; how singular an affair he thinks he must omit. When the mathematician would solve a difficult problem, he first frees the equation of all incumbrances, and reduces it to its simplest terms. So simplify the problem of life, distinguish the necessary and the real. Probe the earth to see where your main roots run.

Henry David Thoreau

3.3 Unexpected Reactions

As you start to simplify, you might find that your team gets nervous and begins to show signs of resistance. You think you are making things better and you may be baffled when your team is either just lukewarm or openly opposing your efforts.

Here's why: Just asking the question about what can be shed will evoke anxiety in your team. Although the questions may not get asked openly, the ones that are likely include:

- Does eliminating work mean people will also be eliminated?
- Does eliminating the work I do mean I am less valued?
- Does this mean that we are doing poorly?
- Does this mean I'll have to learn something new?
- Don't they trust that I'm doing the best I can?

As a leader, be open about your intention to only focus on the most important things. Acknowledge some of the underlying thoughts that some might be experiencing and discuss them openly. Know that in our "more is better" culture, asking what could be eliminated or simplified will be a counter cultural act that will engender surprise, confusion and perhaps resistance.

Let's review the same list of things you considered removing from your personal life in the lens of work. This will provide some thought starters for things you and your team might consider to eliminate.

The more simple we are, the more complete we become.

August Rodin

In your personal life you might shed	In your work life you might shed
Thoughts & Beliefs that no longer serve you well or get in your way	Beliefs about your work, your industry, your team or your company that get in the way
Relationships that are toxic or at the least non-nurturing	Toxic clients, customers, suppliers or employees
Routines and habits that you engage in "just because you always have"	Non value adding work Routine meetings Routine reports Inviting too many people to meetings
Expectations that are not yours or are unrealistic	Products that are in decline
Things, clutter, material possessions	Old files and paperwork Clutter Lingering projects (either close them out or kill them)
Household chores that can be eliminated or simplified	Specialty or customized work that cannot be done efficiently Steps in work processes that add no value to the customer
Social obligations (obligations being the key word)	Meetings for the sake of meetings Meetings without clear outcomes and agendas Belief that all meetings fill one hour
Time on social media, email and other electronic communications	Copying too many people on email Overreliance on email Long email threads when a face to face meeting would be more effective

4   Focus and Direction

One of the most important leadership actions you can take is establishing focus and direction. It has always been true, but is even more so in a scattered, distracted and fast paced world. Not being clear wastes effort, causes frustration and creates confusion for your customers, whether they are internal or external. It bogs you and your team down, diffusing energy and the ability to accomplish what really needs to be done.

 ## Putting it in Practice

Identify three (and only three) areas of focus for your team. You may be in a situation where company initiatives can provide guidance. You might take this opportunity to have a solid conversation with your leader about priorities. You'll want to be certain that your list of three has some balance. Most likely one will be about doing your current work well, one will be about preparing for the future, and one might be improving an internal capability.

My team's top priorities:

1.

2.

3.

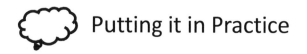 # Putting it in Practice

Share your list with your team. Elicit their reaction. Check to see that they are comfortable with the list and understand the rationale. Then have them list all the activities currently done to support these three priorities.

Then have them list everything else they are doing. With the "everything else" – ask if there are ways to eliminate them? Automate them? Outsource them? Reduce effort or level of quality? Ways to spend less time and energy on them? Integrate or consolidate them? Simplify them?

When going through this exercise, people tend to forget to look at shedding negative things. Often times, people just carry on, shouldering these heavy loads. Ask yourself:

- Are there customers who consume far more in effort and energy than they return?
- Are there types of work that you can do, but are not in your sweet spot?
- Is there an employee who is technically brilliant but sucks the life from everyone?
- Is the team spending energy and time on grudges, worry and past hurts and it's time to move on?

Remember to examine habits and long standing traditions. Stretch hard to consider:

- Are there things we are doing out of habit which are past their prime?
- Are there ways to reduce the effort we take to do some of these routine things?
- Have we asked our customers (internal or external) if the work we are doing is needed or valued?
- Are we doing any processes or procedures that were instituted long ago and are no longer needed?

And don't forget the positive things:

- Do you have high maintenance surroundings that could be simplified?
- Are there community support activities that could be consolidated or simplified?
- Do you have "nice to do" things on your "to do" list that just should be dropped?
- Are there things you are doing that add value but could be outsourced?

4.1 Simplify Your Focus

We live in a world that thrives on multi-tasking. There have been times I've been driving the car, eating my lunch, talking on the phone and listening to the radio – all at the same time. Not so smart – but I'm not alone. I've actually seen someone doing all those things AND applying makeup.

Those that study the brain tell us that multi-tasking is a myth – that our brains really can only handle one task at a time. As such, when we are engaged in simultaneous activities, our brain switches back and forth continually and quickly. And with each switch comes the price of leaving one activity and picking up the next. We may not notice it, but studies show that we are distracted, less productive and consume more time and mental energy by doing so. And the negative consequences show up in the quality of our work, the quality of our relationships, our ability to have sustained focus and our emotional state.

I'm not naïve to think that you can totally eliminate multi-tasking in favor of singular focus. I do however think, as a leader, you can take some actions that help you and the people you lead to focus and be less distracted. Here are some ideas:

- Block quiet time at the beginning of the day to gather your thoughts, review the upcoming day and prepare

- Block quiet time at the end of the day to summarize, reflect, learn and then to plan for the upcoming day

- Create quiet spaces in the work area where folks can go to unplug, recharge and think

- Get comfortable with silence. Allow some quiet time in meetings for people to think.

Letting go means to come to the realization that some people are a part of your history, but not a part of your destiny.

Steve Maraboli

Motivation is what gets you started. Habit is what keeps you going.

Jim Ryun

- Ask that others put away technology when the conversation requires face to face.

- Create some "no meeting" time routinely so that people can have a dedicated amount of time to do their work. It can be either certain times of the day (no meetings before 9 and after 4) or a regular time (no meetings on Wednesday morning).

- Create some ground rules about email / texting with your team. Who gets copied? What is the expected response time? When do you talk rather than email?

- Be clear about your expectations on responsiveness. If folks don't need to be plugged in during off hours – make that clear.

- Find ways to allow your team to take vacations and unplug.

.

> *The chains of habit are too weak to be felt until they are too strong to be broken.*
>
> Samuel Johnson

4.2   Use Habits to Your Advantage

It is true that we are creatures of habit. And for good reason. Habits eliminate the need to think, decide or take valuable brain time in consciousness. We just act and act routinely. It feels natural because it is. It is a well-practiced routine that we can execute smoothly and almost effortlessly. And without thinking.

In fact, if you have an established habit and there is a day you can't exercise the habit, your mind and body rebel. They push you to do it. If you have a running routine and you don't run for a week, your body aches to get outside and run. Your thoughts turn to running. You seek ways to get back in the routine.

> *Cry. Forgive. Learn. Move on. Let your tears water the seeds of your future happiness.*
>
> Steve Maraboli

Habits are powerful, they prompt us to do certain things. We sometimes think of habits only in the negative, such as smoking or watching too much TV or being messy. The reality is that a habit is only a finely ingrained and repeated behavior – and habits can prompt us to do things that complement our lives and our goals, or detract from them. As such, it is important to cultivate habits that serve you well, that help guide you to your higher purpose. For your habits are powerful and shape the outcomes of your life.

This quote is so true:

"Watch your thoughts, they become words;
watch your words, they become actions;
watch your actions, they become habits;
watch your habits, they become character;
watch your character, for it becomes your destiny."
Frank Outlaw, Late President of the Bi-Lo Stores

Take some time to examine your habits and routines. Which ones serve you well? Which ones don't? What habits might you cultivate that will allow you to simplify and focus?

Some people believe holding on and hanging in there are signs of great strength. However, there are times when it takes much more strength to know when to let go and then do it.

Ann Laders

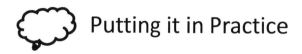 # Putting it in Practice

Observe your habits for a week. Which serve you well? Which ones need replaced? What should replace them?

A few examples are provided.

My Current Habits	Keep or Shed	Actions I can Take	Habits I can Substitute
Eat dinner late at night	Shed	Plan for dinner the night before so it is ready when I get home	6:00 pm dinner time
Exercise 3X week	Keep	Continue to block time in my schedule	

Habits I Wish to Cultivate	Actions I can Take
Unplug from email on Sunday	State my intention to my team and let them know Use "Out of Office" autoreply on Sunday Close the door to my home office on Saturday night and shut down my PC

4.3 Deeper Things You Might Shed

Our natural tendency when thinking about simplifying is to think about "things" – clutter, things we no longer need or want to use, excess belongings and other "stuff". I encourage you to learn to shed things on the inside as well as things on the outside. Things on the inside include beliefs, thoughts and emotions. Often these create more drag in our lives than any physical object.

What would happen if you shed the belief that you had to have all the answers? That you had to do all the work? That you are inadequate? That others might ridicule you if you took a risk?

What might be freed in you if you let go of the long standing grudge? If you let go of expectations (your own or others) that were unrealistic, unattainable or not worth the price? What might happen if you let go of a need for perfection when excellent might do just fine?

We all carry certain beliefs and thoughts that hold us back and weigh us down. That drain our energy and our time. That burden us rather than lift us. At times we are aware of the load; at other times we are unaware of their invisible hand.

Surfacing these emotions, thoughts and beliefs takes some time and effort. But once examined with a cooler, more collected head in the light of day, you'll find that you are able to let go of many of them. At a minimum, you can acknowledge their existence and put them in perspective.

The work to shed thoughts and beliefs that no longer serve you or your team well brings you full circle back to the work on the stories you wrote in Chapter 2. Revisit the stories you tell yourself, your work, your team, your customers and your product. For it is in those stories, that our inner thoughts and core beliefs

And I learned what is obvious to a child. That life is simply a collection of little lives, each lived one day at a time. That each day should be spent finding beauty in flowers and poetry and talking to animals. That a day spent with dreaming and sunsets and refreshing breezes cannot be bettered. But most of all, I learned that life is about sitting on benches next to ancient creeks with my hand on her knee and sometimes, on good days, for falling in love.

Nicholas Sparks

become discernable. And once you can see them, you can decide if they are keepers or should be shed.

 ## Putting it in Practice

Reexamine the stories you tell about yourself and the work stories your team tells. See if you can find some underlying thoughts or beliefs that could be shed.

Which ones bog you down?

Which ones could free you if you shed them?

5   When to Give Up

The thought of shedding may evoke some nervousness in you. Because for many, the idea of shedding may seem to indicate "giving up" or throwing in the towel. Make no doubt, it is much harder to give up on things that you are striving for and are not making progress. Or things that once worked beautifully but now are not. In these situations, I wonder if I should work harder rather than eliminating them from my life. Am I giving up and failing rather than giving in to the hard reality that it is beyond salvaging. The saying: "Winners don't quit and quitters don't win." plays in my head as I struggle with whether to double down, walk away or continue plodding.

Here are some examples:

- New ventures or businesses that aren't getting traction

- Relationships that are important to you but are broken
- Businesses, products or services that were once viable but now are tanking
- Team members whose performance has slipped
- Old friendships that don't have the same tenor
- High expectations that appear undoable
- A job that is no longer satisfying or has become unmanageable
- Dreams that seem unreachable

How do you determine if you spend more energy, time and effort to salvage something? And when is it time to shed it, to move on, to eliminate it from your life?

I've not found an easy answer. At times, persistence does turn situations around and the effort is well worth it. I think of Jeff Bezos and the long path to making Amazon viable. Virtually every hero's story has a climax where they fight on rather than accepting defeat.

Yet, I recall many times I've held on to things way too long, putting time, energy and money into things that I really needed to abandon long ago.

Here are some questions that may guide your decision:

- Are there any viable options left to salvage it or make it whole?
- Are you doing this because you think you "should" or because of other's expectations?
- Have you done your level best?
- Is there any movement or positive momentum?
- What does optimal look like? Is it even feasible to get there?

Don't own so much clutter that you will be relieved to see your house catch fire.

Wendell Berry

Our life is frittered away by detail. Simplify, simplify.

Henry David Thoreau

- What is the worst thing that could happen if you walked away?

- What is the best thing that could happen if you gave up and moved on?

- What is holding you back from giving up? Is your reason legitimate?

- How will you feel a year from now about your decision? Ten years from now?

Giving up is not always the easy path. If you're like me, it is terribly difficult to let go, to move on, to admit that something is no longer working or worth doing. But only by giving up can we allow the space for something new.

Additional Resources:

Covey, Stephen R. *The seven habits of highly effective people: restoring the charac-ter ethic.* New York: Simon and Schuster, 1989.

St. James, Elaine. *Simplify your life: 100 ways to slow down and enjoy the things that really matter.* New York: Hyperion, 1994.

St. James, Elaine. *Simplify your work life: ways to change the way you work so you have more time to live.* New York: Hyperion, 2001.

CHAPTER 14
Gratitude

In this chapter I want to share a practice that has changed my life – and for the better. It has improved the quality of my relationships, has upped my leadership game and brought me inner peace and joy. This is a pretty big claim for a very simple idea, but I am testament to the difference a practice of gratitude can make.

1   Gratitude

I began a simple practice of gratitude over 15 years ago. I merely spent a few minutes every evening jotting down 5 things I was grateful for – night after night. The transformation was not immediate, but slowly I began to see the patterns. I began to realize how much good was in my life. I began to develop an eye for what was whole and good rather than what was wrong and broken. I began to know what really mattered to me.

My practice of gratitude was challenged a few years later as I entered a very difficult time. My marriage was on the rocks, and we were barely escaping bankruptcy – bill by bill and month by month. It was much harder to be grateful for this place and these circumstances. Yet I continued to persist and again gained perspective that even with so much wrong, there was so much right.

In this chapter I want to share this practice of gratitude with you, in the hopes that you too will benefit from it. It truly is especially easy and amazingly transforming.

> *Silent gratitude isn't much use to anyone.*
>
> G.B. Stern

1.1   Some Semantics

As I did the research to write this chapter, so that it was grounded in more than my own experience, I found there are some fine hairs to be split over the difference between gratitude and appreciation:

Appreciate *is a verb and is the act of being grateful for something.*

Gratitude *is a noun and is the emotional state of being thankful; readiness to show appreciation for and to return kindness.*

While some argue that one is a higher level state than the others, for our purposes here, I am going to use them interchangeably.

If the only prayer you said in your whole life was, "thank you," that would suffice.

Meister Eckhart

1.2   A High Emotional State

It's easy to identify some of our lowest emotional states – despair, depression, sadness, frustration, anger. We are vividly aware of when we are in these states. We also would admit that we are not our best in these states. We act out of anger or impulse. We can do hurtful things to ourselves and others. We make rash and hasty decisions.

We operate much better when we are in higher level emotional states; times when we are open, aware, calm, insightful, creative, curious, patient or resourceful. When we experience these emotions, outcomes are better. Relationships flourish. We are at peace. Decision making is solid. Life is good.

As humans, we cannot avoid some of the lower state feelings. We will experience loss and be sad. Something will happen that offends our sensibilities, and we will be angry. Someone will do something that is hurtful – perhaps unintentional, but hurtful none the

Be thankful for what you have; you'll end up having more. If you concentrate on what you don't have, you will never, ever have enough.

Oprah Winfrey

less. Our best efforts fail. Misfortune is an equal opportunity employer.

So while we cannot avoid them, we can take some positive action so that we don't make these states a habit. It becomes problematic for us and for those around us when we "get stuck" in the lower mood states and they begin to magnify and consume us.

As a person who could get "stuck," who could hold a grudge for years and who had a hard time getting past things in my life, I can solidly affirm that practicing gratitude can get you "unstuck" – and that the lows are not as low or as long lasting.

When we are in the dumps, we have the propensity to magnify the misfortune. It was not enough to have a bad day at work; I would collect stories and incidents that turned my bad day into a miserable, terrible, horrible, wreck of a day. When I am looking for it, I can find LOTS of examples to support that viewpoint.

As you practice gratitude, you turn the "poor me" focus upside down. Your lens switches to "lucky me." And over time, even when you experience a setback, you look for the silver lining in that black cloud.

> *I would maintain that thanks are the highest form of thought; and that gratitude is happiness doubled by wonder.*
>
> G.K. Chesterton

1.3   There is Scientific Proof

I am a sample size of one. You may want a bit more evidence on the subject.

Up until the 1990s, research about mental health and human psychology began to shift from studying dysfunction to understanding optimal mental health and high performance. This is called positive psychology. Multiple academic studies show us that gratitude can be learned and cultivated. And those that have a grateful mindset and express appreciation to others experience:

> *There is more to life than simply increasing its speed.*
>
> Mahatma Gandhi

- Increased levels of well-being and life satisfaction
- More happiness
- Better energy
- More optimism
- Less depression
- Improved health, specifically lower blood pressure
- Higher levels of control of their environment
- More personal growth
- Higher sense of purpose
- Better ability to deal with difficulties
- Fewer negative coping strategies (think drugs, alcohol, and other harmful habits)
- Better sleep
- Increased longevity

The impacts also spill over to your work team, family and community. They include a more positive work environment, higher performance, more loyalty, increased citizenship behavior, and higher levels of commitment.

As each day comes to us refreshed and anew, so does my gratitude renew itself daily. The breaking of the sun over the horizon is my grateful heart dawning upon a blessed world.

Terri Guillemets

2   Why Does It Work?

I have to admit that I was a skeptic at first. It seemed a bit foolish and hokey. But for some reason, I stayed with the gratitude journal. Honestly, at first, it was a big effort. I'd spend anxious moments playing back my day, searching (at times in vain) for something to note in my journal. And some days, I would only write one thing. Others days, I would write things like:

- It's Friday

- I have a roof over my head

- I made it through the day

- The meeting was not as bad as I expected

After a week or so of agonizing, I realized that I needed to pay more attention throughout the day for those things I was grateful for. I scanned for good things. I noticed. Sometimes I wrote them down. It was at this point that magic began to happen.

When I began to consciously look for the good things in my life, I found them. And then I found more. And then more. And then even more. I began to go through the day looking for what was working, rather than what was not. And amazingly, I began to see that there were many things in my life that I was grateful for.

In addition to fine tuning my attention, I also began to see patterns in what I was grateful for. I was more aware of what brought me happiness. With that knowledge, it was easy to do more to build that into my day. I was grateful for time with friends; therefore, I was more intentional about making time to spend with them. I was grateful for nature and the outdoors, so I spent more time outside, even if it meant taking

> *Appreciation is a wonderful thing. It makes what is excellent in others belong to us as well.*
>
> Voltaire

> *The unthankful heart... discovers no mercies; but let the thankful heart sweep through the day and, as the magnet finds the iron, so it will find, in every hour, some heavenly blessings!*
>
> Henry Ward Beecher

the long way in the parking lot to enjoy the sunshine for 2 more minutes.

I also gained perspective. When bad things happened, as they do, I felt more balanced and less off kilter. I might not like my current situation, but invariably I could find some glimmer, somewhere to be grateful for.

One of my biggest challenges was when my husband's business took a dramatic downturn and threatened to take us under financially. I struggled with anger, frustration and a sense of unfairness, especially since most of my earnings were going to pay off what I considered to be *his* business debt. It was a tough time, and one I don't care to repeat.

Gratitude got me through this. Being *grateful* for the non-monetary blessings – friends, family, and health; being *grateful* that we still had our home, that there was food on the table. The big shift for me came when I could be truly *grateful* that I had the financial resources to write the check needed to pay off the bills for a business long gone.

There is also a ripple effect to gratitude. When I am grateful for others or for what they had done, I become increasingly willing to show them appreciation. I write thank you notes. I tell others how what they've done is appreciated. I am much less stingy with appreciation and sharing gratitude.

Grace isn't a little prayer you chant before receiving a meal. It's a way to live.

Attributed to Jacqueline Winspear

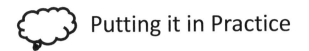 Putting it in Practice

Gratitude Journal

Find a beautiful notebook for your gratitude journal. Every day, at a set time, write in your gratitude journal a list of 3 to 5 things you are grateful for. Good times are at the conclusion of your work day (the last thing you do before you leave your work area) or just before you go to bed. Dedicate your journal to gratitude. If you journal about other things, keep that separate.

There will be days where you may be hard pressed to find 3 things. On those days, remind yourself about your gratitude for basics (food, clothing, housing) or recall gratitude for something that happened in the past (a person that showed you kindness or taught you something, your parents, your education).

The key to realizing benefits is repetition; make it a priority to complete daily for at least two months.

1 **I'm thankful for:**

2

3

4

5

3   What about Work?

So that raises a good question: does gratitude work at work? Here is what the research would tell us. According to a survey of 2,000 Americans released in 2012 by the John Templeton Foundation, people are less likely to feel or express gratitude at work than anyplace else. And they're not thankful for their current jobs, ranking them dead last in a list of things they're grateful for.

It's not because people don't crave gratitude at work, both giving and receiving. Ninety-three percent agreed that grateful bosses are more likely to succeed, and only 18 percent thought that gratitude made bosses "weak." Most reported that hearing "thank you" at work made them feel good and motivated.

In addition, gratitude may drop right to the bottom line. The simple act of writing thank you on a restaurant check increased tips in one study. In another experiment, customers of jewelry stores who were called and thanked upped subsequent purchases by 70%. That's significantly more bling! The control group that was called and thanked just like the first group and then were told about a sale. This group, which was prompted to buy only registered a 30% increase (which is not insignificant). Those customers who were not called remained flat.

The jewelry store study points to the conclusion that gratitude that appears done for personal gain becomes suspect (as does thanking your boss when it seems to be garnering favor or archiving all positive comments about your work as ammunition in the annual review for raises).

> *The invariable mark of wisdom is to see the miraculous in the common.*
>
> Ralph Waldo Emerson

> *If you count all your assets, you always show a profit.*
>
> Robert Quillen

So here are a few take-aways relative to gratitude at work:

- It is sorely needed. Work is a wasteland when it comes to gratitude.
- It will lift spirits, improve work outcomes and motivate performance.

It is best done in the purest form – simple gratitude without links to economic gain or quid pro quo.

> *He is a wise man who does not grieve for the things which he has not, but rejoices for those which he has.*
>
> Epictetus

4   Why Practice Gratitude?

There are many reasons that leaders would want to practice gratitude. Let's summarize them here:

- When you practice gratitude, you are keenly aware of what you value. The more you know and the more you notice, the closer you are to honoring your inner core. And the stronger your inner core, the more stability and balance you have in turbulent times.

- Good leaders are truth tellers. Often we think that only means being honest about the challenges faced. Yet, we often omit the truth that there are many, many good things in our life or in a particular situation. Gratitude enables you to create a more balanced worldview.

- Strong leaders envision a better future and then create it. This work does not happen in lower emotional states. Innovation, creativity and envisioning are more likely to happen or to occur more easily in the higher emotional states that accompany gratitude.

> *If we had no winter, the spring would not be so pleasant: if we did not sometimes taste of adversity, prosperity would not be so welcome.*
>
> Anne Bradstreet

- Leaders who engage others in creating a better future get better results. Blame and negativity squash engagement. Appreciation and gratitude attract it.

- The best leaders grow others. By expressing gratitude and showing appreciation for what others are doing that is positive, helpful and directionally correct – you encourage people to take a risk and grow, you signal what is important. You build confidence and encouragement.

Gratitude is the best attitude.

Unknown

 # Putting it in Practice

Appreciative Feedback (Written)

Make a list of 10 people in your life you appreciate. It may be family members, friends or co-workers. Your list may have people from your past or present. You may be grateful for big things they did over time (like raising you) or a small gesture that was meaningful.

In a two week time span, write a note to each of them about what it is that they have done that your appreciate. Be clear about what they did and the impact it made. Your note may be three sentences or three pages – totally up to you.

Choose the way you would like to deliver your notes. You can deliver them in person, attach them to a small gift, put them in a place where they will find them, or drop them in the mail. The key here is ensuring they are written and then received.

Week 1   **Week 2**

	Person / Appreciation		Person / Appreciation
1		6	
2		7	
3		8	
4		9	
5		10	

 ## Putting it in Practice

Appreciate Others (Verbal)

Again, for a period of two weeks, consciously choose to tell at least one person a day what you appreciate about them – sincerely, specifically and deliberately. I am not talking about a hasty, distracted or vague thank you here.

You can be brief – but be sincere. You might experiment with a mix of folks; family, friends, co-workers, your boss, a customer, or a service provider. Here are some examples to show just how simple this can be:

- Spouse, I really appreciate the time and effort you put into making meals for our entire family.

- Friend, I so appreciate the way your sense of humor can lift me out of a bad mood.

- Friend, I'm grateful for your friendship. You've stuck by me through thick and thin and helped me get through many a tough time.
- Boss, I want to thank you for the opportunity you gave me with the XYZ assignment. It was a vote of confidence in me, I learned a lot and I appreciate it.
- Customer, we appreciate your business. I know it would be very easy to order online or shop in the big box down the street – so your effort to support local business is really appreciated.
- Son, I know taking the trash out is not much fun. I really appreciate that you did that this week without reminders or complaining.
- Direct Report, I want to thank you for the extra time and effort you put into the XYZ project. I know you sacrificed family time to do that, but you hung in there and delivered a great product. Our customer was thrilled.

Week 1   **Week 2**

	Person / Appreciation		Person / Appreciation
1		6	
2		7	
3		8	
4		9	
5		10	

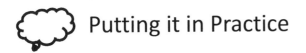 # Putting it in Practice

Share Your Bounty

One way to show gratitude is to "pay forward" our good fortune and bounty. If you have an overflowing pantry, give some to the food bank. If you are grateful for the roof over your head, spend a day on a Habitat for Humanity project. For a period of 5 years, I spent 2 hours a week helping in a Domestic Violence Shelter. Even though we were going through some really tough stuff at home, every single time I walked away counting my blessings and realizing how much I had to be grateful for.

You may want to do something on a regularly scheduled basis or merely seize opportunities as they come. I encourage you to spend your time with a cause that speaks deeply to you and what you care about.

Make a list here of some possibilities.

Count Your Blessings & Pay It Forward

Issues or causes I care deeply about:	Special skills or talents I have that might be put to use:

5   Ending with Gratitude

It seems a fitting conclusion for me to end on a note of gratitude. I am truly and deeply grateful for:

- Leaders who want to lead better and who make the effort to do something about it. (That means you!)

- Today's turbulent environment – which presents both challenges and opportunities.

- People like you who envision a better future and are willing to take a risk to realize it.

- The opportunities that I have to do amazing work with amazing people.

- The great support team around me (you know who you are).

- Life – messy, busy, chaotic life.

> *The struggle ends when the gratitude begins.*
>
> Neale Donald Walsch

Be Thankful

Be thankful that you don't already have everything you desire.
If you did, what would there be to look forward to?

Be thankful when you don't know something
For it gives you the opportunity to learn.

Be thankful for the difficult times.
During those times you grow.

Be thankful for your limitations
Because they give you opportunities for improvement.

Be thankful for each new challenge
Because it will build your strength and character.

Be thankful for your mistakes
They will teach you valuable lessons.

Be thankful when you're tired and weary
Because it means you've made a difference.

It is easy to be thankful for the good things.
A life of rich fulfilment comes to those who are
also thankful for the setbacks.

GRATITUDE can turn a negative into a positive.
Find a way to be thankful for your troubles
and they can become your blessings.

~ Author Unknown ~

Additional Resources:

Breathnach, Sarah. *The simple abundance: journal of gratitude*. New York: Warner
Books, 1996.

So Now What?

The fourteen chapters you've just worked through distill a lifetime of learning, working, and testing for me. They draw on the works of many thought leaders in the field and my implementation of their work into the lives of my clients and myself. This book takes forty years of my life, keen observation, serious study, voracious reading and actual application over time and drops it neatly into this volume. It was my goal to take that rich learning and make it accessible and easy to grasp. However, know that it is not easy for me and won't be easy for you.

But I can assure you that these approaches work. That they make a difference. That implementing them will be transformational. And that actually pulling these leadership actions into your daily life is possible and is ripe with potential. I can also assure you that this is not an overnight process or one that can happen all at once.

As such, here are few parting thoughts to guide your progress.

Slow Down

It is a paradox, but taking time to slow down can really help you go faster. I'm not talking about every minute of every day. Nor am I talking about dragging your feet. What I am suggesting is that taking as little as 10 minutes during the day (although more is better) to pause, breathe, reflect and thing enables you to maintain the faster pace that is required today with more energy, focus and direction. It may be at the end of the day or at the beginning. You might write or doodle or meditate or sit in a quiet place. Find what works for you are create a small daily oasis of space and sanity.

Create Personal Accountability

As you determine what you would like to implement from this book, create a mechanism that helps you be accountable for actually doing so. Otherwise your intention never moves into action. There are many ways to do this. Some of my favorites include:

- Writing my intention prominently on the whiteboard in my office.
- Making a public statement to others who will ask me about it
- Putting it in writing
- Making it a part of my performance goals
- Blocking time on my calendar
- Finding a buddy coach (someone who can support and coach you)
- Taking an action that forces me to follow through (book the flight, schedule the meeting, etc.)
- Leverage a coach or a peer group
- Share your intention with your team and ask them to provide you feedback on progress (or the lack of)

Practice

Recognize that no first attempts are anywhere near perfect. And then recognize that when you are dealing with people in organizations in a complex and changing environment, there are very few perfect outcomes and clearly not a defined and repeatable formula. Give yourself the grace and space to be clumsy at first. Know that your discomfort is a sign of growth. Aim for progress, not perfection. Recognize that you may be brilliant one day and horrendous the next day. And that it is OK. Keep trying and learning. Over and over and over again.

Actually Do the Practice Exercises

If you are like me, I can tend to race through a book and skip the activities, exercise or applications. Yet, each and every time that I have resisted that urge and actually do the work, it has been magic. So if you have skipped over the exercises, go back, with pen or pencil in hand, and actually do the work. It will be slower, but richer. It will walk you through the process, a step at a time. You'll be able to immediately apply what your work in your work. Trust me – it is worth the time and effort.

Dive Deeper

Each of the fourteen chapters is only a very short summary that I've collapsed from my reading, learning and practicing. I've listed those additional resources at the end of the chapter. Use them for the topics that you are unclear about or that you want to learn more deeply.

Move Forward, but get your Bearings Often

Just as with the creative process that you've learned in this book, create dynamic tension to move you along. Create a future focus and then get grounded in your current reality. Take a few steps and then pause to assess. What have you learned? Is your direction correct? What adjustments do you need to make? Is your target still the proper one?

Take a Step at a Time

There most likely is a concept that resonated with you as you read the book. It may be that your team is mired in conflict, or that they are in non-work. It may be that you need to create something new. It may be that you have a strong desire to work more from your inner core. Although the book is laid out in an order that makes perfect sense, it is less important to do this in order than to "just start". Do something, then a little more and then a little more. Just Do SOMETHING!!

Create a Support Network

I've observed high performing individuals closely. And without exception, they are not self-made. They have a support network around them, which includes people who are focused on helping them improve their performance. High performers find others who can teach them. Who can provide them unvarnished feedback. Who can be thought partners. Who can pull them up when they are down and ground them when they are flying too high, too fast. Who can create a safe space where tough stuff gets pulled out into the light of the day in order to be addressed. Your support network might include your boss, your peers, your team, a coach, mentor, guide or teacher. If you are fortunate, it will be rich with people in multiple categories and varying viewpoints. Be intentional about building out your support network. Ask – and you'll be surprised how wiling others are to help you grow. Seek and find those you trust with this important work. Be willing to invest in yourself – in time and money and you will reap the rewards.

A Bit about Evergreen Leadership

This book is based on the leadership development work done in our Evergreen Leadership Programs. We offer a variety of programs to support leaders to provide clarity and direction in the midst of uncertainty, to build strong yet agile teams, to create capacity and capability within their organizations and to create better futures.

Our services include:

- Key Note Speaking
- Leadership Workshops
- Leadership Coaching
- Leadership Circles –intensive peer group based development programs
    - **Lead Boldly** – Executive Leadership
    - **Lead at the Next Level** – High Potential Leadership Development
    - **Shape the Future** – For those wanting to create something better for themselves and those they lead

We'd love to explore with you how to prepare yourself and others in your organization to lead well in turbulent times.

Call us: (765) 404 -8950

E-mail us: info@evergreenleadership.com

Visit our web site: www.evergreenleadership.com

Subscribe to our blog: www.ktaylorandassoc.com/blog/

A Word from Those Who Have Worked With Us

There are few leadership resources that are going to challenge us and provide us with the necessary honesty required for growth. As a coach, Kris provided me with that very thing during our very first meeting. Her writing captures that same mixture and balance of self-reflection, inspiration and call to action that leaders need to move the needle on their potential to grow and thrive.

- Carroll Nelligan, President, Tx:Team

The Leader's Guide to Turbulent Times: could there be a more appropriate title for Kris's book? This is what Kris has been for me, first when I was a CIO and she provided change-management leadership as a critical component of our company-wide organizational and technological transformation. In the years since, I have been pleasantly surprised at how many of her blog entries were so engaging for me. In a few paragraphs I would find myself not merely nodding in agreement, but engaging in a dialogue by responding on her web site; taking what I learned into my work day. I look forward to her continuing to be my guide in these turbulent times.

- Keith Ensroth, Executive Program Manager, Teradata

I have had the privilege to know and work with Kris for over 15 years. Watching her facilitate a leadership or team training session always makes me a more effective leader in the workplace and at home. Her writing challenges my thinking, encourages me to improve myself, and fills me with optimism. Kris offers powerful insights, actionable coaching, and engaging dialogue. I look forward to any interaction with Kris because I know I'll leave a better person.

- Craig Andrews, Senn-Delaney Certified Facilitator / Continuous Improvement Director for ConAgra

Evergreen Leadership™
Developing leaders for the 21st Century

Made in the USA
Middletown, DE
08 May 2015